HORSE OF THE YEAR SHOW

— *Ode to the Horse* —

RONALD DUNCAN

Where in this wide world can man find nobility without pride,

Friendship without envy,

Or beauty without vanity?

Here, where grace is laced with muscle and strength by gentleness confined.

He serves without servility; he has fought without enmity.

There is nothing so powerful, nothing less violent;

There is nothing so quick, nothing more patient.

England's past has been borne on his back.

All our history is in his industry:

We are his heirs, he our inheritance.

The Horse!

HORSE
OF THE YEAR SHOW
UNDER THE SPOTLIGHT

GILLIAN NEWSUM

J.A. ALLEN · LONDON

This publication is dedicated to the memory of my dear father,
Sam Anderson, who sadly died on 28 December 2010.
All profits from the sale of this book will be donated
to Cancer Research UK.

SANDY ANDERSON

© J.A. Allen 2011
First published in Great Britain in 2011

ISBN 978 0 85131 982 7

J.A. Allen
Clerkenwell House
Clerkenwell Green
London EC1R 0HT

J.A. Allen is an imprint of Robert Hale Limited

www.allenbooks.co.uk

A catalogue record for this book is available from the British Library

Designed and typeset by Paul Saunders
Edited by Marion Paull

Printed by Midas Printing International Limited, China

Photos on Preceding Pages

Page 1: Sitting pretty at Horse of the Year Show.
Page 2: Proud winners of the Heavyweight Show Hunter of the Year title in 2009 and 2010,
Robert Oliver and Loughkeen Dancing Lord.
Page 3: Hainton Charlie Girl enjoying the spotlight after being crowned the 2009 Shire Horse of the Year.

CONTENTS

FOREWORD

We at Grandstand Media feel exceptionally privileged to be the present custodians of Horse of the Year Show, or HOYS as it is almost universally known. We take great pride in producing the show and are very aware of its illustrious heritage. The last book to chronicle its history was written in 1976, long before many of the present competitors were born, and it therefore seemed appropriate to put down another marker, to bring the story up to date and provide an insight into the background of this remarkable occasion.

Children and professionals alike dream about that magic ride under the spotlight, signifying they have won at HOYS. The excitement, tension and joy, as well as the inevitable disappointments, just add to the show. Central to all these emotions, of course, are the horses, from the smallest pony to the largest Shire horse. They are the real stars and they have made HOYS the world's most famous horse show.

Besides the horses and the all-important competitors, other people, too, are mainstays of HOYS – officials, volunteers, visitors, supporters. Year after year people come back to savour the unique atmosphere that the show creates, so much so that HOYS has now become an iconic brand in its own right.

Some of the most memorable moments from the last sixty years or so are to be found here. We hope that you enjoy the read, and look forward to sharing the continuing story at another Horse of the Year Show.

SANDY ANDERSON, CHAIRMAN, GRANDSTAND MEDIA LTD

ACKNOWLEDGEMENTS

Particular thanks go to Sarah Briscoe at Grandstand Media Ltd, who spent much time compiling the results section and providing me with recent photographs from the show. We have done our best to ensure that the results are accurate and complete, but a fire at the Stoneleigh offices some years ago destroyed many of the original HOYS files. Since the show began in 1949 various competitions and classes have come and gone, and others have changed their name, making the task even more complex than we had initially anticipated.

During my research for the book a great many people took the time to talk to me, to provide me with information and stories, and to search out old photographs. I am indebted to all of them for their help and patience. I should like to thank the following people: Jane Holderness-Roddam, Jennie Loriston-Clarke, Lady Kitson, Jennifer Williams, Vicki Keen, Robert Oliver, Davina Whiteman, Nigel and Stuart Hollings, Richard Ramsay, David Tatlow and Lorraine Homer, Jayne Webber, Carole Gilbert-Scott, Guy Landau, Lynn Russell, Robert Walker, Alistair Hood, Katie Jerram, Sue Rawding, Jane McHugh, Jean Andrews, Alan Smith, Jenny MacArthur, Michael Clayton, Mary Allison, John and Clare Whitaker, Harvey Smith, David Broome, Tim Stockdale, Jon Doney, Jeff Osborne, Pat and Sarah Cooke, Mark Wein, Mike Gill, John and Betty Peacock, Mike Tucker, Frank Grunnill, Bob Ellis, Kevin Bywater, Val Turner, Frances Young, Pete Harnett, Trevor Meeks, Kit Houghton, Bob Langrish, Stephen Hadley, Jane Wallace, Emma Horton-Barr, Enice Vennard, Alison Hughes, Maureen Thomas, Tom Best and Trisha Tolchard.

I should also like to thank Lucy Higginson, Editor of *Horse and Hound*, for letting me use the *Horse and Hound* archives; Jayne Toyne for scanning photographs for me, and David Barker at Waugh & Co solicitors for allowing me access to Leslie Lane's photograph archives.

Most of all my thanks go to Lesley Gowers at J.A. Allen for asking me to write this book, and to Sandy Anderson for having the vision to suggest the book in the first place.

GILLIAN NEWSUM

PHOTOGRAPH CREDITS

KEY: B = bottom, T = top, L = left, R = right

Artograffi (Gabrielle Goma): 139; Baron Studios (Rex Coleman): 37, 82; Andrew Bennison: 118, 138, 141, 208, 223, 224; Sarah Briscoe: 164B; Roberto Cubeddu: 18T, 83, 94, 98, 121, 170, 172, 179BL, 180, 212T, 231T&B, 237BL; Srdja Djukanovic: 186; Equinational: 196, 206, 230; The Event Photographer: 120, 241R; John Eveson: 126B, 215; Caroline Finch: 17B; Gwen Harris: 1T&B, 12, 13, 14B, 15T,R&B, 144, 145T&B, 146, 147, 156T&B, 159, 160, 164T, 165T&B, 166T&B, 168, 169, 174B, 175, 176, 178, 179TL, 170BR, 183T, 192, 212B; Clive Hills: 48; Lorraine Homer: 49; *Horse and Hound* archives: 23, 89; Kit Houghton: 113B, 155BR; Aly Hughes: 183B; IPC Media (Trevor Meeks): 14, 69, 76, 108T, 110, 117, 119, 124, 125, 126T, 131T&B, 132, 207, 219, 229T, 234, 235, 237, 245L; Vicki Keen (courtesy of): 29TR; Keystone Press: 39; Kicksports: 79; Bob Langrish: 80, 84, 85, 90, 99, 102T&B, 106, 107, 116, 225, 232; Leslie Lane: 38, 44R, 55, 59, 62T, 67T&B, 68, 72T&B, 77, 97, 103L&R, 104, 105, 108B, 111, 113T, 150, 155BL, 189T, 194, 201, 204; M&K Photography: 95, 135, 136, 140, 188, 220; Jim Meads: 155; Trevor Meeks: 79T; Miles Bros: 29L, 45, 70T; Monty: 189B; Sebastian Oakley: 157, 179TR, 187, 138, 139B; Odhams Press (Topham): 26R, 35, 36; PA Photos: 75; Simon Palmer: 86, 250; Kathryn Pearn: 11, 92, 148, 210, 214, 217T, 218, 249; Real Time Imaging: 2, 18B, 19L&R, 93, 115, 123, 130, 133, 161, 163T, 173, 174T, 205, 221, 235T, 237R, 239T, 241L, 243; Anthony Reynolds: 227, 229BR; W.W. Rouch: 29BR, 43, 62B; Jacqueline Sanders: 53. Nico Morgan: 128, 191, 217B, 229BL, 240; Lesley Skipper: 245R; Sport & General: 28, 44L; Topical: 26L; Kevin Wright: 3.

Every effort has been made to trace the copyright owners of the photographs used in this book, but if there are any omissions or inaccuracies the author and publishers apologise.

INTRODUCTION

The memories live on, over fifty years later. Hanging on the wall just inside the entrance to Terry Pinner's house at his livery yard near Huntingdon are the two plaques he received for qualifying for Horse of the Year Show in 1957 and 1966. These were fixed to the wall with great pride after his return from the show and have never been moved. Nearby hangs a photograph of Terry competing in a regional qualifier for the Foxhunter Championship; on the dresser he still keeps the miniature trophy that was given to all the Foxhunter finalists at Harringay in 1957, and in a drawer he still has his old programmes. He talks about it as if it happened yesterday.

All over Britain there are thousands of people like Terry, not necessarily well known but who nonetheless cherish their memories of competing at Horse of the Year Show. They may have qualified just once in their life, but the excitement and the sense of achievement is still palpable. They each have their own story to tell, their own successes or disappointments, but they are all connected by the common bond of having qualified and competed at the ultimate show of the year, the final of finals to find the champion of champions.

For Terry Pinner that first qualification had not been easy. His parents were not horsey, and when Terry wanted to buy a horse that he had heard of locally, his father said it was too expensive. So the seventeen year old saved up his money in an Oxo tin, borrowed the last £5 from his mother, and cycled the five miles to

► Terry Pinner competing with The Stoneyman at the regional Foxhunter qualifier at Dagenham in 1957.

Brampton to buy The Stoneyman, an Irish import from Stoney Cross. He left his Oxo tin behind, but rode his new horse home, and the following year qualified the six-year-old gelding for Harringay after coming third behind Alan Oliver at the Foxhunter regional final held on the Ford Motor company's sports field at Dagenham. At that time, Alan Oliver and his horse Red Link were being featured on 'The Archers' radio programme and had received a tremendous build-up to Horse of the Year Show, but ultimately the pair finished second in the championship to Anne Barker on Lucky Sam. Terry came a creditable equal fourth, having already tied for first place in the Newcomers.

Although this is only one of myriad stories of people qualifying against the odds, overcoming accidents and injuries to get to Horse of the Year Show, it illustrates just how much this show means to the participants, even to those who now appear at the show on a regular basis. Tim Stockdale was so nervous in his first show-jumping competition there that he was relieved to have one fence down, which meant he did not have to go back into the arena for the jump-off. When the eight-year-old Ellen Whitaker qualified to compete in the 12.2hh show jumping, she was so excited she spent hours grooming her pony. 'I thought I'd really made it when I got to my first Horse of the Year Show,' says Ellen.

◄ Tim Stockdale finds a fan. The first time Tim competed at HOYS he was so nervous he was glad to have one fence down so that he would not have to go back into the arena.

This now six-day show, held at the National Exhibition Centre (NEC) near Birmingham, brings together the best from the equestrian world; whether it is in showing classes, dressage displays, Pony Club games or show jumping, only the top horses and riders in the country take part. Around 150,000 competitors set out to qualify for the show each year, but only a tiny fraction of those get through. Thus every qualification is, in itself, a major achievement. For the showing world it is the ultimate goal of a busy season, and these days nearly every type of horse has its place, from Shires to miniatures, from hacks to Highland ponies. The kudos of qualifying is the same for the show jumpers, and although the international riders now have other big overseas shows during the winter, Horse of the Year Show, these days referred to as HOYS, remains the pinnacle of the national show-jumping calendar.

HOYS is a show that never sleeps; from the early hours of the morning until late at night the stables and arenas are a hive of activity, the atmosphere highly charged with excitement, exhaustion and, for the lucky ones, jubilation. For nearly a week the NEC becomes a horsey enclave, a world of its own, with everyone wrapped up in the show and focused entirely on their horses or, in the case of the officials and organisers, focused on the smooth running of the show. If the North Pole caught fire during HOYS week, it is unlikely that anyone at the NEC would realise it.

The 50-acre site near Birmingham has a more rural and spacious feel to it than the show's original London homes of Harringay and Wembley, but it is nonetheless an extraordinary environment for the horses – a busy concrete jungle with bright lights and cheering crowds. For the show horses in particular, it is unlike anything they will have experienced at the outdoor county shows during the summer where they will have gained their precious qualifications. Jayne Webber, one of the most successful show exhibitors in recent years, likens it to asking a horse to walk into Harrods. 'It's a surreal, artificial environment and completely out of the ordinary for the average horse. Some love it; some have trouble coping with it.'

▼ A surreal environment – the international arena at HOYS.

These unusual surroundings can upset the form of some of the best show horses, even those that have done well all season and may be expected to sweep the board at HOYS. The showing at HOYS is sometimes described as a lottery.

This is not a slight on the judges; it is because some horses simply do not perform as well indoors in the autumn as they do in the big grass arenas at the summer shows. Some find it difficult to settle in the strange atmosphere, others have perhaps lost some of their sparkle after a long summer season. The hunters, in particular, can feel confined at an indoor show, especially if they are not well enough collected and balanced to cope with the smaller arena. Sometimes it is the riders who cannot cope with the pressure of this all-important end-of-season show and who perhaps freeze when their big moment arrives. Whatever the reason may be, the one certainty is that the showing results are not predictable.

In addition, the task of judging is not an easy one, for the judges have no time to procrastinate. The timetable requires them to sort out their classes effectively and efficiently and not too slowly; otherwise they will incur the wrath of the senior steward for upsetting the programme for the rest of the day. The horses, likewise, do not get much time to adjust to their new environment. Riders are allowed to exercise them for a short time in either the international arena or the showing arena, depending on where their class is to be held. The international arena is open for exercising at 5 a.m., before the competitions get under way, but there is no audience at this hour of the day, so the atmosphere is not the same as it will be during the class itself. Those due to compete in the showing arena must exercise late in the evening, once the day's classes are over.

▲ Judging, like everything else at the show, runs to a tight schedule. Judge – Ann Fowler, steward – Joy Hall.

Each morning the show classes begin at 7.30 a.m. or earlier, by which time exhibitors must have exercised their horses and have them plaited and looking immaculate. They are often plaiting by torchlight or under the floodlights in the stable area, and if it is raining, the task of producing a horse in tip-top condition is even more difficult, particularly for the showing arena, which is a long walk from the stables. When these horses appear under the lights looking sleek and shiny, beautifully presented and well behaved, it is easy to forget just how much work has been going on behind the scenes.

The scale of HOYS is daunting. Although many spectators think of it as a single occasion in a big indoor arena, with show-jumping competitions, a glimpse of the showing, a display or two, the scurry driving and Pony Club mounted games, in fact there is an enormous amount going on all the time. After the pre-dawn

▲ An exhausting week – Robert Oliver chats to David Tatlow while their horses take a well-earned rest.

▲ Stirrups for sale.

exercising sessions and the early show classes, two performances are staged each day in the international arena, the last one ending at 11 p.m. Meanwhile, a satellite of the show, this one dominated by ponies of all varieties, shapes and sizes, is revolving on its own axis in the showing arena at the far end of the indoor complex. In between the two arenas is the retail village, which includes the Hall of Fame gallery and an Interactive Feature Area where spectators can come into contact with different breeds of horses – and enough equestrian shops to fill Oxford Street.

Over 10,000 people flood through the gates on each day of the show. There are four restaurants, numerous food outlets and at least four bars – over 2,000 bottles of champagne are consumed during the week. Around 1,500 competitors take part in the show and at least 2,000 rosettes are handed out. It is estimated that the economic impact on the local community is in excess of £10 million, but a less obvious economic gain for the nation's equine industry stretches well beyond the doors of the NEC. Anyone who has a horse with the potential to compete at HOYS has a valuable commodity, and the desire to own a particular type or breed of horse increases significantly if that type or breed has a championship to contest at HOYS. Thus, since show classes for mountain and moorland ponies were introduced in 1999, these types have become considerably more popular, and good mountain and moorland ponies exchange hands for much more money than they did twelve years ago. A win for any horse at HOYS can double its value overnight. In addition, because all the horses competing at HOYS have to qualify, those spring and summer shows that hold qualifying competitions receive strong entries for the relevant classes, which in turn benefits these shows by bringing in more money in entry fees. As long as exhibitors continue to hold on to the ambition of riding down the centre line at HOYS under the spotlight, showing classes will continue to flourish.

Economics aside, HOYS has acted as an inspiration and springboard for many of our top riders. John Whitaker was determined to become a show jumper after watching the show on television as a young boy; Jennie Loriston-Clarke was inspired to pursue a career in dressage after watching a display by Lis Hartel, and, as a boy, David Tatlow learned much about his profession from watching the best showmen at HOYS, Harry Bonner and Count Robert Orssich among them.

▲ Rush hour in the retail village – souvenirs for sale.

◄ Tunnel vision – the view from the hospitality suite in the international arena.

Many outstanding riders have come through the ranks of the show pony classes: Jane Holderness-Roddam (winner of Badminton), Jayne Webber (one of the top ladies in showing) and Laura Collett (winner of nine gold medals in pony, junior and young rider eventing championships) all began their equestrian careers in the pony classes at HOYS. 'Traditionally, the show pony has been responsible for producing very high-class riders because you have to be extra sensitive to ride them,' explains Davina Whiteman, top pony producer in the 1960s and seventies. 'The ponies are so quick and light in their tread; it takes an exceptionally talented rider to show them at their best. HOYS is also a great training ground for learning to cope under pressure in an intense atmosphere.'

The show has influenced the careers of many riders and breeders, and has been enormously important in promoting equestrianism, stimulating international success and providing a huge melting pot for competitors from all walks of life. It brings together international and national show jumpers, junior show jumpers, showing people, driving people, Pony Club children, dressage riders and a diverse range of people involved in displays. The opportunity is there to watch, and rub shoulders with, some of the best riders in the world, who are producing some of the greatest horses. Milton, Beethoven, Firecrest, Hopscotch, Marius Claudius, to name but a few, have all come through the ranks of the Newcomers and Foxhunter finals at Horse of the Year Show before making a name for themselves on the world stage. Even well-known event horses, such as HRH Princess Anne's Goodwill and Judy Bradwell's Castlewellan, first showcased their potential in the working hunter classes at HOYS.

This book tells the story of this remarkable show, which was dreamed up by a man in his bath and brought to reality by a blind ex-army officer. Captain Tony Collings, a renowned trainer of horses, whose life was cut short in his prime, allegedly had a 'eureka' moment in the bath one evening while staying with his sister and brother-in-law. Rushing downstairs, wrapped in a towel and still dripping with water, he shouted, 'I've got it,' to his bemused family.[1] His idea was to hold a show at the end of the season in which all the winners that year at county level would compete against each other to find the champion of champions, the horse of the year. It would be the climax of the showing season, the crowning glory of the best horses in the country.

Colonel Mike Ansell, blinded by gunfire (a result of mistaken identity) during the Second World War, was the man who took hold of Tony Collings' dream and

News Chronicle, Saturday, October 8, 1960

'Perishing Horse of the Year Show!'

◄ A Thelwell cartoon, published in 1960.

◄ Is this a competition for the longest mane? Coloured horse class in 2008.

made it reality, albeit with the addition of show-jumping classes. Thus developed a show that for more than sixty years has remained true to Tony Collings' original concept – Horse of the Year Show is indeed the climax of the showing season and its winners are the horses of the year. It is also an international show-jumping event and the home of the national show-jumping finals for both seniors and juniors. It is the show for which everyone wants to qualify.

Horse of the Year Show has touched the lives of so many people over the years, and some of their stories and memories may be relived through the pages of this book. The personalities, the horses, the fun, the drama, the trials and tribulations, both behind the scenes and in the ring, are brought together in this tribute to 'the world's most famous horse show'.

▲ It's nerve-wracking …

► emotional …

▲ dramatic …

▲ ecstatic!

CHAPTER ONE

A PROMISING START

'That was wonderful!' said Harry Llewellyn to the ten-year-old Elizabeth Spencer as she left the arena at Harringay after winning the Show Pony Championship on her 13.1½hh gelding Legend. It had already been an exciting evening for the young girl – staying up late, receiving her cup from Mrs R.S. Summerhays and then riding under the spotlight. Now the famous Harry Llewellyn, whom she had admired from the ringside at the big shows around the country, was shaking her hand and congratulating her. And it got better. 'Do you want to ride a real horse now?' he asked. In no time she found herself being legged up on to the mighty Foxhunter and put over a small fence in the collecting ring, where some of the top show jumpers were warming up their horses for the next class. Elizabeth Spencer (now Lady Kitson) still remembers that evening vividly.

It was 13 September 1949, the first night of the first Horse of the Year Show. Britain was moving on resolutely, and sometimes at a breathtaking pace, from the aftermath of the Second World War. Bread rationing was over, the first laundrette had opened in Queensway, London (coinciding neatly with the end of clothes rationing), Laurence Olivier's 'Hamlet' had become the first British film to win an Oscar, and in the sporting arena the nation was still buoyed by its success in staging the first post-war Olympic Games.

▼ Legend, 'a true child's pony' and winner of the Show Pony Championship at the first Horse of the Year Show in 1949 with Elizabeth Spencer (now Lady Kitson).

Those Olympics had had a catalytic effect on Britain's equestrian development, in two ways: the event riders had performed so dismally at Aldershot that the Duke of Beaufort felt moved to do something about it, so in April 1949 he started the Badminton Horse Trials and British event riders have never looked back. The show jumpers, on the other hand, were lauded as heroes, having won an Olympic team bronze medal (Harry Llewellyn on Foxhunter, Henry Nicoll on Kilgeddin and Arthur Carr on Monty), stimulating yet greater interest in their sport. Indeed, the International Horse Show had already been revived at the White City in 1947 and was proving successful, so when Captain Tony Collings, director of the then highly regarded Porlock Vale Riding School, suggested creating another major London show, he was somewhat taken aback by the negative response he received from the British Horse Society (BHS).

Fortunately, the BHS chairman at that time, Colonel V.D.S. Williams (father of the late Dorian Williams, who was to become the famous television commentator), liked Tony Collings' idea of staging a late autumn event that would serve as a climax to the showing season and produce the champion of champions. Unperturbed by the understandable reluctance of his BHS council to back another big show, Colonel Williams approached Mike Ansell, who was already directing the show-jumping events at the White City and who was well known to Williams – when the nine-year-old Mike Ansell had lost his father, Colonel Williams had taken over much of the responsibility for his upbringing.

As this new show would almost certainly have to be held indoors, the pair decided that a trip to Paris to see 'Le Jumping' in the Palais des Sports was called for. This was quite an eye-opener for them. 'Le Jumping' was not just a horse show for equine enthusiasts; it was entertainment for the masses, and the Parisians were unreserved in their expressions of appreciation and enjoyment. Rapturous applause greeted the appearance of their favourite riders, and even Harry Llewellyn, making his first visit to Paris with the now famous Foxhunter (having recently won the King George V Gold Cup at the White City) received a wildly enthusiastic reception every time he entered the ring, and particularly when he succeeded in winning the Grand Prix.

'The real favourites, of course, were the French riders,' wrote Dorian Williams,[1] 'Jean d'Orgeix and the effervescent Jonquier d'Oriola, a brilliant cabaret artist, together with the irresistible, petite, but outstandingly efficient horsewoman, Michele Cancre, only just seventeen years old. These were the darlings of the crowd and they were given the kind of reception reserved a decade later for the Beatles.'

If this heady atmosphere could be re-created at an indoor show in London, surely even the rather reserved British would join in the fun and become as intensely involved in the competitions? But, of course, the Paris show centred on show jumping, and Captain Collings' idea had been to stage an event that brought together the best horses from all the different showing classes – hunters, hacks, cobs, ponies – he had not intended this new venture to be devoted to show jumping. Mike Ansell, however, sensed that the show classes

SIR HARRY LLEWELLYN

It would be unfair to describe Harry Llewellyn as a 'one horse man' – he had a number of good horses and was an excellent rider – but he will always be remembered as the man who rode Foxhunter. Their achievements together were legendary: three King George V Gold Cup wins, two Olympic medals and members of 12 winning Nations Cup teams. At the height of Foxhunter's career, at the beginning of the 1950s, the pair gained 37 international wins in nine countries over two years, culminating in their memorable performance at the Helsinki Olympics in 1952, when they clinched the gold medal for the British team. Sir Harry was the last team member to jump in the second round, and he knew that the gold medal would be theirs if he could complete the course with just one fence down. Foxhunter proceeded to jump a foot-perfect clear round, and the show-jumping team duly claimed Britain's only gold medal of the entire Games – won on the final day in the final round of the show jumping.

To this day, it remains the only Olympic gold medal ever won by Britain for show jumping, and Foxhunter's name lives on in the competition for young horses devised by Sir Harry. The idea, he said, was to give away some of the numerous silver trophies his horse had won and which his wife refused to clean! Thus the Foxhunter Championship became a regular competition at Horse of the Year Show from 1954 onwards, and it remains the most famous and prestigious novice competition in the country.

Harry Llewellyn's sense of humour as well as his obvious talent as a rider (he competed twice in the Grand National) made him enormously popular with the crowds, and he and Foxhunter competed regularly and with great success at Harringay. The pair made a rare mistake at the 1953 show, and Llewellyn took a crashing fall coming out of the double. Foxhunter, who had caught one of the poles between his legs, fell with his rider and appeared to roll on him. Although Foxhunter leapt to his feet, Harry lay still for a few seconds and the crowd watched anxiously as he slowly pulled himself on to his hands and knees and began fumbling his way to the side of the arena. Two men from the St John's Ambulance team rushed into the arena, but Harry waved them away. He looked up at the commentary box and called out to Dorian Williams, 'I'm not hurt. I'm just looking for a tooth I've lost. You'd better tell them.'[1] Sir Harry received his knighthood in 1977.

◄ Harry Llewellyn and Foxhunter on their way to securing Britain's team gold medal at the Helsinki Olympics in 1952.

alone would not excite spectators as much as 'Le Jumping', and he persuaded Captain Collings to let the British Show Jumping Association (BSJA),* of which Mike Ansell was chairman, run the show and include showing classes in the programme. It would still be a champion of champions show, open only to those horses and ponies that had won at qualifying shows during the season, and thus the winner of each class would be a 'horse of the year'. It was a clever idea and a clever name – one that has come to mean so much to the thousands of riders and exhibitors whose horses have qualified for this pinnacle of the showing world.

▼ The cover from the programme for the first Horse of the Year Show in 1949.

The basic format for the new show having been agreed, the next task was to find a venue, and options were limited. When the idea of the Harringay arena was first mooted, it was greeted with little enthusiasm. How would people be persuaded to come to a horse show held at a greyhound stadium that was also a well-known venue for circuses and Wild West shows, and, furthermore, was situated in some unknown and undesirable district in north London? Two important factors in its favour put it on the map – its proximity to the Hunter Show in Islington and the fact that it was only twenty minutes by underground from Piccadilly to the nearest tube station, Manor House. One other major advantage, and undoubtedly the most significant, was that the Greyhound Racing Association

* In 2009 the BSJA became known as British Showjumping, but for most of this book it is referred to as the BSJA

—but no one refuses a

GUINNESS

THE 'GUINNESS TIME' CHAMPIONSHIP

Arthur Guinness Son and Co. (Park Royal) Ltd. are pleased to announce that they will be sponsoring this new Championship next year. There will be regional Qualifying Competitions and the Championship will be held at the Horse of the Year Show, Wembley 1962.

Page 44

G.E.3421.A

Riding Clothes
. . . and Saddlery. Send for our fully illustrated Price List.

MOSS BROS
OF COVENT GARDEN & CO. LTD.

Junction of Garrick & Bedford Streets,
Temple Bar 4477

Horses are particular . . .

about their appearance and about the appearance of their riders too! Harry Hall of Regent Street has everything the fastidious rider—and horse could wish for.

HARRY HALL
The Greatest Name in Riding Wear

The champion of drinks —

THE DRINK OF CHAMPIONS!

OVALTINE

The makers of 'Ovaltine' take pride in sponsoring the Leading Show Jumper Championship at this year's Horse of the Year Show. Earlier in 1963 they sponsored the King George V Cup and the Queen Elizabeth Cup —and in 1962 the European Show Jumping Champion-

'Ovaltine' is the only food drink which has been officially recognized at every British Empire Games since their inception and at every Olympic

(GRA) were persuaded to underwrite the show in its first year. The chairman of the GRA, Frank Gentle, who had taken on the backing of the International Horse Show two years earlier, agreed to become joint director of the show with Mike Ansell, who was now convinced that he was 'on to a winner'.[2]

Colonel Ansell put together an able and enthusiastic team of supporters, which included Dorian Williams, Captain Collings, Colonel Harry Llewellyn, Bob Hanson, Ruby Holland-Martin, Colonel Guy Cubitt, Brigadier John Allen and Mr A.H. Payne. The dates for the first show were fixed – 13–15 September 1949 – and it was billed as the first indoor show since the war. There were to be two performances each day, at 2.15 p.m. and 7 p.m. Riders from six countries were expected, and Henry Wynmalen would give a dressage display with his 'best trained horse'. Prize money for the show classes was generous and on a par with the show jumpers: the winner of the Pony of the Year title would receive £100, for example, while £120 would go to the winner of the Horse and Hound Cup (under BSJA rules).

Entries for the first show were impressive – close to 400 including the show horses and all the show jumpers. It was a pity that not many spectators turned up to watch them. Fortunately, attendance did improve as word got around that the show was worth seeing, so by the end of the three days a reasonable crowd was there to generate some atmosphere for the final night, even if it was not quite the same as Paris.

It was the show jumpers who wooed the crowd. Friendly rivalry between France and England, combined with a battle of the sexes, gave spectators plenty to cheer about. Harry Llewellyn won the first class from Jean d'Orgeix, but the diminutive Michele Cancre pipped them both in a subsequent competition. Ireland's Iris Kellett dismissed both French and English contenders to win the ladies' event, but the French had the last word with a win for d'Orgeix in the final class. However, it was a national class that created the most interest and brought to the attention of the British public the talents of a certain Pat Smythe, destined to become one of the most successful show jumpers of her day. She was undoubtedly the 'darling' of that first show at Harringay.

To start with, there was the tear-jerking story behind her reunion with the 15hh Finality, the little bay mare bred from Kitty, a horse that used to pull a milk float. Pat's previous success with the mare had brought the young rider to the attention of the British team selectors, and in 1947, at the age of eighteen, she competed in Ostend and Le Zoute. But just as the pair seemed to have an exciting

◄ (opposite page)
Advertisements from 1950s show programmes.

international career ahead of them, the horse was sold. Perhaps fortunately for Pat, the new owner, Jimmy Snodgrass, did not have much success with Finality, and just before this first Horse of the Year Show, Jimmy asked Pat if she would ride the mare for him. Reunited, after more than a year, Pat soon re-established her unique rapport with Finality and succeeded in winning the main event, Leading Show Jumper of the Year, on the second day of the show, from none other than Ted Williams on his good horse, Tim. The spectators loved her and her little horse, giving her a standing ovation for her performance, which probably sealed the fate of the show.

▼ Iris Kellet riding Rusty and leading Starlet. This brilliant Irish rider was a regular competitor at HOYS in the 1950s.

▲ ► (above right) Leading Show Jumper of the Year in 1960, Ted Williams riding Pegasus, with Walter Cass (*left*), editor of *Horse and Hound*, and (*right*) Australian rider Laurie Morgan, winner of the individual gold medal in the three-day event at the Rome Olympics.

TEETHING PROBLEMS

In view of such obvious spectator enthusiasm, the organisers felt it was just a matter of ironing out a few initial problems and the show could surely be made a success. There was also, of course, the rather more serious issue of finance. The show had made a loss of some £2,500, a hefty sum at that time, but the GRA were happy with the way things had gone; they picked up the bill and even agreed to support the show for another year. As for the teething problems, there was still work to be done, but Mike Ansell was never short of ideas and inspiration, and he certainly had the force of personality to make changes where he thought they were needed.

The first of these would be the music, which was clearly a central ingredient of the entertainment and the general ambience of the show. The organist from Blackpool, hired on the basis that he would be much cheaper than a band, had not been a success. To start with, his organ had been lost *en route* from Blackpool to Harringay, and arrived too late for a rehearsal. 'At the first performance it was not only excessively loud,' recalls Dorian Williams,[3] 'but it went through the whole gamut of appearing and disappearing, emitting a profusion of coloured lights – not perhaps the most dignified accompaniment to a horse show, as the audience made all too clear.' The following year the Morris Motors Band took on the task, but was subsequently replaced by a military band. This proved to be much more suitable and the music continued to be provided by a live military band for many years until it gave way to pre-recorded music.

The next task was to tighten up the programme to avoid large gaps between classes. Somewhat ambitiously, three jumping events had been scheduled for every performance, and as it took at least twenty minutes to build each course (the materials being brought in on large trucks loaned by the circus), spectators became a little restless, particularly as they had only the dubious organ music, a dressage display and a Pony Club activity ride to keep them entertained between jumping classes. At one point, a slow handclap of disapproval could be heard from the impatient audience – never a good moment for an organiser.

TROUBLE WITH THE TRAINS

When David Broome and his father, Fred, competed at Harringay in the 1950s, David recalls that his grandfather had made a special advance trip to the area to try to find some cheap stabling, having decided that the stables on offer at the Harringay stadium cost far too much. He managed to strike a deal with the station master at Harringay railway station, and Fred's horses and David's ponies were duly stabled in the old railway stables on the other side of the track to the stadium. The system worked well until one evening the horses got blocked in. 'We hadn't banked on the shunting of the trains just before the 7 p.m. class,' explains David. 'We couldn't get Dad's horse out of the stable in time for the class because there was a train blocking it in.'

Then there were the show classes – was there really any point in them being at Harringay? The audience was enthused mostly by the show jumping; not many of them were privy to the finer points of conformation and movement, or even knew the difference between a hack and a hunter, so for them the show classes seemed long-winded and tedious. But finding the champion of champions had been the *raison d'être* for the show in the first place, and many committee members felt that abandoning these classes would betray Tony Collings' original idea. So a compromise was reached: the classes would be judged in an outside arena (in an area normally used for greyhound and dirt-track racing) and the horses would come into the main arena only for final judging and presentation of awards. Thus the system of preliminary judging came into being, and it soon became a tremendous accolade simply to make it through to the final judging and to have a chance to exhibit your horse in front of the big crowds in the main arena.

Another showing issue facing the committee was the method of judging the champion of champions. A points system was introduced, which, with various adjustments, has remained in place, but has always been the subject of controversy. At the first show, two awards were made in each class; one for the horse adjudged the best on the day and another for the most consistent, i.e. the horse that had won the most points during the season. The latter lead to complaints that people were simply pot-hunting by chasing points up and down the country. The two awards were then amalgamated, using a very complicated system of adding together the points accrued during the year and the points won on the day at HOYS. The problem with this system was that the winner on the day was not always the overall winner on points, which had the effect of making the judges look a little foolish.

'The matter came to a head in 1952, when one of the hunter judges was the Duke of Beaufort,' explains Dorian Williams.[4] 'His co-judge was the Earl of Halifax and quite apart from their knowledge and experience as judges of hunters, they were men of considerable stature who commanded respect from every point of view. Their own selection in the Hunter Championship did not coincide with the horse which had collected the greatest number of points, and which was there-

▲ Mighty Fine – the first Hunter Champion at Horse of the Year Show. He was initially produced in Ireland by Nat Galway-Greer and won the supreme championship in Dublin before being sold to Reg Hindley. In 1949 he won nine championships, including the Hunter of the Year title.

fore, officially, the Hunter of the Year … On this occasion the title winner stood about fifth in the class.'

The Duke of Beaufort was not happy with the outcome: surely the horse he had selected as the best of all those qualified should be the Hunter of the Year, not some other horse that happened to have gained more points during the season, probably because his owner had entered him in as many qualifiers as possible? His Grace made his feelings quite clear, and the old system was soon replaced with one in which points were allocated only at HOYS (although horses still had to qualify for the show) and were divided between the judging of the conformation and action, and the judging of the ride.

▼ Mighty Grand, winner of the Hunter Championship in 1955 and 1956, ridden by Patricia Cope, who was only seventeen years old when the pair won their first Hunter of the Year title at Harringay. At the same show they also took reserve place in the Riding Horse Championship.

▲ Rajah III, winner of the Hunter Championship in 1952, the last year in which the original points system (whereby show horses accumulated points throughout the year) was used. He also won the Working Hunter Championship twice, and was a very successful Ladies Hunter.

► Mr W.H. Cooper's heavyweight Mighty Atom, Hunter of the Year in 1950 and 1951. He was also champion at the International Horse Show four times, and twice won the Winston Churchill Cup for the supreme champion riding horse.

Soon after the new judging system was adopted in 1954, Tony Collings, the man whose original idea for a champion of champions show had set the wheels in motion for the founding of HOYS, was killed in an aeroplane crash, the Comet 1 air disaster, while on his way to judge in South Africa. A talented and successful horseman, he had won Badminton in 1950 on Remus, having been second the year before at the first-ever Badminton Horse Trials. As a professional instructor, he was not eligible to ride in the Olympics. Instead, he trained Britain's eventing team for the 1952 Helsinki Games at the Porlock Vale Riding School in Somerset, which he had by then established as a training centre of international repute.

It was around the time of Tony Collings' tragic death that the Harringay committee, now without the benefit of Collings' energy and commitment, finally persuaded the 'old guard' at the BSJA to accept the use of international rules for the show-jumping classes. The BSJA committee, and many of the riders, had fought hard to retain the national rules at what was, after all, their own show, even though it now featured more international than national classes. Their particular concern was that, under the rules set out by the International Equestrian Federation (FEI), the time limit was much tighter and, worse still, competitors incurred penalties for exceeding the time allowance (half the time limit). It was felt that these rules would encourage riders to jump big fences at speed, which was considered not only bad for the horses but also dangerous. There was some justification for their concern, but the problem for the show organisers was that under BSJA rules, which had no time penalties and no jump-off against the clock, classes were dragging on for hours. Furthermore, the rules for awarding jumping penalties were complex and confusing for the international riders, whose presence was an important aspect of the show.

SHOW JUMPING COMES OF AGE

The international (FEI) rules were finally accepted in 1954, the year that eighteen-year-old Dawn Palethorpe won the Leading Show Jumper of the Year class and the same year that the Foxhunter competition was inaugurated. Dawn Palethorpe, who later married Warren Wofford, another international show jumper, had taken over the ride on the 15.2hh Earlsrath Rambler from her sister Jill earlier in 1954, and following her success at HOYS, was selected to compete for the British team in Paris and Germany the following year. The pair covered themselves in glory on this tour, culminating with wins in Aachen in the ladies' class

ABRIDGED RULES FOR THE JUDGING OF JUMPING COMPETITIONS

Rules of the British Show Jumping Association

(1) Rider must not commence his round until ordered to do so by the Judge.

(2) If a Horse/Pony turns round, circles or refuses after having commenced its round,

1st turn round, circle or refusal	
2nd turn round, circle or refusal	2 Faults.
3rd turn round, circle or refusal	4 Faults.
The above are cumulative on the entire round.	Elimination.

(3) If a Horse/Pony causes all or any part of the obstacle to fall,

with fore-legs	
with hind-legs	4 Faults.
	2 Faults.

(4) If Rider's foot or leg causes any part of the obstacle to fall   4 Faults.

(5) If Horse/Pony jumps Wing, whether Wing is knocked down or not   4 Faults.

(6) If Horse/Pony and Rider, or Horse/Pony or Rider falls   4 Faults.

(7) Exceeding the Time limit   Elimination.
Time limit is worked out at 300 yards per minute on the track that a trained horse would take.

Rules of the Federation-Equestre, Internationale (F.E.I.)

(1)
First turn round, circle, run out or refusal   3 Faults.
Second turn round, circle, run out or refusal   6 Faults.
Third turn round, circle, run out or refusal   Elimination.
The above are cumulative on the entire round.

(2) Obstacle knocked down   4 Faults.

(3) Fall of Horse and Rider or Rider only   8 Faults.

(4) Jumping an obstacle out of its correct order   Elimination.

(5) Jumping an obstacle before it is re-set   Elimination.

(6) Horse leaves the Arena whether mounted or riderless   Elimination.

(7) Time allowed for the Course
Worked out on a basis of 436 yards per minute measured on the track that a well-trained horse would take.

(8) The "Time Limit" is twice the time allowed.

(9) Faults for time. For every second or part of a second exceeding the Time Allowed   ¼ Fault.

(10) Exceeding the Time Limit   Elimination.

27

◄ The rules for show jumping taken from the 1949 HOYS programme. The BSJA rules were considered too complex, and because there were no time penalties and no jump-off against the clock, classes sometimes went on for far too long.

and the Puissance, and producing a double clear round in the Nations Cup, so that Dawn left the show with a new fur coat – her prize as the leading lady rider.

The other outstanding lady rider of this time was, of course, Pat Smythe, who had set the audience alight with her brave win against Ted Williams at HOYS in 1949 and helped ensure the success of that first show. The following year, Pat and Finality again won the hearts of the Harringay crowd – which was, by now,

THE FOXHUNTER CHAMPIONSHIP

'The class everyone wants to win' is how Michael Whitaker, twice holder of the title, has described the Foxhunter Championship, which is one of the largest and most prestigious novice competitions in the world. Thousands of horses take part and winning is indeed the top accolade for a novice horse, and sometimes the pinnacle of a career for an unknown rider.

The competition was set up in 1954 with the objective of bringing new blood into show jumping to increase the pool from which to find future international horses. Sir Harry Llewellyn, its instigator, who named the competition after his famous horse Foxhunter, believed that a lot of untapped talent was to be found in the hunting field, in racing and at riding schools, and that people needed to be encouraged to have a go at show jumping. The idea was to hold classes around the country, culminating in a championship final at Horse of the Year Show. Both established riders and those relatively new to show jumping would aspire to qualify their novice horses to compete for the title. 'I insisted in the early days that the course was rustic and no more than three foot three inches in height, but soon coloured poles were introduced, which was good because it conditioned horses for tests over larger courses. Many hunters turned out to be better show jumpers than their owners had thought.'[2]

The competition soon became enormously popular, and many successful international horses first came into the spotlight with a good result in the Foxhunter. The first person to win the competition was Frances Stanbury on her own horse, Dreamboat. The pair had the only clear round in a jump-off against well-known riders such as Seamus Hayes, Pat Smythe, Douglas Bunn and Ted Williams. Tragically, Dreamboat never got the chance to shine internationally because two years later, while competing at Harringay, she died in her stable of a twisted gut.

In 1962, Douglas Bunn won the class with the four-year-old Beethoven, a future world champion partner for David Broome, who took the Foxhunter title himself in 1966 with Top of the Morning. This horse had been sent over from Ireland especially for the competition. 'A great friend of mine, Frank Kernan, was at the 1965 Horse of the Year Show and told me that he had a horse that would win the Foxhunter next year,' recalls David. 'What I didn't know until recently was that Harvey Smith had a bet with Frank for a hundred pounds – a lot of money in those days – that it wouldn't happen. Anyway, I drove to Liverpool early in 1966, collected the horse from the cattle boat, brought him home, qualified, went to Wembley and jumped the only clear round in the competition. That's what dreams are made of – and Harvey duly paid up!'

Although the great Milton did not even make it through to the final when he contested the series, his granddam, Pennywort, ridden by Paula Graham, won in 1970, and three years later Marius (then called Middle Road), Milton's sire, would probably have won if Caroline Bradley had not made the mistake of jumping an extra fence at the end of the course, which resulted, somewhat controversially, in their elimination.

The list of winners includes many well-known horses, and plenty of others can be found in the placings – Ann Moore's Psalm was second in 1966, Warren Point second in 1981, Everest Rapier second in 1984, Brook Street Clover second in 1988. From time to time letters have appeared in *Horse and Hound* complaining that it is unfair for novice riders to have to compete against the professionals, but the objective of the Foxhunter class is to showcase potential international horses, not riders. Besides, there have been a good number of relatively unknown winners, and the satisfaction of beating the top riders is very apparent. In the 2003 Foxhunter, the first three places were all filled by relatively inexperienced competitors, and the title was won by twenty-four-year-old Helen Tredwell on Opportunity B. Furthermore, three of the top five horses were British bred. When *Horse and Hound* took over the sponsorship of the championship in 1994, an award was introduced for the best British-bred horse to encourage more home-bred talent into the top end of the sport. The Foxhunter is achieving its objectives and providing a fascinating competition, which even the top riders still want to win.

► David Broome and Top of the Morning. Harvey Smith bet the horse's owner, Frank Kernan, £100 that it would not win the 1966 Foxhunter title. Harvey lost his money.

growing – when they came up against the formidable duo of Colonel Harry Llewellyn and Foxhunter in the Puissance. After two rounds, she and Harry Llewellyn were the only two riders left in the competition, and the spectators were mesmerised as these two seemingly unfairly matched pairs battled it out. The cheers reached a crescendo when the two riders entered the arena side by side and shook hands, having decided to share the title.

Television viewers had found the competition as compelling as the Harringay spectators, even though it had gone on for more than an hour over the allotted transmission time. Telephone lines to the BBC and to the Harringay arena were jammed with people ringing in to say how much they had enjoyed the contest, and it was at this point that the BBC realised that show jumping could be a winner for them.

PAT SMYTHE

Pat Smythe can be credited with inspiring a generation of horse-mad girls. For them, her story was a fairytale come true; a hard-working girl whose family was struggling to make ends meet learnt to ride on a one-eyed pony called Pixie in Richmond Park and discovered she had a talent for creating good show jumpers out of horses that other people had found impossible to ride. Her first major success came with a 15hh mare whose mother used to pull a milk float. Soon Pat was chosen to represent Britain at international shows. She competed alongside famous British cavalry officers, and when women were finally allowed to participate in show jumping at the Olympic Games, she became the first woman to win an Olympic show-jumping medal (team bronze, Stockholm 1956).

Born on 22 November 1928, Pat was the darling of British show jumping throughout the 1950s, and a role model for the young riders following in her wake. After various mishaps, she and Pixie eventually won the children's jumping class at the Richmond Royal Show. Her first top horse, Finality, was sent to the Smythes by Johnny Traill, for whom Pat's mother trained polo ponies, and this was the horse Pat rode when she was first selected to represent Britain at overseas shows.

Among the other horses that came Pat's way, her three best were the ex-racehorse Prince Hal, the mare Tosca and her Olympic horse, Flanagan. With them, she became a regular member of the British team, winning thirteen Nations Cup competitions, four Ladies' European Championship titles, eight National Championship titles and a team Olympic bronze medal, for which she was awarded the OBE. As well as that, she set a ladies' high-jump record of 7 feet 3½ inches. At HOYS, her numerous wins include the Leading Show Jumper of the Year title in 1949, 1958 and 1962. Probably the most memorable of her performances there was the dual with Harry Lewellyn and Foxhunter in the Puissance in 1950, in which they eventually shared first prize.

Indeed, for the next thirty years the BBC regarded show jumping as one of their major sports and gave it substantive coverage up until the late 1980s, when viewing figures began to slump and show jumping was no longer shown on prime-time television. Its popularity in those early days was helped by spectators' appreciation of some of the great partnerships of the time – Harry Llewellyn and Foxhunter; Pat Smythe and Finality (followed by Prince Hal and Tosca); Dawn Palethorpe and Earlsrath Rambler; Andrew Fielder, who at the age of sixteen won the first of three Leading Show Jumper of the Year titles with the massive, back-kicking Vibart; the brave Irish rider Iris Kellett and Rusty, and her compatriots Seamus Hayes and Planet, and Tommy Wade with the popular little Dundrum, 'a veritable power-packed midget'.[5]

In the 1950s, Seamus Hayes was thrilling the crowds with many good wins, one of them being notable for its dramatic finish. He was riding Tommy Makin's Planet in the jump-off for the Gordon Richards Stakes, a competition he had

won the previous year (1951), narrowly beating Alan Oliver. This time the same two riders were once again battling it out for top place, and Alan, renowned for his unorthodox style of seemingly launching himself over the big fences before his horse, had set a fast time on Red Star. Seamus, with his engaging smile and happy-go-lucky outlook, was already a favourite with the HOYS spectators, and they were ready to cheer him home as soon as they realised he was slightly up on time with only two fences to go. But as Planet landed over the second element of a pair of railway gates, he tripped and went down on his knees with his nose on the ground. Just as it looked like game over for Seamus, the Irishman picked the horse up with the reins, held him together and somehow managed to persuade him to take off over the last fence. They crossed the finish line one fifth of a second faster than Alan Oliver and Red Star.

Alan Oliver may have had a somewhat unusual style of jumping but he certainly got results. Like Ted Edgar and Harvey Smith, he was more or less self-taught, although he did at least get plenty of advice from his father, Phil. In fact, the pair of them were often referred to as Steptoe and Son. One of Phil's training

▲ ◄ (above left) Pat Smythe riding Tosca, one of her best horses in the 1950s. Pat won the Leading Show Jumper of the Year title at the first show, in 1949, and on two other occasions. She also won the Victor Ludorum (Grand Prix) twice.

▲ Tommy Wade, riding the 'power-packed midget' Dundrum, receives the Guinness Time trophy from Viscount Elveden, Chairman of Guinness, in 1962.

► Champion jockey Gordon Richards presenting his own trophy to Seamus Hayes on Planet, winners of the Gordon Richards Stakes for the second year in succession in 1952.

strategies was to place his cloth hat on the ground in front of a practice fence and make Alan place his horse's feet on the hat every time he came in to the fence. The hat would be moved nearer or farther from the fence, but wherever it was, the horse's front feet had to touch it on the stride before take-off. It was no wonder that Alan had such a brilliant eye for placing a horse at a fence.

Show jumping's popularity had shot into the stratosphere. Buoyed by the euphoria of Britain's team gold medal at the 1952 Helsinki Olympics (Wilf White with Nizefella, Duggi Steward with Aherlow and Harry Llewellyn with Foxhunter) – Britain's only gold medal of the Games – the organisers of Horse of the Year Show, now running over four days, could expect a full house for nearly every performance. Millions more were watching the show on television, albeit

ALAN OLIVER

Alan started competing as a child in the late 1940s, when children were still allowed to ride in adult classes. It was not long before he was beating some of the top adults. He developed a somewhat alarming style of throwing himself out of the saddle at take-off, but it seemed to work for him. He became a prolific winner, particularly at national level, and in 1953 claimed his first Leading Show Jumper of the Year title with Red Admiral. Eighteen years later he won again on Pitz Palu, with whom he had won the Grand Prix at HOYS from 1968 to 1970.

After a successful career in show jumping, Alan turned his attention to course designing, serving time under Jack Talbot-Ponsonby and John Gross, and designing the courses at HOYS for two years.

on 15-inch black and white screens, and the voice of Dorian Williams was becoming familiar in households up and down the country. 'We had the great advantage over other sports of being able to run live during peak viewing hours,' explained Colonel Ansell.[6] Indeed, in those early years the show frequently overran its allotted time, but if it was an exciting class, the BBC seemed reasonably happy to adjust its timetable – once to the extent of continuing HOYS coverage in place of a scheduled transmission from Brighton of a political party conference.

Press coverage was also extensive, and newspapers were falling over themselves to support major classes at the show. The Foxhunter Championship, inaugurated in 1954 to commemorate Harry Llewellyn's famous horse, was initially sponsored by the *Evening Standard* and then taken over by the *Daily Express* in 1957; there was also a Sunday Times Cup, a Daily Telegraph Cup, and a Country Life and Riding Cup. Nowadays, *Horse and Hound* has its name associated with the prestigious Foxhunter Championship, but sponsorship from newspapers is long gone.

Such was the success of the show that when the Greyhound Racing Association withdrew their financial backing after the first two years, it was not difficult to find private supporters and, anyway, the show soon began to pay its own way and return a profit for the BSJA. However, the first year without a major financial backer was not without mishap. Eight hundred tons of soil for the indoor arena

▲ Alan Oliver competing on Red Admiral. The pair won Leading Show Jumper of the Year at Harringay in 1953, when Alan was seventeen years old.

▲ Wilf White competing with Nizefella at the White City in 1958. He was a member of Britain's victorious show-jumping team at the 1952 Olympics, and won Leading Show Jumper of the Year at Harringay in 1956.

had been brought under cover a week before the opening of the show, but the night before it was due to be laid there was a flood. 'Rain poured down, drains were blocked, and although under cover, the soil became sodden,' wrote Colonel Ansell.[7] 'Our contractors laid the floor, but when David Satow [who was nearly always at Colonel Ansell's side, to guide him] and I came down a day or two before "take-off" we could hardly walk across without gumboots … Jumping started in the morning, and by four o'clock in the afternoon there hadn't been a single clear round. I was in despair.' At last, Dawn Palethorpe put the Colonel out of his misery when she managed a clear round on Earlsrath Rambler, to a great cheer from the crowd.

The arena was still a bit tacky when their Royal Highnesses Princess Elizabeth and Prince Philip attended the show on the Thursday evening, but luckily they were entertained by an exciting dual between Harry Llewellyn and Jean d'Orgeix. Even better, Harry Llewellyn came out the winner. Sitting in the royal box, Colonel Ansell was fascinated to discover that Prince Philip used opera glasses when watching the show and 'obviously missed nothing'. Four years later, when the two men met at the Badminton Horse Trials, Prince Philip commented to Colonel Ansell that he was tired of watching the youngsters 'trotting and cantering around the ring on their show ponies and obviously getting into trouble from the parents if they did not win'.[8] His suggestion was that there should be competitions for them in the form of gymkhana races, which would be much more fun and, furthermore, negate the need for a smart show pony in order to compete.

▲ Alan Oliver's younger brother Paul riding the brilliant jumping pony Kangaroo. This pony won the Leading Jumper of the Year title in 1966 and 1967 when ridden by Nicola Loffett.

This was a brilliant idea as far as Colonel Ansell was concerned. He was already struggling to find good displays to keep the audience entertained between show-jumping classes, and some of these displays were both time consuming and expensive to organise. Here was the perfect solution – create a good competition for children with no cash prizes, just rosettes, and entertain the crowds at the same time. The first Prince Philip mounted games were held at Harringay in 1957, and have subsequently taken place every year. (See Chapter Seven.)

It was clear from the start that children's competitions would be hugely popular at Harringay; there were always impressive entries in the show pony classes (unlike some of the other show classes), and the entries for Leading Juvenile Show Jumper of the Year were incredible – 175 entered in 1953. It was the popularity of show jumping that really carried the show in those first ten years, just as it still does today, although it would be fair to say that many spectators find the displays and other contests equally as exciting to watch. The showing classes, after a rather slow start at Harringay where they came close to being dropped altogether, have gradually gained momentum over the years, with more and more classes being added to the programme. The majority of spectators may not choose to watch the showing classes in their entirety, but there is certainly an interest in seeing the best horses being put through their paces in the main arena.

SHOWING

At the first HOYS, there were just four showing classes. Tony Collings wrote about the show in the 1949/1950 *Horseman's Year*:

The final feature that made 1949 a remarkable showing season was the institution of a new show of international calibre, held indoors and in London. This was the 'Horse of the Year' show at Harringay. It is primarily a show-jumping festival, but in addition there were four championship classes, all carrying with them extremely generous prize money and immense prestige. These were for the Show Hunter of the Year, won by Mighty Fine; the Hack of the Year, won by Liberty Light; the Cob of the Year, won by Knobby; and the Pony of the Year, won by Legend. In the first three classes there was a subsidiary competition for the Most Consistent Hunter, Hack and Cob of the Year, won by Unique, Liberty Light and Knobby respectively. (There was no competition for the Most Consistent Pony of the Year as it was felt that certain ponies could not have been shown throughout the summer because their young riders would, quite properly, have been at school and it would have been unfair to have penalised these to the advantage of those children who, by some means or other, appear able to miss most of their school work.)

The show pony classes were popular from the start, with big entries (there were thirty-six entries in the first year of the show). It was no great surprise that the first championship went to the chestnut pony Legend, already winner of three successive championships at the International Horse Show (1946–48), and undoubtedly the best pony on the showing scene in the late 1940s. He was bred by Mrs Ruth Howard at Huckworthy Lodge, on the edge of Dartmoor, out of a mare called Melody, and by Lyric, who was a son of Love Song. A sensitive and lively pony, he was not easy to break, but was given by Mrs Howard to her granddaughter, Elizabeth Spencer, on the child's fifth birthday – the day that the plucky little girl had finally managed to ride the four-year-old pony without being bucked off.

Legend was retired after his third win at the International, but with the announcement of the new Horse of the Year Show starting in 1949, Dick and Millicent Spencer, Elizabeth's parents, were persuaded to bring out the almost

COLONEL 'HANDY' HURRELL

An influential figure and driving force in the equestrian world, Colonel Hurrell was an instructor at the famous army centre at Weedon before the war, and was the last equestrian officer instructor at Sandhurst. He wrote the first Pony Club Handbook and was president of the Hunter Improvement Society and the Hack and Cob Society. He helped Colonel Ansell to found Horse of the Year Show in 1949, and as assistant show director took responsibility for all the show classes – a responsibility that grew bigger nearly every year as the number of classes and entries increased.

LEGEND

When I watch classes for children's ponies at the big shows I often see animals of obvious quality and excellent conformation but lacking that indescribable gaiety and friendliness which make a child's pony also a child's friend. I see show ponies and not, in the real sense of the word, children's ponies. And then I recall Legend and the magic impact of this famous pony and his young rider … though many times a champion, in recollection he seems to stand out as much for the extraordinary sense of mutual enjoyment between him and his young owner, Elizabeth Spencer, as for his lovely conformation and brilliant action. He was a true child's pony.

Extract from an article by Stella A. Walker, *Riding*, July 1956

unbeaten Legend for one final show – a decision that was well rewarded. This exceptional pony, renowned for his gaiety and natural movement, was as much liked at the indoor London show as he had been elsewhere, and the judges, Mrs Oliver Gilbey and Lieutenant Colonel J. Hume Dudgeon, had little difficulty in choosing him as champion. The Legend trophy is still presented each year at the Bath and West Show.

Legend's retirement from the show ring left the way open for Pretty Polly to make her mark at HOYS. Ridden by Davina Lee-Smith (now Davina Whiteman, chairman of Ponies UK), this lovely mare held sway at Harringay for the next two years and, through her progeny, continued to have an influence on the showing world for many more years. In 1952, Jennie Bullen (now Loriston-Clarke) claimed the Show Pony of the Year title with Royal Show, and Davina rode Pretty Polly's sister, My Pretty Maid, who was then sold to the Coates family. Gaye Coates won the championship with her in 1953 and again in 1955.

'My first memories of Harringay were of how close everyone was to the arena, especially around the entrance,' says Davina. 'I can remember coming down the shoot after winning and my father was shouting at everyone to mind their backs, as it was quite a crush. I leaned down to him and said, "Shut up, Daddy. That's my headmistress!" She and another teacher had come to support me.

'It was difficult getting from the stables to the main arena because you had to ride past the railway line, which ran just above us, so if you were on a spooky pony it was quite nerve-wracking. You had to hope that a train wouldn't come along.'

► Royal Show, ridden by Jennie Bullen, winner of the Show Pony Championship at Harringay in 1952 and 1956.

Following the 1950 show at Harringay, a letter was published in *Horse and Hound* asking why Hackney horses and ponies were not represented at Harringay. Two years later they were, and, the highly acclaimed stallion Bossy, owned by Mr and Mrs G. Kimpton and driven by James Black, a famous producer of Hackneys, took the first Hackney Pony of the Year award at Harringay. The dark-brown Bossy, only 11.2hh, was a great favourite with the crowds because of his engaging personality and presence, and because he loved applause. By Little Chief out of Ascot Belle, he was bred at Broadlands, Ascot, by Frank Minoprio, and was initially brought out by the Haydons for Mrs Barbara Harcourt-Wood. By the end of his career in 1954, he had won nearly a thousand prizes.

Frank and Cynthia Haydon had already started to make their mark on the Hackney world from their Hurstwood stud, and they went on to dominate the scene for the next thirty years (see page 63), making frequent appearances at HOYS as exhibitors and in some of the wonderful displays.

Another leading personality from this period was Count Robert Orssich who produced show hacks. He won the Hack Championship at the first HOYS with the brown gelding Liberty Light, who had been purchased earlier that season by Mrs Selwyn Butcher for 'what was rumoured to be a record price for any Show Hack'.[9] An ex-racehorse (registered as Pearl Harbour, he won twice on the flat and once over hurdles), Liberty Light was 'spotted' in the trainer's yard by

PRETTY POLLY

A 'perfectly made' pony, according to Pamela Magcregor-Morris,[3] Pretty Polly was a 14hh chestnut mare bred by Mrs S. Nicholson in County Meath; her sire, Naseel, was an Arab stallion and she was out of a Welsh mare, Gypsy Gold. As a four-year-old she won the Pony Championship at the Dublin Horse Show, and the following year, under the ownership of Mr Albert Deptford (better known at the time as a breeder of Suffolk Punches and cattle), won the R.S. Summerhays Cup for Pony of the Year at Horse of the Year Show from thirty-four entries. She retained the title in 1951, and was champion pony at the Royal Show and the International Horse Show for the next three years. Unfortunately, she could not be shown at HOYS again after 1951 because a rule was introduced (although soon rescinded) barring the previous year's champions from competing.

She did, however, return twice more to take part in the parade of champions. Stuart Hollings recalls seeing her as a brood mare in her second parade: 'I was fascinated to see this legendary pony in the flesh. She must have been about twenty-three years old, and was just being ridden for the occasion, but as soon as the spotlight went on she pricked up her ears and you could see her eyes light up. It was quite an emotional moment.'

Pretty Polly came from an exceptional family of

show ponies, and went on to create her own impressive dynasty. When she won the title at HOYS in 1951, her brother, Eureka, ridden by Janet Richardson, was second to her in her class, and her sister, My Pretty Maid, was third. Pretty Polly subsequently bred eleven foals, nine of which became champions. The Pretty Polly lines were later crossed with the famous Bwlch strain (stemming from the celebrated stallion Bwlch Valentino) creating a formidable line of show ponies. Her name lives on in the Pretty Polly Championship at the Royal International Horse Show.

Colonel Dan Corry of the Irish Army show-jumping team and then bought by Mrs Barbara Harcourt-Wood, who sent him to Count Orssich to produce. The horse won the championship again in 1950, before being usurped by Mrs F. Phelps-Penry's Festival Maid.

The Austro-Hungarian Count Orssich had arrived in England in the 1930s and, having studied under instructors from the Spanish Riding School in Vienna, he had the advantage of a far greater knowledge of classical training than the

▲ Pretty Polly ridden by Davina Lee-Smith (now Whiteman), winners of the Show Pony Championship in 1950 and 1951 at Harringay. Pretty Polly produced a dynasty of great show ponies.

average showman in Britain at that time. Count Orssich produced numerous champions, including Honeysuckle, Lucky Strike and Free as Air. Lucky Strike, ridden by Anne Davy, was Hack of the Year in 1962 and then went into show jumping, sharing the Puissance title at HOYS in 1971, ridden by Malcolm Pyrah.

The cob scene was initially dominated by Mrs Rosemary Cooke from Tetbury, who had started showing ponies in 1922 at the age of seven. She owned the grey

SERIOUS SHOWMANSHIP

Count Robert Orssich, a famous producer of hacks in the late 1940s and fifties, was a master of showmanship. In the Hack Championship at HOYS one year he was seen cantering around the ring holding his reins in one hand and twirling his show cane in the other. When he came across the middle of the arena to change legs, he threw his spinning cane up into the air, like a majorette at the front of a marching band, and caught it as it came down. His horse, unperturbed by this flamboyant display of showmanship, completed a perfect flying change and continued to canter elegantly on its way.

▲ Count Robert Orssich riding Liberty Light, champion hack at Harringay in both 1949 and 1950. Count Orssich was one of the most successful show riders of his time, and trained many top showmen and women, including Richard Ramsay.

► Former Champion Hack Lucky Strike ridden by Malcolm Pyrah. The pair jointly won the Puissance in 1971 with Piero d'Inzeo on Believe.

cob Knobby, 'an old-fashioned sort in a class of his own'.[10] Knobby won the Most Consistent Cob of the Year at the first HOYS as well as the Cob of the Year title, in the days when cobs still had docked tails. Mrs Cooke then brought out Alexander, said to have been purchased originally for £32 from a tinker at a fair in Ireland and later produced for her by Count Orssich. The smart chestnut, with four white socks, was one of the most successful show cobs in the early 1950s; he won Most Consistent Cob of the Year in 1951, and Cob of the Year in 1952, and he regularly hunted with the Duke of Beaufort's hounds. After her success with showing cobs, Mrs Cooke moved on to small hunters.

Hunters at Harringay were thin on the ground, partly because many riders objected to having a 'practical test' – a few jumps – included in the show class. In 1950, nine of the thirty-four hunter entries were presented at Harringay, and Pamela Macgregor-Morris was moved to write in *Horse and Hound*, 'One wonders if this event will be discontinued since it is so badly supported.' In 1954, it was even worse and only four hunters came forward for judging.

The emphasis at the early shows was very much on performance; the hacks did a small practical test, the hunters had a few jumps, even the ponies had a practical test. In 1951, a working hunter class and a Prix Caprilli competition (later to be called Combined Training) were introduced. Some of the horses already selected for the eventing team for the 1952 Olympic Games were entered in the Prix Caprilli, but it was won by Pat Smythe and Tosca.

◄ Rosemary Cooke with Alexander, one of the most successful cobs of the 1950s. He won at HOYS in 1952, the same year that he won the Winston Churchill Trophy at the International Horse Show.

One hunter that really made its mark at this time was the middleweight Rajah III, largely because of his outstanding versatility. Owned by Mr Ronnie Marmont, the horse had run over hurdles and, as a seven year old, won the hunt race at the North Warwickshire point-to-point. A very successful show career followed, in which he was almost unbeatable in ladies' classes. At Harringay, he was twice Most Consistent Hunter of the Year, and in 1952 won the Show Hunter of the Year title on overall points. This was the year the new scoring system was introduced and discredited, since the winner 'on the day' was High Court. However, Rajah III also won the Working Hunter title at Harringay (1951), and was generally highly regarded for his performance and character. Once, when being judged in a ladies' class by the Hon. Mrs James Baird, the side-saddle slipped round under his tummy while he was at full gallop, 'but he stopped instantly of his own accord, averting what could have been a perilous situation.'[11]

Ronnie Marmont owned many other successful show horses including the 1957 and 1958 Working Hunter champion Gowran Boy, Cufflink (Show Hunter champion in 1954) and the small hunter Burrough Hills, bred in Northamptonshire by Major R. Bourne, and often ridden by Miss Ailsa Smith-Maxwell (daughter of the hunting correspondent of *The Field*) in the days when the classes were often referred to as young people's or juvenile hunters. Burrough Hills won the Small Hunter of the Year title three years in succession, from 1957 to 1959.

During those first ten years some of the greatest early showmen of our time rode at Harringay: Norman Crow, renowned for producing top-quality young-sters and, later, ridden horses from his farm near Wellington, Shropshire; Irishman Nat Galway-Greer, who produced the prolific winners Mighty Fine

TRAMELLA

One of the most versatile horses of her era, Tramella was a successful event horse – she partnered Diana Mason to a team gold at the 1954 European Championships, which was the first time women had been allowed to compete in an international eventing championship. She was also a successful dressage horse (European team gold medal 1963), and a successful show horse. Diana Mason regularly competed on her talented 15hh mare at Horse of the Year Show. For two years in succession (1954 and 1955) they won the Combined Training title, and in 1955 they also qualified for the final of the Foxhunter Championship. In show classes, their achievements included a second in the Working Hunter, a second and third in the Small Hacks and a third in the Small Hunter.

(the first horse to win the Show Hunter of the Year title) and Mighty Atom; Count Orssich, an outstanding producer of hacks and a close rival to popular showman Harry Tatlow.

Tatlow's son, David, who followed in his father's footsteps and became a successful showman in his own right, remembers watching, as a young boy, some of great showing riders of the age. As well as Robert Orssich, he saw Sam Marsh and Harry Bonner – the latter a legendary producer of hunters. 'My father once told me that I was to watch everything that Harry Bonner did when he was in the arena. He was an artist in the show ring, and he used to produce horses in a lovely manner.' Then there were the ladies: Mrs Jane McHugh, 'one of the greatest lady producers I have every come across', who rode hunters, hacks and Arabs, and Nora Bourne, the 'queen' of side-saddle riding. A small, neat lady, she rode with such presence and poise that all eyes would be drawn to her whenever she entered a show ring.

David used to accompany his father to Harringay in their old Landrover and trailer, and after the excitement of staying up late to watch the show, he would fall asleep across the Landrover's front seat. He remembers, too, early mornings

▲ Ronnie Marmont's prolific winner Burrough Hills, seen here with Mrs Ailsa Pease (nee Smith-Maxwell) on board. He won the inaugural Riding Horse class at HOYS in 1955 (the class was later dropped from the programme), and was Champion Small Hunter from 1957 to 1959.

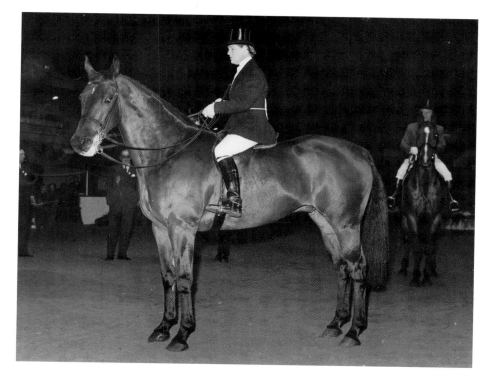

◄ Tudor Line – Middleweight Hunter of the Year and Champion Show Hunter of the year 1967. Owned by the late Mrs S. Sexton, USA; produced and ridden by Mrs Jane McHugh.

POSTMAN TAT

David Tatlow recalls going to Harringay as a child to watch his father, Harry, compete in the Hack of the Year class on a horse called Lovely Boy. 'At that time you had to perform a number of duties in the hack competition, such as posting a letter and opening a gate. I remember seeing my dad put the envelope between his teeth so he had both hands free to open the gate, before posting the letter!'

On another occasion, Harry was competing in the arena at Harringay in a Hack Pairs class, a competition in which a male and female rider teamed up to be judged as a pair, with the lady, riding side-saddle, on the left of the man. 'My father was competing with Mrs Joan Flemming,' recalls David. 'They were riding a matching pair of greys, and as they did their show together you could hear Dad telling her to turn right, and then Joan could be heard saying, "No, left Tat, left," and then he said, "No Joan! Right, turn right." They were like an old married couple having a row, and I don't think they realised we could all hear them. It was hysterical. They still won the class.'

► Robert Oliver on Catherston Credit and Sarah Bullen on Tenterk receive their award after winning the Hack Pairs Championship. These classes were once a regular feature of the show.

filled with fog like 'pea soup' as he struggled over to the stables to help prepare the horses. 'My father always said that one of the worst innovations of the showing world has been the horsebox,' says David, 'because it has ruined the social side of the show. After each performance at HOYS, everyone used to meet in the members [lounge] or in the bars or restaurants – show jumpers, showing people, driving people – so everyone got to know each other. You certainly didn't want to spend the evening in an old, leaky lorry or trailer. In those days, you often saw lorries parked with tarpaulin sheets thrown over the top of them to stop the rain coming in. There was a great sense of camaraderie.'

In fact, Harry Tatlow, who was good friends with well-known show jumper Wilf White, another farming man, was such a regular visitor to the Foxhunter Bar at Harringay that when the show moved to Wembley in 1959, the bar staff presented him with a silver whiskey measurer engraved 'To Tat, Foxhunter Lounge, 1948–1958'.

By 1958, the show was running over five days with a full programme of competitions and activities. The great thing about it was its intense atmosphere. Unlike the International Show (which gained its Royal prefix later) at the White City, where the outdoor arena was separated from the stands by the greyhound track, at Harringay spectators were indoors and were so close to the arena that the front rows were almost in touching distance of the horses. This created a tremendous sense of spectator participation, and when the crowds roared their approval of a horse and rider, or of some impressive achievement, the noise was deafening. Thus when the news came in 1958 that Harringay was to be sold as a food depot and Horse of the Year Show would have to find a new home, it was a bitter blow for the organisers and the fans. In hindsight, it was probably a blessing in disguise. Harringay had its limitations, and the show was forced to find a new and better venue. But it was not an easy task, and even as the 1958 show was being advertised as 'the last show at Harringay', it was still not known where, or even if, the 1959 show would take place.

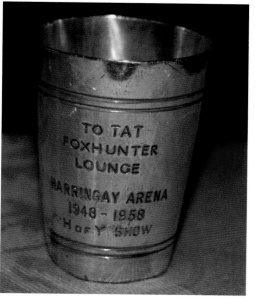

▲ The silver whiskey measurer given to Harry Tatlow by the staff of the Foxhunter Bar at Harringay.

That tenth anniversary show was 'fraught with nostalgia',[12] but produced a memorable five days of competition. Ted Williams was once again the star of the show jumping with Pegasus, retaining the Horse and Hound Cup and winning the BSJA Spurs (best national rider) for the fourth successive year. Alan Oliver topped the bill by winning the Puissance and collecting the Harringay Spurs

The finale in 1958, the last year that Horse of the Year Show was held at Harringay.

TED WILLIAMS

One of the all-time favourites, Ted Williams continued to compete into his sixties, although he would never admit his age. His numerous successes were mostly on the national circuit, and he won Leading Show Jumper of the Year at HOYS three times, in 1955, 1957 and again in 1960. His most famous partnership was with Pegasus, a horse that was only just over 15hh and ridden by Ted with exceptionally short stirrups. With this plucky little

horse Ted won the BSJA Spurs on five occasions. The BSJA Spurs were awarded to the riders gaining the greatest number of points in jumping competitions held under BSJA rules, on one horse. There was also a contest for the Harringay Spurs, presented by Garrard & Co, for the rider gaining the greatest number of points in jumping competitions held under FEI rules on two horses.

(best international rider) for the first time in his career. Over 100 horses had qualified for the Leading Show Jumper of the Year by winning £100 or more during the season, and the competition eventually ended in a draw between Pat Smythe and Ted Edgar.

Dorian Williams wrote:[13]

> The final performance at Harringay on 11 October was for many a sad occasion, but it went through just as any ordinary performance: the musical drive, the dressage display by Willie Schultheis, the Pony Club games, the parade of personalities, which that year included the palomino stallion Bubbly, three of Miss Broderick's lovely Coed Coch ponies, Pretty Polly, the Hackney pony stallion Oakwell Sir James and, for the last time, the pit ponies and the cavalcade. At the end I introduced the Duke of Norfolk, the president of the BSJA, who spoke briefly but effectively and was able finally to announce to an apprehensive public that the show would carry on the following year at Wembley.

CHAPTER TWO

HALCYON DAYS

It did not take long for the nostalgia for Harringay to be replaced by a general approval for the superior facilities at Wembley's Empire Pool, although the showing fraternity had a difficult time of it in the first year at the new venue. A prolonged drought had turned the outdoor arena into a dust-bowl, and local water conservation restrictions prohibited the organisers from watering it. The Hackney exhibitors, being closest to their horses' heels, suffered the most – apart from Cynthia Haydon, star of the driving fraternity, who dealt with the problem with her usual aplomb by wearing a pair of goggles.

Essentially, Wembley provided much more space, allowing for plenty of outdoor trade stands and a larger selection of bars and restaurants, many of them named after famous horses. There was room for a covered collecting ring, and a more spacious stable area and caravan park, which no longer resembled a 'shanty town'.[1] However, the one big drawback was that the main ring no longer had a separate entrance and exit; there was only one way in and out. This put greater pressure on the collecting-ring steward to avoid collisions between riders going into the arena and those coming out of it, particularly as the latter would often be exiting at speed and in large volume – the Household Cavalry, for example.

The first show at the new venue certainly got off to a good start. The show jumping had a strong international flavour with riders from Italy (including the reigning European champion Piero d'Inzeo, who became a regular visitor to

COLONEL SIR MIKE ANSELL

There could never be any doubt that the success of Horse of the Year Show in its first twenty-six years, and indeed the enormous popularity of British show jumping in post-war Britain, was due in large part to the drive, determination and sheer hard work of Colonel Sir Mike Ansell. He was chairman of the BSJA for nearly two decades, and of the British Horse Society for almost as long, and director of the Royal International Horse Show and Horse of the Year Show. After retiring from the latter, he became chairman of the British Equestrian Federation.

An imposing man, sometimes autocratic and dominating but usually regarded as fair, he left no stone unturned in his pursuit of perfection for Horse of the Year Show, which ran like clockwork under his control. He commanded the utmost respect from the efficient team he had brought together to help him – Captain Jack Webber, Gerald Barnes, Colonel 'Handy' Hurrell, Dorian Williams, Christopher Hall, Tom Hudson and Raymond Brooks-Ward – but there was never any doubt who was in charge. Described by Dorian Williams as a 'benevolent dictator',[1] Colonel Ansell 'towered over the whole show both in physique and authority'. Even his closest friends and colleagues sometimes forgot that he was blind.

His blindness was the result of 'friendly' gunfire during the Second World War. Retreating British troops had entered a farm building near St Valery where Colonel Ansell was already hiding with a few of his men and, thinking they were Germans, opened fire on them. Colonel Ansell was shot in the face and subsequently spent close to four years in various prisoner of war camps, finally being reunited with his wife, Victoria, at the end of 1943. Returning to his home in Bideford, Devon, and still with a little sight from the corner of one eye, he decided to set up a market garden, but in December 1944 he was drawn back into the world of equestrianism when he was persuaded to stand for chairman of the BSJA. The following year he organised the Victory Championship at the White City.

Colonel Ansell's love of horses went back to his days with the Inniskillings; he played polo for his regiment and was a successful point-to-point rider and show jumper (he used to jump a horse called Leopard without a bridle). He became his regiment's equitation officer and later attended the famous Cavalry School at Weedon. When blindness brought an end to his army career, Colonel Ansell retained his love of show jumping. It was something he had spent many hours thinking about while a prisoner of war. 'The secret was to keep oneself fully occupied,' he wrote in his memoirs.[2] 'I shall always remember lecturing [to other prisoners] on the horse show of the future, because it was then that I began putting my ideas in order to promote show-jumping as a spectator sport after the War.'

Soon after establishing Horse of the Year Show at Harringay, Colonel Ansell lost what remaining vision he had, but it never held him back. 'Being blind, I have the advantage I'm always thinking ahead, and always have my finger on my watch,' he wrote. His ears became his eyes, and he always knew what was going on. Harvey Smith has described him as the best organiser in the world. 'It was our luck that he was

◀ Colonel Mike Ansell at his desk with the miniature show jumps he used to design the early show-jumping courses.

continues ▶

blind, because it meant that the show-jumping world got the benefit of his skills. Otherwise he would probably have continued his career in the army.'

After receiving a knighthood in 1968, many people thought that Colonel Ansell might retire – he had already run the show for twenty years – but that was not something he was prepared to contemplate. If anything, it strengthened his resolve to remain in full control of the show and to give it all his energy and attention. He continued at the helm for another seven years and although there were times when his dominant personality met with dissent, few would deny it was his strength of character that had been the driving force behind the success of HOYS, and of British show jumping, for over a quarter of a century.

Michael Clayton, editor of *Horse and Hound* for twenty-three years, recalls Colonel Ansell going into the ring at the end of a big show-jumping competition, usually on the arm of David Satow, and while the presentations were being made he would quietly go down the line chatting to the riders waiting to be given rosettes. 'Oh look, dear old Mike is patting the horses,' said someone in the royal box. 'Oh no he's not,' said someone in the know. 'He's feeling behind the saddle to find out if the riders who have ridden for the British team are wearing their British team saddle-cloths. If not, they are going to be on the carpet tomorrow morning.'

Such was his grip on the show and his attention to detail that nothing got past him unnoticed. When he retired in 1975, Dorian Williams asked Ronald Duncan, the poet who had composed the 'Ode to the Horse', if he would write a tribute to Colonel Ansell, and he duly obliged:

Taller than his shadow: a man
   who is patient with servants,
   impatient only with his friends;
   we like him for his virtues,
   love him for his faults. A man
   who knows the difference between fortitude
   and courage; discipline
   and obedience. Who
   to a rude age brings a consistent gentleness.
   His perceptive hands sign kindness
   on flank, girth or flower.
   He, grateful for our sight; we for his vision.
   There is a bright candle burning in his mind.

HOYS), Holland (Harry J. Wouters van den Oudenweijer) and Ireland (Iris Kellett, Seamus Hayes and Tommy Wade). Indeed, Piero d'Inzeo won the opening class on his famous horse The Rock, finishing a clear two seconds ahead of Lady Sarah FitzAlan-Howard on her little South African polo pony Oorskiet, said to have been under 15hh. Throughout the week, d'Inzeo and the eighteen-year-old Lady Sarah, a joint winner of the European Junior Jumping Championship, were battling it out for top honours – a David and Goliath scenario that enthralled the crowds. Lady Sarah dealt the final blow to the Italian by narrowly claiming the Harringay Spurs (for the most points won in international classes), having seen off another Goliath in-the-making in the form of David Broome in the Hit and Hurry competition.

This was the year, 1959, that the Puissance wall first went up to 7 feet at HOYS (the competition was won by d'Inzeo on The Rock from Alan Oliver and Red Admiral) but, more significantly, it was also the year that Harvey Smith, 'the bricklayer from Yorkshire',[2] and David Broome first made their marks at HOYS. Nineteen-year-old David's foray into senior level at the show resulted in him winning an impressive four competitions, and initiating an outstanding career. He went on to become arguably the best show jumper in the world.

Harvey Smith had already been competing at HOYS for four years, but in 1959 he achieved his first major win by taking the Leading Show Jumper of the Year title on Farmer's Boy. Harvey Smith soon became a household name. Outspoken and sometimes outrageous, he was often the centre of attention and he brought colour and entertainment to the show-jumping world. Best known for his controversial 'V for Victory' sign in front of the members' stand at Hickstead after winning the

▲ Sarah FitzAlan-Howard competing on the diminutive Oorskiet in 1960.

DAVID BROOME

Horse of the Year Show was always a happy hunting ground for Welshman David Broome, and he has many fond memories of the show both from Harringay, where as a child he watched his father compete and also jumped ponies himself, and from Wembley where he held sway as one of the top riders for over thirty years. David's long and extremely successful career included representing Britain at six Olympic Games, bringing home individual bronze medals at two of them (Rome 1960 with Sunsalve and Mexico 1968 with Mister Softee); winning the King George V Gold Cup a record six times, becoming European champion three times, and world champion once.

His first success at HOYS came at the age of fourteen, when he won the Trial Stakes with the 13.2hh Ballan Lad. Then in 1959, the year the show moved to Wembley, David was successful in four competitions, including the Country Life and Riding

Cup and the Lonsdale Memorial Stakes (on Wildfire), which he won from two other talented young riders, Lady Sarah FitzAlan-Howard and Jane Kidd (better known now for her involvement in dressage). The following year he established himself firmly at international level by gaining the first of his two Olympic bronze medals, winning the King George V Gold Cup and then claiming the Victor Ludorum (Grand Prix) at HOYS on his Olympic horse Sunsalve. As he turned for the last three fences in the Grand Prix, the crowd suddenly became aware that is was possible for him to beat the time and 'an extraordinary crescendo of cheering started, mounting to a mighty climax as he cleared the last fence'.[3] After the presentation, David and Sunsalve embarked on a lap of honour around the Wembley arena as the band played 'Rule Britannia'. The victory helped him to

continues ▶

secure the Harringay Spurs that year, the prize for the rider gaining the most points in international classes.

From that time onwards, David was rarely out of the spotlight at HOYS. He won both the Leading Show Jumper of the Year and the Grand Prix four times – in 1981 he won them both with Mr Ross. But the highlight of his Wembley appearances came in 1975 when he entered ten competitions, won seven of them, including Leading Show Jumper of the Year and the Sunday Times Cup, and was second and third in two others. David had three outstanding horses at this time – Sportsman, Philco and Heatwave – all owned by Lady Harris. Such was David's dominance during this period that one evening while he was waiting in the arena to receive one of his many prizes, he turned to Alwyn Schockemohle, who was next in line, and said that he could not make up his mind which horse to ride in the big class the next day, Philco or Sportsman. The German rider replied that it would not matter which one David rode since he would win anyway. 'They were two of the best indoor horses of all time,' says David.

Perhaps David's worst memory of HOYS was losing out on the £25,000 first prize in the Masters competition, the first time it was staged in 1988.

It was a tough competition because the winner took all, and David, who finished in second place behind John Whitaker and Milton, came away with just £1,000 in his pocket after going five rounds in the competition on Countryman and jumping clear when the planks stood at about 5 feet 9 inches. 'I had done everything I was asked to do and I still got beaten. To be sitting on £25,000 and to lose it all did me in. It took me about eight weeks to get over that.'

In 1993 David competed at his last Horse of the Year Show. He had not made a conscious decision to retire at that stage ('I was never going to do the blubby bit,' he says) but when he won the World Cup qualifier on Millstreet shortly after HOYS that year, he sensed that it would be his last big win and that this was the twilight of his career. The following April he formally announced his retirement from international competition and sold his top horse, Lannegan. Together with two of his three sons, Matthew and James, David is now involved in running a busy equestrian centre in Wales, the David Broome Event Centre, and he is still a frequent visitor to HOYS. He is one of the best ambassadors for show jumping that the sport has ever had.

Derby there for the second successive year in 1971, he also caused a few headaches for the authorities at HOYS.

The furore over Harvey's 'V' sign was still the talking point of show jumping when Horse of the Year Show got under way the following October. Harvey began another successful trip to Wembley by winning the Cortina Crown, a class for which the winner received a red Cortina car, the second-placed rider won a blue Cortina and, of course, third place got the yellow Cortina. He then contested the Basildon Bond Championship for the Leading Show Jumper title and managed to get two horses, Mattie Brown and Evan Jones, through to the third round (only seven horses had jumped double clears to reach this stage). Alan Oliver gained a third clear round on Pitz Palu to win on time from Ann Moore and April Love, while Harvey took third with one mistake on Mattie Brown.

◄ Harvey Smith and Farmer's Boy, winners of the Leading Show Jumper of the Year title in 1959, the year the show moved to Wembley.

On Evan Jones things had gone less well, and he had knocked down each part of the treble as well as the wall. Nevertheless, Harvey elected to ride this horse for the prize giving and, as he left the arena after the presentation of awards, he jumped Evan Jones through the treble again – ostensibly to allow photographers to take a picture. According to the rules at that time, a rider was permitted to jump a fence in the arena, other than when competing, only for the benefit of photographers; but since none had availed themselves of the opportunity, and anyway Evan Jones was not in the first three, the judges ordered an enquiry.

Harvey's explanation of providing a photographic opportunity was eventually accepted, reluctantly, by the HOYS officials, but it had caused a certain amount of bad feeling among the other riders. The chairman of the rules committee, George Hobbs, winner of the Horse and Hound Cup at Wembley that year, lodged an objection to the decision, and the story rumbled on in the press for sometime after the show had ended, although Harvey was eventually let off the hook.

Harvey was not the only person to cause trouble at HOYS. In the 1960s some riders were upset by the 'related distances' in the show jumping, introduced with

HARVEY SMITH

One of the most colourful characters on the show-jumping circuit, Yorkshireman Harvey Smith was at the top of the sport for nearly three decades. Self-taught as a rider, and a natural self-publicist, he was often regarded as a troublesome rebel by the sport's authorities, but there was no doubting his talent and his keen competitive instincts. Initially, he came to the public's attention as the best-placed British rider in the King's Cup at Hickstead in 1958, but his first major win was at HOYS the following year when he claimed the Leading Show Jumper of the Year title on Farmer's Boy, a horse he had bought for £40 at York sales.

He was a member of Britain's Olympic team in 1968 and 1972, and won a bronze medal at the world championships in 1970, as well as two silver medals and a bronze at European championships. He won the Hickstead Derby four times.

A master of Puissance competitions, Harvey made history at HOYS by twice sharing first prize with himself. The first time this happened was in 1962, when both O'Malley and Warpaint cleared the wall at 6 feet 11 inches. The second time was in 1967 (the same year that Harvey claimed his third Leading Show Jumper title) with Harvester and O'Malley. The wall was put up to 7 feet 2 inches and five riders attempted it, but none succeeded in clearing it. Harvey's horses both collected four faults for a knock down, as did Fritz Ligges' horse Weisel, so the three of them shared first prize. Harvey took first and second place in the HOYS Puissance in 1970 and won it on two further occasions.

► Robert Hanson, owner of many good show jumpers and show horses, with Harvey Smith, on O'Malley, and Anneli Drummond-Hay, riding Merely-a-Monarch, the horse she took show jumping having won the Burghley three-day event on him in 1961 and Badminton in 1962.

JUMPING ON ICE

'Harvey Smith, who has a habit of putting his foot in it, fell through the floor of the Wembley stadium last night,' wrote Colin Hart in the *Sun* in October 1969. In fact, it was Harvey's horse that had put its feet through the wooden boards covering the ice rink during the opening class of the show. Luckily, the horse was unharmed by the incident, and Colonel Ansell immediately decided to make Harvey a joint winner of the class as compensation for the mishap.

varying degrees of success by Colonel Jack Talbot-Ponsonby, the course designer at Wembley, who at least had the foresight to realise the need to make the tracks more testing without simply building the fences higher and higher. His courses certainly proved more difficult, partly because riders and horses were not used to coping with so many fences in such a small arena, and partly because it took a little while for Colonel Talbot-Ponsonby to perfect the distances. Nonetheless, most competitors accepted that this course designing technique was the way forward.

One rider who was particularly unhappy with the designs was Douglas Bunn, owner of Hickstead. He was so appalled by the difficulty of the courses at the 1967 Horse of the Year Show that he left Wembley in protest, taking his top horse Beethoven with him and later commenting to the press that if Colonel Talbot-Ponsonby tried to ride his own courses, he would be in hospital within a week –

▼ Douglas Bunn competing on Beethoven, the horse he took home from the 1967 HOYS in protest at the difficulty of the show-jumping courses. Beethoven was later ridden by David Broome, who won the World Championship on him in 1970.

or in the cemetery. 'He insists on placing all those obstacles in the ring, yet the riders know a lot more about this than he does …'[3]

Unfortunately for Douglas Bunn, not many of the other riders agreed with him. Hans Winkler (the German Olympic gold medallist) said the courses were 'difficult but fair' and horses did need to be 'absolutely under control'.[4] Jack Talbot-Ponsonby, who died in a hunting accident two years after this incident, had been a successful show jumper himself, winning the King George V Gold Cup three times, so Douglas Bunn's objections were not taken too seriously. Dorian Williams, writing under the pseudonym of Loriner in *Horse and Hound*, even penned a short poem about the incident:

> Bunn, Bunn, away he's run
> Censoring T.P.'s courses.
> 'Problems related',
> He's angrily stated,
> Aren't suited to Bunnworthy horses.
>
> But the 'problems' involved
> Jack says can be solved,
> And I say it can't be too soon!
> So will someone instruct
> Maestro Bunn to conduct
> His Beethoven less out of Tune?

There were more problems for the authorities the following year when Ted Edgar caused a stir late one night at HOYS by hitting fellow competitor Norton Brooks over the head with a bottle, knocking him out cold. Alan Smith, writing for the *Daily Telegraph* at that time, recalls the incident:

> After the show had finished each evening we would often go back to someone's caravan for a drink. On this particular night, Colin Hart [from the *Sun*], Jenny Murphy [the *Observer*] and I were having a glass or two in Alison Westwood's caravan when Alan Oliver came rushing in demanding a blanket. We all followed him out of the caravan to find a large group of people surrounding poor Norton Brooks who was lying unconscious on the floor with his head bleeding, having been hit over the head with a bottle by Ted Edgar, who thought Norton was chatting up his wife, Liz.

I remember Dr Nichols, the show doctor, was going around telling everyone to keep quiet about it. 'We don't want the press to hear about this,' he said. Colin, Jenny and I looked at each other, but we agreed that, as it was already three o'clock in the morning, we wouldn't attempt to get the story into our late editions. Of course, it did come out eventually, and Ted was suspended for at least six months.

There were few high-profile controversies in the showing world; it was more a case of quiet rumblings about the points system of judging, the dust and the footing in the outdoor arena, despite the stoic efforts of the showing steward Colonel 'Handy' Hurrell to provide good going. In 1962, two top middleweight hunters, Marksman and Spencer, both had to withdraw from the final judging after they had come off the outdoor arena lame, and in 1969 the dust was so bad that the preliminary in-hand judging took place on the concrete, a policy that was to continue until 2003. More drama occurred in 1975, when the middleweight Dublin champion Gralla slipped up on the sand in the outdoor arena, deposited his rider and proceeded to buck his way around the ring until he was finally caught. Worse was to follow when Seta Pike was led from the ring with the sole of his foot pumping blood at an alarming rate. The going could not be blamed for this accident, however, since it transpired that his foot had been badly cut by a shoe cast by a horse in the preceding lightweight class.

It was remarkable what the showing fraternity put up with in order to compete at Wembley – plaiting ponies in the dark for early morning classes, cramped accommodation for horses and grooms, and in 1974 the ongoing building developments at Wembley made things even worse. With nowhere for the show horses to exercise, it was question of walking around on the concrete in front of the arena among the cars and buses, or riding around the caravan park and dodging the dumper trucks and cranes. 'Tub' Ivens, one of the most successful showmen of his time, kept his horses in the horsebox for three nights rather than use the stabling, even though he had already paid for it. He was at least compensated for the inconvenience by winning the Lloyds Bank In-Hand championship that year with Sammy Dasher.

The showing world at HOYS continued to expand. In 1965, one of the new classes was the Fredericks In-hand Championship, which brought together qualifiers from all the different classes to find the supreme in-hand champion of the year, irrespective of breed or type. There were nine entries in the first year,

▶ Sammy Dasher, shown by 'Tub' Ivens, won the Lloyds Bank In-hand Championship in 1974. That year, building developments at Wembley caused problems for the showing fraternity.

▼ Mary Rose Peddie with Arden Tittle Tattle, winners of the Show Pony Championship in 1959 and 1960.

including two pony mares exhibited by Lieutenant Colonel Williams-Wynn from the famous Coed Coch Pony stud in North Wales, and the successful show pony Arden Tittle Tattle (now ten years old), who finished reserve to first-ever in-hand champion Prince's Grace. This 16.2hh hunter mare by Prince's Game was bred by Rex Chappell from Lincolnshire and exhibited by Mrs A. Wood from Chaddesley Corbett in Worcestershire, who collected £100 first prize and a trophy.

From the start, the new championship evoked a great deal of controversy. Many people claimed it was impossible to ask a judge to select the best in-hand exhibit from a line-up of such diverse types, for example a Welsh Section A, a young hunter, an Arab stallion and show pony brood mare. The same problem still remains, although the final classes are now split between horses and ponies, but it is nonetheless a popular competition, and serves to create greater interest in the breeding classes. It is unlikely that some of the in-hand classes at county shows would survive today if they were not HOYS qualifiers.

One of the first stars to emerge from the in-hand competition was Colonel Rosser John's Treharne Tomboy, a Section A shown by David Reynolds. He won in both 1968 and 1969, the last year that the competition was held until it was resurrected three years later as the Lloyds In-hand Championship. Other dual winners include the pony Rosevean Eagle Hill, who won as a yearling and again as a three year old; Llanarth Flying Comet, the Welsh Section D, who won in 1979 and 1980; and the outstanding hunter mare, Hunting Eve, owned by Miss A. Murray and shown by John Rawding, who won three years in succession from 1987 to 1989. (See Chapter Three.)

CYNTHIA HAYDON

In the world of driving, Cynthia Haydon will never be forgotten. Her skills as a whip were unmatched and her success in the show ring unrivalled. A stylist and a perfectionist, her horses were always immaculately turned out, well schooled and moving beautifully, whether in single harness, pairs, tandems, unicorns or four-in-hand. Few have matched her flair and expertise as a driver or as a breeder and trainer of Hackneys.

In the early seventies, Mrs Haydon took part in the early combined driving competitions, and with a team of four Hackneys competed in the first FEI world championships in Munster, Germany (1972). She was the only woman at the championships, and she competed on the British team, which, with Douglas Nicholson and Sir John Miller, won the gold medal. After another successful world championships in 1974, Mrs Haydon decided to call it a day in this demanding sport, which she described as having no 'artistry', and to concentrate instead on showing. She was fifty-six years old.

Working with Hackneys had become a way of life for Cynthia Haydon from the time when, as a small child in York, she would sit with her uncle as he drove his horses. She left boarding school at sixteen because she was always bottom of the class and 'my father got fed up with paying the fees'.[4] Her father was Robert Black, the leading professional Hackney trainer in England at that time, and Cynthia met her husband Frank when two of his horses came to the Black's yard to be trained and produced.

After the war, there was a growing interest in Hackneys, born out of their use as harness horses to offset petrol shortages. The Haydons already had a small nucleus of good horses and people began contacting them for advice. It was not long before the Hackney business took over, and Frank Haydon's organisational flair and energy found a new direction (his first career was as a master butcher with a small chain of shops). The success of the Hurstwood stud in breeding good-quality horses and in producing them to the highest standards was brought to the attention of a wider audience by the brilliant driving and showing skills of Cynthia Haydon. She won the Supreme Champion Harness Horse at the National Hackney Horse Show no fewer than thirty times, and the Supreme Champion Harness Pony twenty-nine times. In 1984 she was awarded the MBE.

Cynthia Haydon was a regular winner at HOYS, but will probably be best remembered for some of the wonderful displays put on by her driving teams. She was the 'raffish and dashing'[5] Lady Scattercash in the 1964 production of 'Jorrocks Rides Again', nonchalantly smoking a large cigar as she drove a pair of hackneys. In 1969, she led the popular Hackney Ride and Drive, and the following year she and Frank produced the memorable Hackney quadrille. The Haydons were renowned for their friendly hospitality, and their presence in the Wembley arena could always be relied upon to heighten the atmosphere of the show.

► A cartoon of Cynthia Haydon, one of the world's greatest whips and an enormous influence on the Hackney scene. She had a penchant for cigars.

'Setting the Style'

▲ Jane Soutar on the 1967 Champion Pony, Favorita, owned by Alicia Stubbings. Jane was one of three people who rode champion ponies at HOYS and who later went on to win the Burghley Horse Trials.

Arden Tittle Tattle was one of the top show ponies of her time. Owned by Miss Coates and Miss Stubbings, and ridden by Mary Rose Peddie, she was HOYS champion in 1959 and 1960. There was a triumphant moment for the pony breeder Glenda Spooner when the 13.2hh Arden Tittle Tattle won her first HOYS title, for in reserve place for the second year was Arden Bronze, and both these ponies were by Mrs Spooner's stallion Ardencaple, who had pulled off a similar double the previous year when Enoch Arden took top honours. Ardencaple also sired some successful hacks, including Rio Grande.

Another top pony was Gems Signet, a champion both in-hand and under saddle. He won the Pony of the Year title in 1971 when ridden by Sophie Waddilove. Bred by Albert Deptford out of Polly's Gem, a daughter of Pretty Polly by Bwlch Valentino, he stood at stud as a three year old and was then gelded and sold as a ridden show pony for a record £8,000. The alliance that Albert Deptford had instigated between the Pretty Polly family and Nell Pennell's Bwlch strain created an almost unbeatable dynasty during the 1960s and seventies.

Famous names of the future were emerging among the riders on the show pony scene at this time, including three riders who would go on to win at the Burghley Horse Trials: Judy Bradwell, who rode the grey pony Creden Lucky Charm, HOYS champion in 1964; Jane Soutar (now Wallace), who rode the champion Favorita in 1967; and Aly Pattinson, who rode the 1963 champion Pollyanna. Jane Soutar rode ponies for Davina Whiteman for nine years, and she recalls the high profile that these classes had in the sixties. Pony champions would often make headline news in the sports pages of the *Telegraph*, and their young jockeys enjoyed enormous kudos. 'It was a wonderful grounding in learning how to present a pony immaculately, and to cope with a big occasion,' says Jane.

There was even greater kudos for Nigel Hollings (current chairman of the British Show Horse Association) when he won the Pony Championship on Snailwell Charles in 1972, as he was the first boy ever to claim the title. As youngsters, both Nigel and his older brother Stuart were based for about four years with Davina Whiteman, one of the top producers of show ponies.

'We had such fun at Davina's,' recalls Stuart. 'And we were lucky to have the opportunity to watch and listen to some of the great showmen of our time – Vin Toulson, Roy Trigg and Harry Tatlow.' The two boys would spend all summer at Davina's yard in Leicester, riding ponies and going to shows – and causing trouble for Mrs Lee-Smith, Davina's mother. 'We used to hate salads,' recalls Stuart, 'so whenever we were given salad for lunch we would chuck it out of the kitchen window when no one was looking. I think the sheep in the field next to the kitchen got to know that whenever the window opened there would be some food coming out, because one day Mrs Lee-Smith opened the window to empty some crumbs out of her apron and a big sheep with horrible yellow eyes jumped up at her and caught its front feet in her apron pocket. You should have heard the scream!'

◄ Snailwell Charles ridden by Nigel Hollings, who, in 1972, became the first boy to win the Pony Championship at HOYS, and was awarded a gold Blue Peter badge.

A BLUE PETER BADGE

At the age of twelve Nigel Hollings became the first boy to win the Show Pony Championship at HOYS, twenty-three years after the show first began. It was a momentous occasion and received an enormous amount of publicity. Nigel was awarded a gold Blue Peter badge for his achievement. 'I don't think I really appreciated what it all meant at the time,' says Nigel, who can remember being absolutely terrified when he was called forward to receive his award on Snailwell Charles. But it was clearly destiny. Nigel and his brother Stuart were based with Davina Whiteman at the time, and Davina's groom had held a séance with the boys before the show, in which an upside-down eggcup had glided across her coffee table to spell out Nigel's impending win. Furthermore, driving down to Wembley with Davina, a stranger in a left-hand-drive car had pulled alongside Davina's car on the motorway, lowered his window and handed her a rose, which she took as a good omen.

The hullabaloo that surrounded his win in 1972 certainly gave Nigel some street cred at home, where he received a special achievement award from his town council, and his success was splashed across the front pages of the local newspaper. He was eventually brought back down to earth one morning as he was travelling on the school bus to Clitheroe Grammar. Some girls in the year above him were messing about on the bus, and one of them took an exercise book out of his school bag, looked at the name on the front cover, and asked him, 'Why have you got Nigel Hollings' book in your bag?' 'Because I am Nigel Hollings,' came the reply from the shy twelve year old. 'What! A little squirt like you? You won Horse of the Year Show?'

Since those early days, Nigel and Stuart (a regular contributor to *Horse and Hound*) have gone on to become very successful producers themselves. Nigel won the Riding Horse of the Year with Fair Breeze in 1989, also claiming the Champion of Champions title, judged that year by David Broome. They have produced many successful ponies, both in-hand and under saddle, and continue to be very involved in the pony world. In 2003, thirty-one years after Nigel won the Show Pony Championship, his daughter Alexandra won two pony titles at HOYS, the Mini (lead rein) Mountain and Moorland and the Mini Show Pony Championships.

The Cob Championship at HOYS was dominated in the sixties and early seventies by two great cobs, Sport and Jonathon, who between them collected ten HOYS titles out of a possible twelve from 1962 to 1973. Sport, a grey gelding who won in Dublin before being purchased by Mrs Z. Clark, gained six of them – a record equalled only by Super Ted in the eighties and nineties. Then Roy Trigg started to make his mark on the cob world when he produced the grey Jonathon for Mrs A. Baldry, winner of the Wembley title four times. Later, he produced champions Huggy Bear and Just William, the latter being owned by top race-horse trainer John Dunlop.

By the sixties the hunter classes at HOYS had become very competitive, with entries having increased enormously since the early days of the show and a

◄ Prolific winner Sport, owned by Mrs Z. Clark, was Cob of the Year six times, a record equalled only by Super Ted.

◄ Mrs A. Baldry's Jonathon, four-times winner of the Cob of the Year title, ridden by Roy Trigg.

Wembley title becoming the most sought-after accolade (due, to some extent, to generous sponsorship of the classes). The 17hh heavyweight Gold Dust, owned by Major C.S. Drabble, stormed onto the hunter scene in 1960, winning the HOYS title – his eighth successive championship of the season, having been unbeaten since arriving from Ireland the previous year.

Producer Bill Bryan was in his heyday, collecting the HOYS title for two years in a row (1963 and 1964) with the ex-point-to-point horse Romeo VI, owned by Mrs P. Morris. In 1963, he had also headed the class of heavyweights with five-year-old Killala, having produced both horses from his yard in Herefordshire. Killala won the heavyweight classes three times during the early sixties. Norman Crow was still a major exhibitor of hunters, and won the HOYS championship twice on Top Notch (1969 and 1970), and then hunted the horse three days a fortnight with the North Shropshire until Top Notch was twenty. Roy Trigg was also very successful, winning the Show Hunter of the Year title twice with Admiral (1971 and 1972), and in 1973 Vin Toulson first made his mark at Wembley by winning two championships, Show Hunter with Prince's Street and Small Hunter with Sporting Print – an indication of his impending supremacy in the hunter world.

► Norman Crow's Top Notch, Champion Hunter in 1969 and 1970.

BILL BRYAN

An outstanding showman and a delightful character, Bill Bryan was a regular attendee of HOYS from the show's inception until he retired in 2003. His highlights included winning two Show Hunter of the Year titles with Romeo V in 1963 and 1964, and one with The Showman in 1996, on which he also won the Champion of Champions award. To celebrate the show's golden jubilee in 1998, he won the Small Hunter of the Year with Toy Boy.

Born in 1928, Bill's first job was at Rolf Blakeway's yard, where he would ride and groom the horses for five shillings a week, and although the work was mostly in hunting and show jumping, Bill did get the opportunity to do some showing and won his first hunter class at Moreton-in-the-Marsh in 1945. He later moved to John Tilke's yard and whipped-in for the West Warwickshire, and then set up his own yard at Doreston in Herefordshire, from where his seven children all learnt to ride, and where Leslie Law (Olympic gold medallist in eventing) had his first job. As a student at the local agricultural college, Robert Oliver also took every opportunity to work at Bill's yard and learn from him.

Leslie Law, who was a great friend of Bill's son Willy, remembers the fun they had at the yard. 'Willy and I were riding up to ten horses a day; point-to-pointers, show horses, hunters, youngsters, all sorts. We got plenty of good advice from Bill, and plenty of bollockings as well, and learnt a lot by watching him.'[6] Bill loved hunting and loved working with horses, but most of all it was the showing that kept him going. He described showing as being like a fever – 'the high you get when you are winning is addictive.'

◀ Bill Bryan receives his award from Mr and Mrs Hall after winning the Small Hunter Championship on Jill Ashmole's Toy Boy in 1998.

▲ Harry Tatlow rides Miss de Beaumont's Juniper, Champion Hack in 1960.

Ronnie Marmont's outstanding small hunter, Burrough Hills, won his third and final HOYS title in 1959, the first year the show was held at Wembley. 'He remains the prototype,' wrote Pamela Macgregor-Morris, 'and we may not see the like for some considerable time.' Subsequently, Some Gardener, owned by Mrs Rosemary Cooke, also won the title three times, but not in succession.

The hack scene was largely dominated by David Tatlow, who produced, among others, Mrs B. Samwell's Lady Teller. This mare reigned supreme at HOYS from 1968 to 1970, until her place was taken by Right Royal.

Another very successful producer of hacks was Jennie Loriston-Clarke (then Jennie Bullen), who graduated from ponies to hacks by producing the sensational five-year-old Desert Storm to claim the HOYS title in 1959, and again in 1961. Desert Storm went on to become a successful dressage horse for Jennie, but many more top hacks, riding horses and combined training horses were brought out by Jennie in the sixties and seventies. Jennie also produced Tenterk as a four-year-old, before this successful hack went to Robert Oliver.

▲ Alicia Stubbings, owner of many good show horses and ponies, stands with her Champion Hack Desert Storm, ridden by Jennie Bullen.

Event riders were involved with HOYS through the Spillers Combined Training Championship which, due to its popularity, had been split into novice and open sections. In 1972, one of the contenders in the open class was Mary Gordon Watson on her world champion horse Cornishman, but the class was won by Jennie Loriston-Clarke, riding the stallion Xenocles. Jennie had also been competing at the world championship, in dressage. Combined training was generally dominated by event and dressage competitors, including Pamela Sivewright, Mark Phillips, Richard Walker and Anneli Drummond-Hay, who turned her hand to show jumping after a very successful career in eventing with Merely-a-Monarch.

Mary Gordon Watson and Cornishman also competed in working hunter classes and in 1969, when the pair were already European eventing champions, Cornishman stood second in the Working Hunter Championship to a 'nice

RIGHT ROYAL

A record-holding hack, Right Royal is the only horse to have won the Hack title at HOYS for four years in succession, from 1971 to 1974, and each time with a different rider. Initially produced as a novice by David Tatlow, he was bought by Mr and Mrs Spencer-Cox and shown by their daughter Vicky to win his first HOYS title. After that, he was bought by Marjorie and Richard Ramsay, but shown by Vera Holden to win his second title. Marjorie Ramsay rode him in 1973, and the following year, having been sold to Fiona O'Neill, but still produced from the Ramsay's yard, Right Royal won the championship for the last time when piloted by Fiona. A bay thoroughbred by V-Ray, Right Royal was a large hack with an even bigger personality. 'He used to walk into the show ring like a film star,' recalls Richard Ramsay. 'He had amazing presence.'

◄ Marjorie Ramsay and Right Royal, winner of the Hack Championship for four years in a row, from 1971 to 1974, each time with a different rider.

brown four-year-old from Cumberland'⁵ called Goodwill. This was the horse that was later partnered by HRH Princess Anne.

Between 1959 and Mike Ansell's retirement in 1975, Horse of the Year Show played host to some of the most memorable names in show jumping – Alan Oliver, Seamus Hayes, Ted Williams and Pat Smythe were still competing in the early days at Wembley, while David Broome, Harvey Smith, Ted and Liz Edgar, Paddy McMahon, Anneli Drummond-Hay, Alison Dawes, Marion Coakes and

► Goodwill, winner of the Working Hunter title in 1969 when owned by Reta Burch. The horse was subsequently bought for Princess Anne, who won the Combined Training on him in 1973, and rode him to an individual silver medal at the 1975 European eventing championship.

PRINCESS ANNE

Princess Anne made an early competitive appearance at Horse of the Year Show when in 1968, she took part in the riding club quadrilles, coming second with her team from the Battle and District Riding Club. Then in 1971, the year she won the European championship with Doublet, she joined in the parade of champions at Wembley, together with Ann Moore, winner of the European show-jumping title. In 1973, Princess Anne won the Spillers Open Combined Training competition on Goodwill, and she was also third with Doublet, while Lorna Clarke took second place on Peer Gynt. The dressage phase of the competition was held at Syon Park, and the jumping took place at Wembley. Two years later, Princess Anne and Goodwill won an individual silver medal at the 1975 European championships. Trevor Banks had spotted Goodwill when the horse won the Working Hunter title from Mary Gordon Watson's

Cornishman in 1969, and bought him for Princess Anne. HRH the Princess Royal is still a regular visitor to Horse of the Year Show and has made many presentations there.

▲ Princess Anne with Colonel Mike Ansell at Horse of the Year Show's twenty-first birthday party in 1969.

Ann Moore were all coming along to challenge the old guard; and by 1975 the talents of the two young Whitaker brothers, Michael and John, were just beginning to emerge.

David Broome was immensely popular with both the spectators and his fellow competitors, but the real 'darlings' of the crowd were Ann Moore and Marion Mould (née Coakes) with her remarkable horse Stroller. Ann Moore's success on the international stage – she was ladies' European champion in 1971 and 1973, and Olympic silver medallist in 1972 – brought her to the forefront of the sport, and her victory with Psalm in the Leading Show Jumper of the Year competition at HOYS shortly after her Olympic success was well received.

Some notable overseas riders competed at Wembley in the sixties and early seventies, among them Ireland's Paddy McMahon (1972 Grand Prix winner on Pennwood Forge Mill); Brazilian Nelson Pessoa, winner of the Harringay Spurs in 1963; Swiss rider Hugo Simon; and top German riders Alwyn Schockemohle, Hans Winkler and Hendrik Snoek. Indeed, by the 1970s the foreign contingent was beginning to get the upper hand, and in 1972, German riders won five of the eight international classes. It was left largely to the women to keep the lid on the Germans' success. Besides Ann Moore claiming the Leading Show Jumper of the Year title, a young Caroline Bradley won the Gordon Richards Stakes.

It was a golden era for the horse world; as well as the individual Olympic medals won in show jumping by David Broome, Ann Moore, Marion Coakes and Peter Robeson between 1960 and 1972, Britain's event riders collected an individual gold and two team Olympic gold medals over the same period. In 1972, show

---

ABSENT WITHOUT LEAVE

'John Simms, from New Eastwood, Notts, won the junior jumper title on Ki-Ming and then dealt with a horde of pressmen with formidable sang-froid, almost disconcerting in one of 14 years. He should go far, but now it was only as far as the water trough, where his contemporaries dumped him after carrying him on their shoulders from the collecting ring. Absent without leave from school, his headmaster saw his triumph on television: but the message that came down to Wembley was not one of congratulation.'

Horse and Hound 1969

jumping was said to be the second most popular sport on television (according to a survey by *The Field*); sponsorships were increasing for both riders and competitions – Rothmans, Spillers and Phillips Electrical (with a colour television as first prize) were among HOYS' many supporters – and tickets for Horse of the Year Show Ball (£4.50 for dinner and dancing in the Park Lane Hilton Hotel) were quickly snatched up. Colonel Mike Ansell retired at the end of the 1975 show, having established and presided over one of the best events on the sporting calendar.

▶ David Broome at the 1960 Olympic Games in Rome, where he won the individual bronze medal. With him on the podium are the d'Inzeo brothers from Italy.

LORD HARRIS

Owner of the Carpetright Company, Lord Harris was a long-term supporter of David Broome and provided him with many outstanding horses, including Philco and Sportsman, which Lord Harris often chose himself. Lord Harris has been involved in the sport for some fifty years, having initially owned horses ridden by David Barker and George Hobbs, and he is still one of show jumping's leading owners.

He has owned horses such as Monsanto and Midnight Madness (ridden by Michael Whitaker) and Hopes Are High (Nick Skelton), and in 2009 he bought Hello Sailor and Hello Dandy for Tina Fletcher to ride, followed by the purchase of Unique in 2010. 'He has been the best supporter of British show jumping of all time,' says David. 'He has had so many good horses.'

MARION MOULD AND STROLLER

Probably the smallest partnership in the history of international show jumping and certainly a legendary one, Marion and the 14.2hh Irish-bred Stroller began their remarkable career on junior teams – collecting a team gold and a team silver at European championships – before taking on the seniors at the highest level. Their victories include the Hickstead Derby in 1967, an individual silver medal at the Mexico Olympics (1968), the Queen's Cup (1965 and 1971), the first Ladies' World Championship (1965) and the Hamburg Derby in 1970. At Horse of the Year Show, they won the Sunday Times Cup for two years in succession (1966 and 1967) and the Leading Show Jumper of the Year title in 1970. The following year they won the Country Life and Riding Cup – Stroller's last competition before retiring.

► The legendary Stroller and Marion Mould.

AN EDITOR REMEMBERS

Michael Clayton, editor of *Horse and Hound* from 1974 to 1997, has many memories of Horse of the Year Show. His earliest are from his days as a staff reporter for the *London Evening News*, when the heavy horses were led to the Harringay arena through the streets of London, having been unloaded at one of the railway stations. When he became editor of *Horse and Hound*, Michael realised that 'Horse of the Year Show was a marvellous opportunity to keep my finger on the pulse of the showing and show-jumping worlds … HOYS was the climax of the year's showing, and attending every day meant I had a good opportunity to meet people and see the top end of showing and show jumping at its best. The dinner table [in the viewing restaurant at Wembley] also gave me a great opportunity to entertain significant guests – including some of the leading executives of IPC, owners of *Horse and Hound*, and the largest magazine publishers in Europe. Giving them some idea of the status of *Horse and Hound* was a great help to the editor.

'For me, it was a wearing but enjoyable week, working every day in the office, then changing into a dinner jacket (in the office) and driving to Wembley through the home-going traffic to entertain "whoever" all evening at the show. I was surprised to find that Bob Dean, founder and chairman of British Equestrian Promotions, and formerly head of the advertising company Pearl and Dean, acted as a sort of unofficial "head waiter". He loved going around the tables checking that everyone was happy, and he enjoyed organising the table plans each night to ensure that the great and good were given the best tables, which meant being in the front row. I'm not sure this was always

▲ Michael Clayton, editor of *Horse and Hound* from 1974 to 1997, and Di Lampard of British Showjumping, judging the Supreme Horse of the Show in 2005.

a benefit because the dust from the arena could kick up into your soup! Colonel Mike Ansell, Dorian Williams and Raymond Brooks-Ward also "worked the tables" during the evening, and I'm sure it all helped enormously in making the viewing restaurant a desirable ticket, and in creating new sponsorships.'

TRAIN JOURNEYS AND THE BUTLIN CONNECTION

Colonel Ansell seemed to have a penchant for getting deals done on trains, and he certainly never let an opportunity pass by. In 1954, when travelling with his friend, the poet and playwright Ronald Duncan, on one of his many train journeys to his home in Devon, Colonel Ansell asked the writer if he could compose a tribute to the horse that could be read out at the end of each finale, to bring Horse of the Year Show to a close. By the end of their journey, Ronald Duncan had composed the now famous 'Ode to the Horse', which is still read out every year at the end of the last performance.

Early in 1963, on another train journey home from London, Colonel Ansell met by chance Sir William Butlin, owner of the burgeoning Butlin's holiday camps business. It did not take long for Mike Ansell to raise the subject of show jumping and lay the foundations for what was to become a major involvement by Butlin's in the show-jumping world. Within a month of that train journey, a meeting was arranged at the BSJA office in Bedford Square with Colonel Ansell, Captain Jack Webber, Raymond Brooks-Ward, Major Reg Whitehead (well-known course builder) and Ron Hayter, the general manager of entertainment for Butlin's.

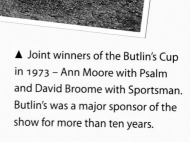

▲ Joint winners of the Butlin's Cup in 1973 – Ann Moore with Psalm and David Broome with Sportsman. Butlin's was a major sponsor of the show for more than ten years.

The first Butlin's Horse Show took place at Pwllheli during the Whitsun holiday later that year, and more followed in the summer at Minehead, Filey, Skegness, Clacton and Mosney in Ireland. The last two competitions at each show – the Butlin Championship and the Butlin Have-a-Gamble – acted as qualifiers for Wembley. The first night of HOYS became known for a while as the Butlin Gala Night, with proceeds going to the Army Benevolent Fund, and the company also sponsored the Pony Club mounted games, making it one of most significant sponsorships in show jumping at that time.

CHAPTER THREE

CHANGING FORTUNES

By 1975, there were already some signs that show jumping's popularity was on the wane but there was little else to indicate that, within twenty years, HOYS would come perilously close to being lost. The show was still enormously popular, both with spectators and competitors, and ticket sales were buoyant. It was when television and sponsorships, which had an enormous influence on the commercial success of the show and upon which HOYS had become increasingly reliant for its own future, began to withdraw their support because of the continuing loss of interest in show jumping, that the show hit hard times.

This was a gradual process, however, and initially the show continued successfully. John Stevens, a talented musician and actor as well as equestrian enthusiast, took over from Mike Ansell as the new director in 1976 and, although there were a few hiccups that year – Harvey Smith fell off while competing in the Dick Turpin Stakes and had to have three stitches in his face; one of the Pony Club riders fell off in the collecting ring and broke her leg; and some of the show jumpers went on strike over the size of the course that had been built for the Horse and Hound Cup (probably something they would not have dared to do when Colonel Ansell was in charge) – nonetheless the show still attracted full houses on most of the days. But the problems brewing for show jumping were to have a devastating effect on Horse of the Year Show. The BBC, encouraged by the excellent viewing figures for show jumping in the 1950s and sixties, had gone into overkill, as it did for snooker years later. Hickstead, the Royal International

Horse Show, a new show at Birmingham, Horse of the Year Show and Olympia were all being televised. So it was hardly surprising that people were beginning to tire of seeing 'the same dull faces, doing the same dull thing with dull commentaries', as Harvey Smith described it.[1]

By the early 1980s, show jumping was becoming a victim of its own success. Its popularity and its exposure on television had made it increasingly commercial, and big money had been pouring in by way of sponsorships for the riders as well as for competitions. But the sponsors expected a return on their investment; thus the best riders were under constant pressure to come up with good results to keep their sponsors happy. On the other hand, because they had financial backing, these same riders were able to afford a string of good horses, which kept them consistently in the

▲ Ted Edgar gives vet John Brazier a lift at the 1985 show.

► Liz Edgar on her brilliant horse Everest Forever in 1985. Ted and Liz Edgar were sponsored for many years by Everest Double Glazing (also supporters of HOYS), and they trained some outstanding riders from their yard in Warwickshire.

prizes. The top end of the sport soon became a closed shop, and it was very diffi-cult for new faces to break through into the 'magic circle'.[2]

The same group of riders were appearing endlessly on television screens, and although Harvey Smith and David Broome were still competing, there seemed to be no new emerging 'characters' in the sport. Show jumping was a more serious matter these days. A few refreshing people burst on to the scene, such as Joe Turi, a Hungarian trick rider who defected to England by jumping off a lorry in Dover, but on the whole it was all fairly tame and predictable. Even the riding was less dramatic; everyone rode so much more tidily. Although a few competi-tors had slightly unorthodox styles – Annette Lewis, for example, would throw her lower legs out like a pair of wings as she jumped – riders such as Alan Oliver and Tommy Wade had had their day, and if they had still been competing, they may well have refined their style and technique to cope with the increasing demands of the sport, as Harvey Smith did.

▼ Malcolm Pyrah and Towerlands Angelzarke were twice winners of the Grand Prix at HOYS, and, in 1987, also took Leading Show Jumper of the Year.

Aware of the problems for up-and-coming riders, and keen to encourage the amateurs, the BSJA introduced a Pro-Am competition at Horse of the Year Show in 1981, in which an amateur rider was teamed with one of the top-ranked riders, and they would both jump a course against the clock (the amateur's

course being easier). It could be argued that in that year one young rider did break through the ranks; seventeen-year-old Lesley McNaught was runner-up to John Whitaker as Leading Show Jumper of the Year, but Lesley had been riding for the Edgars' yard since she was fifteen, and thus had the back-up and support of one of the most successful and experienced teams in the sport, which undoubtedly helped her to make the most of her talents. Not many young riders had the ability and the back-up to take on the top competitors with as much success as she did.

By 1984, Raymond Brooks-Ward was the show's organiser and he managed to persuade the show committee to bring in a rule that allowed four extra riders from the national classes – always such an important part of HOYS – to compete

THE BULLENS

From the early days, the Bullen family have been strong supporters of HOYS, both competitively and in displays, putting their many talents to use for its benefit. As a small child, Jane (now Holderness-Roddam) can remember helping her mother, artist Anne Bullen, to make bodies out of pyjama suits with flower-pot heads for the Pony Club mounted games. Older sister Jennie was already competing successfully in the show pony classes, having won her first championship in 1952 on five-year-old Royal Show, 'a very likely pony even without the added advantage of Jennie Bullen in the plate' wrote Pamela MacGregor-Morris, in her *Horse and Hound* report.

The following year all five of the Bullen children took part in an activity ride by the Cattistock Pony Club – the 'best Pony Club display we have ever seen at the show'.[1] Jane, aged five at the time, was just beginning to ride in show pony classes, and she usually rode side-saddle because her mother was fed up with her falling off all the time. 'Every time my pony put its head down I'd go straight over its ears,' recalls Jane. The solution clearly worked because Jane later claimed the reserve championship at Horse of the Year Show with Prosperity of Catherston. Jane later took part in hack,

combined training and working hunter classes. She won the Working Hunter title in 1986 on Valindrie, Margaret Sherrington's horse that went on to become an advanced eventer. She also competed in the working hunter class with her Badminton winner, Our Nobby.

Jennie had even greater success, initially in the hack classes, winning the Hack of the Year title in 1959 and 1961 with Miss Stubbings' Desert Storm, with whom she went on to compete in dressage. Another very good hack ridden by Jennie was Miss Betsy Profumo's Lemington Moon River, champion in 1975 (when Jennie also won the Dressage Horse of the Year with Kadett and the Novice Dressage with Jumping Championship with Chico II) and again in 1976. Jennie dominated the dressage competition at HOYS between 1975 and 1982, and she won the Combined Training title on countless occasions. In 1983, riding Dutch Gold, she gamely took part in the 'Olympic Show Jumping Relay' with Steven Smith and jockey Bill Smith, which of course they won. Both Jennie and Jane have put in long hours judging at Horse of the Year Show – in 1992, Jennie judged the cobs and Jane rode over a hundred hunters and hacks – to add to their many contributions to this show.

◄ Jane Bullen (now Holderness-Roddam) on Coed Coch Pryderi. Jane learned to ride side-saddle so she wouldn't fall off every time her pony put its head down.

for the remainder of the week in the international competitions. 'It gives riders a last chance to qualify, and broadens the spectrum a bit,' said Raymond at the time of rule change.[3] It was a popular decision, and to this day the four riders who manage to gain the last-minute qualification relish the opportunity to compete in the big international classes. By the time of this rule change, the show was being run for the BSJA by the London-based British Equestrian Promotions (BEP), headed by Bob Dean and managed by Raymond Brooks-Ward, who also organised the Royal International Horse Show and Olympia.

The following year the show lost another of its founding fathers with the death of Dorian Williams, the voice of show jumping, who had been associated with HOYS since its inception in 1949. His influence had been enormous (see Chapter Five), and for thirty years he had closed the show by reading Ronald Duncan's famous 'Ode to the Horse'. But the show went on, and appeared to be doing well enough. Box-office figures showed an eight per cent increase in 1985 and the 'future looks bright', according to the Town and Country page of *Horse and Hound* that year. But from 1986, attendance figures went into a decline that continued almost unabated for the next twenty-one years.

The future was still looking reasonably bright for the riders if sponsorship deals were anything to go by. In 1987, the year after Britain's show-jumping team had won the European championship, the Smith family – Harvey and his sons Steven and Robert – signed a record sponsorship deal, worth £500,000 over three years, with Brook Street Bureau. The Smiths chose the first day of Horse of the Year Show to announce their sponsorship package to ensure maximum press coverage. Meanwhile, the Whitaker brothers were sponsored by Next and the Edgars still had their long-term sponsorship with Everest Double Glazing.

A year later, the valuable Next Masters, a winner-takes-all competition, was introduced at Horse of the Year Show, and John Whitaker on the Bradley family's Milton won the class, collecting £25,000. Much to the sponsor's delight, and

◀ Robert Smith competing at HOYS on Kalusha in 2008. Together with his father Harvey and brother Steven, Robert signed a record sponsorship deal at the 1987 show.

ROBERT SMITH

The elder son of Harvey, Robert has been one of the top riders at HOYS since 1979 when, at the age of eighteen, he won Leading Show Jumper of the Year just months after becoming the youngest rider ever to win the King George V Cup. He has been a regular member of Britain's Nations Cup teams, collecting a team bronze at the 1997 European championships, and he was Britain's sole representative in the show jumping at the Athens Olympics, narrowly missing an individual medal when he came fourth.

Robert won the Puissance at HOYS for two years in a row, in 1994 and 1995, but his best year was 2000, when he won seven competitions – three national and four international classes – including the Grand Prix.

► John Whitaker and the legendary Milton. The pair won the valuable Next Masters competition for three years in succession, and were enormously popular with spectators.

probably even more to John's delight, he and Milton won the same class in the following two years, netting a total of £81,000 over the three years.

John Whitaker and Milton continued to thrill the crowds, and even David Broome was still in the frame, winning his fourth Leading Show Jumper of the Year title in 1990, having achieved his first major victory twenty-four years earlier when he won the Grand Prix. But not everyone was happy with the show and the way it was being run. In an article in *Horse and Hound* in 1987 bluntly entitled 'Here's what we want at Wembley', Harvey Smith had a list of complaints ranging from the lack of international competitors to the unsatisfactory catering facilities.

Generous prize money in the Masters competition and a £20,000 first prize in the Everest-sponsored Grand Prix indicated a reasonable level of commercial

◀ David Broome, still winning at HOYS in 1990, this time collecting his fourth Leading Show Jumper of the Year award, riding Lannegan.

THE SHIRES

During the 1990 show, Roy Bird, then secretary of the Shire Horse Society, received an urgent message that there was 'a problem with the Shires'. He rushed to the control centre at the main arena only to find that there was, after all, no problem; it was merely a ruse to get him into the arena during the judging of the Shire Horse Championship so that a presentation could be made to him to mark his important role in revitalising heavy horse breeding in Britain. He had taken over as secretary of the Shire Horse Society in 1963, at a time when it was close to being wound up and the heavy horse was in danger of becoming obsolete. Since then membership of the society has grown enormously and the breeding stock has increased and improved. Although the Musical Drive of the Heavy Horses is no longer a regular feature at the show, there is a strong turnout each year to contest the title of Shire Horse of the Year, since the class returned at the NEC in 2009. The most outstanding breeders and producers of Shire horses have been the Bedford brothers, Paul and Walter, from York, whose numerous successes include four Horse of the Year Show titles at Wembley, from 1985 to 1988, with the dark bay mare Landcliffe Laura.

▼ The 2010 Shire Horse of the Year, Acle Sabrina, owned by Mr B. Banham.

support at the beginning of the 1990s, but the BBC's coverage of the show painted a different picture. Gone were the days when Horse of the Year Show was shown live on prime-time television, just after the nine o'clock news. Now it was relegated to a late-night slot, often going out after midnight, with a recorded programme showing the day's highlights. In fifteen years, show jumping had gone from a major to a minor sport as far as the BBC was concerned, ultimately making it more difficult to attract big sponsors, and therefore difficult for the organisers to provide good prize money.

Raymond Brooks-Ward had already seen the writing on the wall in the late 1980s when he decided to sell his share of BEP to the other two owners of the company, the BSJA and the British Horse Society. BEP had been formed in the 1970s to bring in sponsorship to show jumping and to run Horse of the Year Show for the BSJA, but in recent years the company had experienced a sharp decline in profits. In 1991, the BSJA and the British Horse Society, now sole owners of BEP, decided to sell the company to Alan Pascoe Associates so that it could be run by professional event managers; but within a year Alan Pascoe Associates had gone bust, Raymond Brooks-Ward had died and the BSJA was left to run its own show.

It was tough call. At short notice, the BSJA had to put on a major international show, together with all the national show-jumping competitions, showing classes and entertainments. In 1992 show jumping was at an all-time low, made worse by a disappointing performance from Britain's show-jumping team at the Barcelona Olympics; ticket sales were already flagging; the BBC had all but withdrawn its coverage of the show, producing just one programme of highlights on Sunday afternoon, and sponsors had drifted away.

ONE TOO MANY

Mark Todd rode Busby Boy and Double Take at the 1989 show, at a time when he was making a bid to take part in both the show jumping and the three-day event at the 1992 Olympics. While at Wembley, Mark also tried his hand at showing, taking part in the working hunter class, a role he was offered at the last minute because Vin Toulson had strained some ligaments in his leg when unloading the small hunter Sir Percival at the show. The horse had taken fright coming off the lorry and landed on Vin. Mark piloted Seabrook on Vin's behalf, but had three fences down and a refusal. 'That's enough of that,' he commented afterwards.[2]

ON TAP

In the days when the musical drive of the Shire horses was still a regular feature of the show, John Whitaker recalls that these massive horses were always stabled in the same area at Wembley, and their grooms always had a barrel of beer on the go. Of course, John frequently found that it was necessary to walk past their stables on the way back to his horsebox …

In a desperate bid to keep the show going, the BSJA sent out a three-line whip to bring in the support of its top riders and ensure their participation in 'the most crucial Horse of the Year Show since it was started in 1949'.[4] In spite of the clash with other big shows in Europe, including the new World Cup Show in Oslo, where considerably more prize money was on offer, the top thirty riders on the British rankings list were told they must jump at Wembley or nowhere. All but one of the top riders turned up at Wembley to support the show.

In spite of all the best efforts of the staff of the BSJA, the officials, judges and supporters, luck went against them on the last day of the 1992 show. Until then things had been going reasonably well; in defiance of the gloomy picture painted by some of the newspapers at the start of the week, enough spectators attended the show each day to bring in a small profit, and although the programme often ran late in the evenings, causing spectators to miss trains and journalists to miss deadlines, a sense of optimism prevailed with the growing idea that nothing was going to stop this show.

It was tragic, therefore, that an imaginative new competition introduced to create greater interest in the show jumping backfired so badly. For the first time in the history of the show, a bank had been constructed in the main arena so that an indoor derby class could be staged. The feature created enormous interest and publicity, but on the night of the competition the third horse to come down the bank, Sir Arkay, ridden by Switzerland's Jurg Friedli, slipped and broke a hind leg. It was a devastating moment for the organisers, the spectators and the competitors, quite apart from Sir Arkay's connections.

There was certainly no shortage of publicity now, but of all the wrong kind. The tabloid press had a field day and the League Against Cruel Sports also jumped on the bandwagon, threatening to prosecute Jurg Friedli for cruelty.

Show jumping had never looked more vulnerable. In England its popularity had sunk so low that the Three Counties Show, one of the country's premier agricultural events, decided to omit show jumping from its programme altogether due to its 'dwindling appeal', claiming that 'Birds of prey, gundog and ferret demonstrations draw a much bigger audience.'[5]

Alongside show jumping's decline in popularity, Horse of the Year Show was now struggling for survival. The BSJA had done its best to keep the show running after losing Alan Pascoe Associates and, in spite of being a little overambitious in the scheduling and its plans to entertain the public, it had, remarkably, broken even financially – a profit of £700 was recorded – which was a great relief to its members. 'There is no question of the show not going ahead next year,' said Michael Bates, chairman of the organising committee.[6]

The BSJA's efforts were supported by its members and by the showing fraternity. This was, after all, their flagship event and no one wanted to see it go under. Despite the massive hike in entry fees (to help pay for the show), the low prize money on offer and the fact that owners had to pay to come to watch their own horses, the top show jumpers continued to make every effort to compete at Wembley, often commuting between London and more lucrative European venues. In 1994, John Whitaker made a pre-dawn start from England to ride in the Bremen International in Germany, returning twelve hours later to win the Grand Prix at HOYS (worth £6,000 to the winner) with Everest Grannusch for the second year running. He then returned to Bremen to contest the German classic, which was offering a first prize of £40,000. This was the kind of support that helped to keep the show alive, for without the top riders there would have been fewer spectators.

That year, 1994, was something of a watershed for the show – *Horse and Hound* even claimed it had recaptured past glories. By now, the BSJA had done a deal with Wembley plc, leasing it the rights to run the show, and thus handing over financial responsibility for it, for a period of seven years. Recapturing past

▲ Michael Bates, chairman of the 1992 show's organising committee, the year the BSJA was left in the lurch and had to run HOYS on its own.

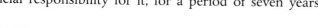

THE HACKNEYS

Cynthia and Frank Haydon dominated the Hackney world in the early years of the show, breeding and producing an enormous number of champions at their Hurstwood stud, which had a great influence on Hackney breeding lines. Later, Yorkshire trainer Denis Midgley produced many champions, including the pony Heathfield George (owned by C.R. Cowan), which won the title for three years in succession, from 1979 to 1981. One of the most successful owners was Noddy Vyse, who had the good horse Whitehavens Step High and also the pony Sunbeam Super Star, both multiple winners of the title. The most outstanding Hackney horse in this period was Jo Quigg's black stallion, Ingfield Black Prince, winner of the championship at Wembley four times. In 1991, the last year that Ingfield Black Prince won the title, Jo Quigg also won the pony title with Northbrook Handy Mac. The Hackney Horse and Pony Championships were held at Horse of the Year Show for the last time in 1993.

glories was perhaps a slight exaggeration, but one thing that did give the show a lift was the introduction of a World Cup qualifier for dressage. In the long history of the show, it has so often been dressage competitions and displays that have enthralled the audience, and this World Cup was no exception. As Alan Smith wrote in the *Daily Telegraph*: 'Just when the gravediggers were assembling to bury Horse of the Year Show, 45 years old and apparently beyond redemption, the corpse rose, dancing, in the Wembley Arena. Led by Holland's Anky van Grunsven and her charismatic stallion Olympic Cocktail, the Volvo Dressage World Cup held a huge audience enraptured.'

Had the terminal decline been halted? On the surface things appeared to be running well enough, but financially the show was still struggling, and Wembley was looking tired and rundown. One upbeat voice came from Jon Smith, chairman of First Artist Corporation, the company that had been brought in by Wembley to promote the show. He appeared keen to make positive changes, promising, among other things, to upgrade the Fibresand Arena for the show classes 'and make it a hip, trendy place to be in its own right',[7] perhaps even creating a stage in the arena for a pop concert.

This might not have been quite what the showing fraternity had in mind, but there was no doubting Jon Smith's enthusiasm, and the 1995 show did indeed have a new look, and a different layout. A Hall of Champions replaced the old Fibresand Arena, catering was improved, and a giant four-sided video screen hung suspended from the roof of the international arena. The organisers had even managed to persuade a reasonable number of foreign riders to participate, including the good-looking young Brazilian show jumper Rodrigo Pessoa. Boosted by Britain's success – a team silver medal – in the European show-jumping championships the previous week, ticket sales were up by about 30 per cent, and Sky Television gave the show some coverage on the last day (though not live). Nerves about the show becoming a little too pacey and glitzy under its new management were largely laid to rest. There was a hint of optimism in the air. But in just over a year it had all gone wrong again.

'Wembley tries to calm fears that HOYS is off' ran the headline in *Horse and Hound* in its 5 December 1996 issue. Wembley had written to showing societies advising them not to allocate Horse of the Year Show qualifiers for 1997 because they may not be accommodated, a message that sent alarm bells ringing in showing circles. There was talk of a six-day show, with two days of showing and four of

▲ Anky van Grunsven and Olympic Cocktail, winners of the Volvo Dressage World Cup at HOYS in 1994.

show jumping, so that only one arena at Wembley would need to be used. Furthermore, although Wembley was contractually responsible for the costs of the show, it had begun to make approaches to the BSJA for financial contributions to the 1997 event. The BSJA was clearly concerned about the show's future, and in a bid to have some form of back-up in the event of the unthinkable, had invited tenders for a new national Festival of Champions to be held in the place of HOYS.

Faced with continuing losses, Wembley plc began to question its commitment to HOYS, and agreed to hand over the running of the show to another company, EPS Ltd, which subsequently set up a subsidiary company, EPS HOYS Ltd, to organise the show. When the parent company, EPS, went bust in the spring of 1997, EPS HOYS Ltd declared it was still able to continue running the show, but the BSJA was not happy with the arrangement, given the company's dubious financial state. Since the deal between Wembley plc and EPS HOYS Ltd had never been ratified with the BSJA, the BSJA refused to accept the arrangement.

In the dispute that followed, EPS HOYS Ltd was removed from the management of the show and the company disappeared from the scene with £200,000 worth of HOYS funds that it had already collected from sponsors and trade-stand holders. It also owed money to Grandstand Media, the company that had been brought in to help secure sponsorship for the show. Wembley plc no longer wanted to run the show and was still at odds with the BSJA over its contractual responsibilities. With two and half months to go before the 1997 show was due to take place, HOYS had never looked more vulnerable.

Grandstand Media, which comprised two directors and a secretary, were the other party involved in the shake-up, and they had been working out of an office in the basement of Wembley Stadium to secure sponsorship for the show. When EPS HOYS Ltd pulled out, owing them a large chunk of money, they were left in a difficult position financially, yet already felt close enough to the show to have the confidence to consider taking on the organisation themselves. It was an extraordinary move by the two directors, Mark Wein and Mike Gill, even to contemplate such an idea, given that this was not an area in which they had much experience, and also that they would be taking on an unprofitable event that was already £200,000 down on its finances. Furthermore, show jumping was still in the doldrums, with Volvo having just withdrawn its long-standing sponsorship of the World Cup series. Mark Wein and Mike Gill had a daunting task on their hands.

► A popular HOYS competitor, Geoff Billington is seen here competing with Pedro VI at the 2009 show.

The sequence of events went like this. Mark Wein and Mike Gill asked the BSJA to give them two weeks to produce a viable business proposal that would include making up the £200,000 deficit left by EPS HOYS Ltd. The two men then began networking fast, and were amazed by the support they received from the equestrian world. Two of the show's sponsors agreed to put up the same money again (their first payment having been lost to EPS HOYS Ltd), but what probably set the seal on the show's fate were two very substantial donations given by people who simply wanted to save the show.

Encouraged by these remarkable and generous gestures, Mark and Mike turned their attention to reducing the expenses and began negotiating with all the contractors, hotels and officials. They also managed to agree a lower rent for the facilities at Wembley. Eventually, they shaved off enough from the costs to enable them to demonstrate to the BSJA that they could make the 1997 show financially viable. Contracts were signed, and Grandstand Media had eight weeks to stage the show.

'The stress was unimaginable,' says Mark Wein. A multitude of things had to be done, and at the same time Grandstand Media needed to recruit more staff to cope with the sudden influx of work, but Mark's biggest headache was to ensure that the costs were controlled rigidly. Neither Mark nor Mike knew how the equestrian side of the show worked, so this was left to Jon Doney, the show's equestrian director, to bring together – a difficult task, since the show's organisation had gone into limbo for a month during the dispute. During this time, both Jon Doney and the BSJA office had been inundated with calls from anxious exhibitors, wanting to know what was happening and whether or not they had qualified in vain.

While Grandstand Media grappled with costs and planning, they were given overwhelming support by an army of unsung heroes who willingly gave their time and money to keep the show on the road; officials, judges, suppliers and competitors all pulled together, often working long hours for free. Without such commitment and sheer hard work from all concerned, Horse of the Year Show

◀ Mark Wein, whose company Grandstand Media took over the running of HOYS in 1997, presents Robert Whitaker and Finbarr V with the Puissance Trophy in 2008.

might easily have sunk into oblivion, or at best become a shadow of its former self. This was the turning point for HOYS.

The show went ahead, and in spite of ticket sales of around 15,000 over the five days, it just broke even. Spurred on by this relative success, Grandstand Media extended their contract with the BSJA for another four years, with the option to extend it for a further ten years after that. Once again, the show appeared to be on firm ground, and could look forward to celebrating its golden jubilee the following year.

SHOW JUMPING

While the show went through changing fortunes, some of the greatest names in show jumping were making an impact on the sport and on the Wembley event. David Broome's sister, Liz, had married Ted Edgar, and the pair had created a formidable team, not just between themselves, but also with a number of very talented and dedicated youngsters who were based at their yard in Warwickshire. With Ted's eye for a horse, and under his and Liz's guidance, riders such as Nick Skelton, Lesley McNaught and Emma-Jane Mac, came on to the show-jumping scene with all the back-up they needed to reach the top. Of these, Nick Skelton has remained in show jumping's top league, and has often been relied upon to bring a HOYS class alive with a dramatic finish in a jump-off. Like

▼ Members of the Whitaker family in front of the wall at the NEC. There has been at least one Whitaker at nearly every show since 1971, when John first competed at HOYS.

Michael Whitaker, he is a master against the clock, and no rider could rest on his laurels until Nick Skelton had completed his round.

Nick, who began riding for the Edgars as soon as he left school at the age of fifteen, competed successfully on junior teams (a team silver and an individual gold) and within three years was holding his own among the best riders of the day – Derek Ricketts, David Broome, Graham Fletcher, Eddie Macken, Harvey Smith and Caroline Bradley. His first major claim to fame came in 1978 when he broke the British high jump record, clearing 7 feet 7 ⁵⁄₁₆ inches on Lastic. Many senior medals followed, although Olympic success has always eluded him.

◄ Nick Skelton competing on Nemo at the 2009 show. Nick has won four Grand Prix at HOYS and four Leading Show Jumper of the Year competitions. In 1984 he won ten classes at the show.

His wins at Horse of the Year Show have been outstanding, and include four Grand Prix and four Leading Show Jumper of the Year titles. He had a run of impressive wins in the 1980s, but his best year was in 1984 when he won an unprecedented ten classes at HOYS, totting up a prize fund of over £11,000. Among the top seven money winners at Wembley that year, four of them were from the Edgar stables, including Everest Forever, ridden by Liz Edgar. Nick's horses were St James, Everest Radius and Apollo.

Skelton continued to hit the headlines at HOYS during the early nineties (in 1991 he won five competitions there), but Michael and John Whitaker were nearly always ready to challenge him, and rarely did a Horse of the Year conclude without at least one Whitaker win. It was perhaps only because the immortal Milton, ridden by John Whitaker, was injured in 1991 that Skelton was able to clean up so successfully that year. Certainly, Milton's appearances at Wembley were one of the biggest crowd pullers of the time. In 1990, when show jumping was losing television coverage and its reputation had been further blighted by the 'rapping' scandal in Germany, Milton rescued the sport with his outstanding performances and his massive fan club. 'I love Milton' signs would be held up by spectators in the stands whenever the legendary grey put in an appearance, and he rarely failed to disappoint. That year, the last in which he competed at Wembley, he won the valuable Masters competition for the third time in succession, collecting £29,000.

John Whitaker had begun to make a name for himself at senior level with the consistent Ryan's Son, the brave Irish horse with a distinctive white blaze, and during the early 1980s the pair was rarely out of the top five money winners at Horse of the Year Show. John's younger brother Michael first impressed the HOYS crowds in 1976 when he completed an unprecedented double by winning both the Young Riders title and the Leading Junior Jumper of the Year.

Twenty years later, Michael's niece, John's daughter Louise, also won the Young Riders title. In 1995, when Louise was fifteen years old, she had set up a remarkable record of qualifying for and competing in the Pony Club mounted games (for the Rockford Harriers) as well as in four show-jumping competitions – the 138cm final, the Junior Show Jumper of the Year, the Young Rider Show Jumper of the Year and the Junior Foxhunter final. These days Louise is very successful in bringing on young horses, while other young members of the Whitaker dynasty – Ellen, Robert and William – have created an enormous following at HOYS and compete with great success against their elders. Indeed, such is the ability and

JOHN WHITAKER MBE

One of the all-time greats of show jumping, John Whitaker has been competing at Horse of the Year Show since 1971, when he rode a pony, Crazy Horse, in the juniors at the age of sixteen, thus fulfilling his first major ambition – to get to HOYS. 'It was watching Horse the Year Show on TV that first got me interested in show jumping,' says John. 'I was about ten years old, and I thought, "that's what I want do." I would stay up late and watch the show jumping, and the next day I'd get my pony out and practise.' All that practising paid off, and in 1972 John qualified Singing Wind for the Foxhunter final, but the horse that first took him to international stardom was the legendary Ryan's Son with whom John established a hugely successful, fourteen-year partnership. The pair won all over the world, including a team silver medal at the Los Angeles Olympics in 1984.

John's tally of medals is phenomenal – Olympic team silver, Alternative Olympics team and individual silver, five world championship medals, including an individual silver, and twelve European medals, four of them individual, including a gold in 1989. He has also won the World Cup final twice and the Hickstead Derby four times. His career has spanned nearly forty years, and he is still thrilling the crowds at Horse of the Year, where his presence is always a threat to other competitors. He has won the Grand Prix twice, the Puissance four times, including sharing the first prize with himself in 2005, and Leading Show Jumper of the Year five times. On Milton, he won the Masters, the most lucrative prize at the show, for three years in succession, from 1988 to 1990.

The striking grey gelding Milton, who entertained spectators with his special 'airs above the ground' displays at prize giving, had a huge following, and his appearance at the show was guaranteed to sell tickets. In his competitive career, this equine superstar won over £900,000 for his owners, Doreen and Tom Bradley. His last performance at the show was in 1990, but he returned in 1995 to parade. 'Milton is the sort of horse you come across once in a lifetime,' says John. 'I am lucky to have had the chance to ride him.'

► John Whitaker's first great partner, Ryan's Son, with whom he won a team silver medal at the Los Angeles Olympics in 1984.

commitment of this family to the sport that it is difficult to imagine a Horse of the Year Show without them. They have been staunch supporters of the show through thick and thin.

Back in the seventies, Caroline Bradley achieved a remarkable record of finishing first, equal second and fourth in the Leading Show Jumper of the Year. It was the first time Caroline had won the title, and she did so emphatically. Her win came on the Dutch stallion Marius (sire of Milton); second place was on Berna, her national champion partner that year; and she was fourth on Tigre. Caroline,

► Michael Whitaker riding Insul Tech Wonami den Aard competing in the Diamond Jubilee Cup 2008.

MICHAEL WHITAKER

Michael may have followed in his older brother's footsteps but certainly not in his shadow. After his exciting debut at the 1976 Horse of the Year Show, in 1980 Michael went on to become the youngest winner of the Hickstead Derby at the age of twenty. Four years later, he won a team silver medal at the Los Angeles Olympics, coming close to winning an individual medal as well. During his career, he has also picked up two world championship team medals, and eleven European championship medals – three of them individual. He has won both the King George V Cup and the Hickstead Derby four times – from 1991 to 1993 he won the Derby for three years in succession on the same horse, Monsanto.

Brilliant against the clock, Michael is rarely out of the prizes at HOYS; he has won the Leading Show Jumper title four times and the Puissance three times. His best year was 1995, when he won five classes, including Leading Show Jumper for the second year in succession, having recently returned from the European championships in St Gallen with a team and individual silver medals.

regarded as one of the best lady show jumpers in the world, was a regular competitor at HOYS – she won the Puissance in 1974 – until her tragic death in 1983, aged thirty-seven, following a heart attack.

One of the most successful horses at the show during the seventies was Eddie Macken's legendary Boomerang, who won the Grand Prix a record four times in five years. No other horse in the history of the show has won this class more than three times. A remarkably consistent and tough horse, the Irish-bred Boomerang won Grand Prix classes all over the world, but is probably best known for his four successive wins in the Hickstead Derby. Another horse that has a special place in Horse of the Year Show records books is Anglezarke, originally bought by Trevor Banks for Mark Phillips to show jump. When Malcolm Pyrah rode him for the Hunnables, the horse twice won the Grand Prix (1984 and 1986) and also had two wins in the Leading Show Jumper of the Year (1980 and 1987).

▼ Caroline Bradley and Marius competing at the show in 1977, the year that Caroline achieved the remarkable record of finishing first, equal second and fourth in the Leading Show Jumper of the Year competition.

SHOWING

The showing fraternity, meanwhile, were still struggling to impress the judges in the outside arena at Wembley, where conditions underfoot were often at the mercy of the weather or affected by alien objects in the sand and rubber. In 1977, the top heavyweight hunter, Lady Zinnia's Balmoral, left the outdoor arena on three legs after treading on a 4-inch nail, which lodged itself in his foot. Fortunately, Vin Toulson managed to remove the nail, return for the final judging and win his class. Such was the concern about the possibility of more hazardous objects in the arena that, according to Pamela Macgregor-Morris in *Horse and Hound*, 'two mine detectors were brought in before the hacks and ponies were judged.' One can only assume she meant metal detectors, or perhaps the arena was more dangerous than the riders realised …

It was a case of tempers exploding in 1985, as the late Elwyn Hartley Edwards' report of the show classes in *Horse and Hound* that year made clear:

> First hint of an impending storm came in the 12 hands 2in class [show ponies], when a flurry of unwanted enthusiasm resulted in a young rider being deposited in no uncertain fashion. Properly, the pony was sent from the ring, although in my view it would have been wise not to have re-mounted the child, who was promptly slung off again.

> That class was won by Cymbeline's Gale Warning (ominously named in view of what was to happen later) … Then came the very strong 13 hands 2in class which was, indeed, to produce the champion pony of the year, Twylands Carillon, a near perfect pattern with a brilliance of movement to match. Next to him in the line-up was placed the gelding Keston Poldark, another exceptional pony.

> A moment later, following one of those infectious furores which threatened to scatter the class round the arena, a steward stepped in to stop the rot and ordered Keston Poldark from the ring. He left, only to return moments later and once more to be summarily dismissed by the stewards. What happened subsequently is best forgotten, since apologies for unseemly outbursts have been made and accepted. An objection was indeed lodged. The judges supported the action of their steward and it was over-ruled.

The Hack Championship also caused a stir that year, although there were no 'unseemly outbursts' by anyone except a horse. Elwyn Hartley Edwards' description of the scene is very entertaining.

> Just as the shock waves of the Poldark affair seemed to be receding, another storm rumbled around the arena. Hack classes, by their nature, are not the

most predictable but they retain always a certain grace and dignity. They ended by providing a topic of conversation for the rest of the week. I hasten to add that the judges, Mrs Michael and Mrs Wakley, having borne the heat of the day, preserved a most commendable composure throughout …

The grey horse Duke of Newcastle won the [small hack] class from the Jerram's Sunrise of Randle, while Robert Oliver, exerting a formidable presence with an old world courtesy, won the large hack class with Mrs Shuck's Rye Tangle from Victoria Smith's Wishful Thinking.

All four then appeared for the championship, and that was when the doors started to open and shut. Robert thinks that Rye Tangle struck himself as he came through the gate but without much doubt he seemed to be sufficiently 'unlevel' at trot to make the usually imperturbable Mr. Oliver express consternation (in the facial sense, that is). Preserving, nonetheless, a courtly demeanour, Mr. Oliver doffed his silk hat and disappeared through the doorway. It was now the turn of the remainder of the cast to express consternation – or was it bewilderment? Two minutes later, Mr. Oliver re-entered the arena at a stirring canter, the vets outside having pronounced Rye Tangle to be sound. After a majestic sweep or two, Rye Tangle was brought into the championship spot with Duke of Newcastle, after certain reluctance on his part, getting the reserve rosette fixed to his bridle.

The grey horse, perhaps resenting being so patently up-staged, then asserted himself by attempting to cross the great divide between the arena and the champagne bar. Enter police dressed as stewards to escort the miscreant from the stage under the judges' disapproving gaze. Victoria Smith, bemused but attempting a gallant smile, moved to centre stage to be made reserve champion.

To add to the upsets that year, Grandstand, winner of the Cob Championship for the past three years, stood down to The Irish RM, shown by Vin Toulson. However, the following year (1978) this outstanding heavyweight, piloted by Roger Stack, another great showman, came back to win his fourth and final Cob Championship, before retiring in front of the HOYS crowds. The most successful cob of this period, though, was undoubtedly Heather Griffiths' Super Ted, who won the title six times between 1987 and 1994 when ridden by Robert Oliver. A hugely popular winner, he was beaten at HOYS only by John Dunlop's

▲ Hack Champion, Rye Tangle, seen here with Ali Oliver on board, in 1986.

► Cob Champion for four years was Keith Luxford's Grandstand, ridden by Roger Stack.

Just William (in 1991) and by Apollo, ridden by Lynn Russell, who finally deposed him in 1995, the last time that Super Ted was shown at Wembley.

The most successful show pony of this period was Holly of Spring, who won the championship for a record four successive years, from 1975 to 1978, when ridden by Cathryn Cooper. By Gems Signet (HOYS champion in 1971) out of Penhill Finola (by Bubbly), the 13.2hh chestnut, who was bred by Albert Deptford and produced by Davina Whiteman, had been unbeaten since Windsor during her first season's showing as a four year old, but in the final judging at HOYS that year it had been necessary for a referee, Mrs Jennifer Williams, to be called in when the two judges, Peter Brookshaw and Mrs Clarke Brown, could not agree on their winner. Holly of Spring, who 'had a lovely floating action and quite impeccable manners, never appearing to have an even slightly mischievous thought in her pretty head',[8] finally got the nod and won the first of her four championships. Ardenhall Royal Secret was the only other pony of this era to win the championship title more than once (1994 and 1997), as the pony classes grew ever more popular and competitive.

▲ Vicki Keen riding Royal Return, Champion Hack in 1980.

► Holly of Spring and Cathryn Cooper, winners of the Show Pony Championship a record four times, from 1975 to 1978.

VIN TOULSON

There was rarely a year at Horse of the Year Show when Vin Toulson did not take home a red rosette, whether from one of the three hunter weight classes or from a small hunter or cob class. Between 1982 and 1987 he won the Show Hunter Championship four times and the Cob Championship once, and he was responsible for producing many other top show horses.

Vin was born in Chipping Norton and grew up surrounded by horses. As a youngster he was more interested in racing than in showing and he worked as an apprentice to Bill Ranson in Lincolnshire, but Bill's wife Rosemary had show ponies and horses, so Vin often found himself on the gallops in the morning and schooling show horses in the afternoon. He rode for three seasons as a professional national hunt jockey before he and his wife Daphne turned their attention to the showing world.

The pair had met when Daphne was injured and looking for someone to take on the ride of her somewhat neurotic horse Denzil Oxby. Vin was recommended, and he not only won seven chases with Daphne's horse but also persuaded her to marry him. A keen hunting man – 'I would hunt every day of the week if I had time' – Vin was always on the lookout for a good showing horse, whether off the racetrack or a failed show jumper.

Jean Andrews, who worked as Vin's groom and co-rider from 1964, remembers his first successful year at the show. Prince's Street was an 'unreliable' racehorse that had come off the track at Easter and was in the show ring within six weeks. Vin won the Show Hunter title with him at the end of that year, 1973, and he also won the Small Hunter class with Lady Inchcape's Sporting Print, a horse he had purchased cheaply (for about £400) at Leicester sales because it would not jump. Two years later, Jean

▲ Vin Toulson receiving his award after winning the 1983 Hunter Championship on the South Essex Insurance Group's Elite.

Andrews swapped one ofher show ponies for Sporting Print, and rode him herself to collect his second HOYS championship.

With Prince's Street, Vin began his long and successful association with sponsor Barry Fehler of South Essex Insurance. More good hunters followed – Magnum, Assurance, Elite and Seabrook – and Vin became a familiar and popular figure at the show. He rode there for the last time in 1998, winning the Reserve Hunter title with Steve Pitt's middleweight Triple Gold.

One of the most important pony sires of this time was Sandbourne Royal Ensign, owned by Robert Cockram. Four HOYS champions – Drayton Penny Royal, Sandbourne Royal Emblem, Glenmoss Juliet and Bradmore Catkin – were sired by him. Among the top pony producers were Simone and Carol Gilbert-Scott, Bob and Julie Templeton, and Ron and Debbie Thomas, but a successful outcome with a show pony at HOYS was, and still is, unpredictable, given that these little 'Ferraris' are ultra sensitive and highly tuned, and need to be handled with kid gloves. They are not easy to ride and their small jockeys must be quiet and gentle, but at the same time must give a nervous pony confidence.

The hack classes were frequented by some of the best showing riders and producers of this time – Stella and Christine Harries (also important pony producers), Allister Hood, Marjorie and Richard Ramsay, to name a few. In 1984, Carol Gilbert-Scott won the inaugural Supreme Championship with the hack Fair Change, the year before Rye Tangle had such a run of success in the Hack Championships with Robert Oliver. Rye Tangle also took the Supreme title in 1986 and 1987. By the late 1980s, Katie Jerram was making a name for herself, particularly in the hacks. One of her greatest triumphs in this period was winning the Hack Championship in 1990 with Piran Pyca, a horse that had in the past found the atmosphere of the indoor arena at Wembley too much to cope with. With help from trainer Ruth McMullen and a large dose of patience, Katie finally achieved the Hack title with this stunning horse.

The following year, the pair won the title again, and in 1992, Katie looked set for a third successive title on Piran Pyca when she headed the large hack class. She had also won the small hacks with Treverva Verity but, not surprisingly, Katie opted to ride Piran Pyca in the championship. So her trainer, Ruth McMullen, found herself back in the limelight as she deputised for Katie on Treverva Verity, a novice at the start of the season, who promptly won the championship. Other successful hacks of this period included memorable horses such as Mrs Goodall's home-bred Tenterk, the Cooper's Brown Buzzard (who deposed Tenterk at HOYS in 1981), Mrs S. Nichol's Valentino, and Lemington Moon River (owned by Miss Betsy Profumo), all of them champions twice at HOYS.

Success in the hunter classes tended to be the domain of the male riders, in particular the 'three musketeers' – Robert Oliver, Vin Toulson and David Tatlow – as they were known among the lady riders of the time. Between them, these riders collected at least fifteen hunter championships between 1975 and 1997. Try

▲ Albert Deptford, breeder of Holly of Spring and many other outstanding show ponies.

ROBERT OLIVER

The most outstanding showman of our time, Robert has been winning championships at Horse of the Year Show since 1970, and continues to do so. His unprecedented record of nine Show Hunter, twelve Cob, two Riding Horse, five Small Hunter and six Hack Championships is unlikely to be surpassed. As well as all those he has ridden himself in the show ring, many other successful horses have been produced from Robert's yard in Herefordshire.

Robert's long association with horses began when, as a schoolboy, he used to visit yards with his uncle, William Watts of Hereford, a leading farrier who was responsible for setting up the system of apprenticeships for farriers in England. Robert's first introduction to showing came through Pat and Vivien Eckley, who owned the famous Cusop show ponies (their breeding went back to Bwlch Valentino); and as a farm student at Vowchurch, in Herefordshire, he spent all his spare time at Bill Bryan's yard.

A keen hunting man, Robert whipped-in for three seasons with the South Herefordshire before becoming Field Master, and he later became Field Master and Master of the Ledbury Foxhounds (from 1990 to 2000). In 1968, he set up his own yard at Harewood End, near Ross on Wye, and from there produced his first HOYS champion, small hunter Lord Sorcerer (1970). More success followed with the heavyweight Flashman, Hunter of the Year in 1979. In fact, from the mid-1970s Robert's career went into overdrive; he produced champion small hunters, working hunters, cobs and hacks as well show hunters, and was rarely out of the spotlight.

▲ Robert Oliver on Seabrook in 1984, when the horse won the Hunter Championship for the first time. He won it twice more with Vin Toulson in the saddle.

In 1977 he broke all records at HOYS by winning the Cob, Small Hunter and Hack titles and taking reserve in the Hunter Championship. Many famous horses are associated with him – Super Ted, Tenterk, King's Warrior, Seabrook and JCB to name a few – and he has dominated the showing world for the last forty years.

THE GILBERT-SCOTT SISTERS

In 1964, in their second year of competing at Horse of the Year Show, Carol Gilbert-Scott took the reserve Show Pony Championship riding her sister Simone's pony, Naseel Namoose II, which their mother Bobbie had bought from Reading market for £95. Subsequently the Gilbert-Scotts owned and produced a whole string of champion ponies – Cusop Pirouette (and the reserve, Whalton Caprice), Lennel Aurora, Christmas Carol of Bennochy (and the reserve, Blythford Chinook), Creden Keepsake, Drayton Penny Royal, Bradmore Catkin, Glenmoss Juliet and Jackets Maybe, the latter being the pony with which they won their last HOYS Show Pony Championship before giving up showing in 2001.

They also produced the first-ever Champion of Champions in 1984, Champion Show Hack Fair Change, and the Intermediate Show Riding Type champion, Radway Small Talk, when these classes were introduced at Horse of the Year Show in 1999. They trained both the champion and reserve in the 2010 Intermediates – Opium Casa Leona and Wesswood Caste a Spell.

Carol and Simone continue to help riders to produce show horses and ponies, and they were responsible for training ladies' hunter Bournebrook Golden Law, champion for three successive years, culminating in the Supreme Horse title in 2005 when ridden by Shelley Perham.

as they might, the ladies struggled to beat them and it was only Gill Oliver (1988) and Moggy Hennessy (1993) who kept the ladies in the frame by taking the Show Hunter titles during this period. Ruth McMullen (better known these days for training top event rider Pippa Funnell) and Davina Whiteman (now chairman of Ponies UK) had given the men a run for their money in the seventies and early eighties, but it was not easy to break through the ranks of showing's own 'magic circle', and amateur riders stood even less chance of getting into the spotlight at HOYS.

King's Warrior (Robert Oliver) and Seabrook (first with Robert Oliver and then Vin Toulson) dominated HOYS in this period, both winning the championship a remarkable three times. Some of the good show hunters also contested the working hunter classes, and successful among these were Supercoin and Dual Gold. Mary Broome (sister of Liz Edgar and David Broome) won the class twice with her parents' Let's Go (1977 and 1978), the only horse to achieve a double win until Mrs Betty Robinson, a former show jumper, made it two in row with Bootleg (1989 and 1990).

► Jayne Hutchinson's outstanding Small Print, ridden by Peter Richmond. He won the Small Hunter Championship five times between 1988 and 1994.

ALLISTER HOOD

Allister made a somewhat inauspicious HOYS debut in 1972 by falling off at the first fence in a working hunter class. He was at least in good company – David Broome, also competing in this class, suffered exactly the same fate. Fortunately, Allister redeemed himself the following year by winning the lightweight hunter class with Field Master and standing reserve to Vin Toulson on Prince's Street in the championship.

Brought up on a farm with horses – his father showed Shires – Allister went to work for Ruth McMullen for six months after leaving school, but stayed for three years. He rode horses belonging to Paul Rackham and, later, Tom Hunnable, through whom he met his wife, Anne, who was producing ponies for the Hunnable children. The Hoods' most memorable year was 1981 when Allister became only the second person (the first was David Tatlow) to win both the Hunter and Hack Championships in the same year, riding Bayleaf and Brown Buzzard, the latter going on to win the Hack Championship again the following year with Cathryn Cooper in the saddle.

▲ Oliver Hood (left) congratulates his father, Allister, after his victory in the Riding Horse Championship in 2006. Allister won on Captain Hastings and Oliver was reserve on Woodfield Alf.

Royal Trooper, twice winner of the Hack Championship, in 2002 and 2003, was also produced by the Hoods; and in 2006, Allister and his eldest son Oliver, then twenty years old, gained a double in the Riding Horse Championship, claiming the title with Captain Hastings (Allister on board) and the reserve with the large division winner Woodfield Alf, ridden by Oliver.

► Mr and Mrs Cooper's Brown Buzzard, winner of the Hack Championship in 1981 and 1982, with Allister Hood.

DAVID TATLOW

Born on the day that the Second World War broke out, David knows all about being brought up on a farm in the 1940s. 'During the war,' he recalls, 'farmers were not allowed to keep horses, other than working animals, because they would eat the valuable grass needed for the stock. We got round this by having a corral in the middle of the wood, so when anyone [official] came round, us children [David was the youngest of five] would take the day off school and move the horses and ponies into the wood. We'd stay with them so they wouldn't whinny and give the game away. Everyone did it.'

Equestrian sports were re-established with remarkable speed after the war. David enjoyed point-to-point riding, and also began to hone his showing skills under the tutelage of his father, Harry, whom he would accompany to Harringay. Here David rubbed shoulders with Harry Bonner and Count Robert Orssich, learning much from watching the great showmen of the time.

Among David's many successes at Wembley was his double win in 1968, when he claimed both the Hunter and Hack Championships – the first time this feat had been accomplished – riding State Visit and Lady Teller. This was the first of three successive Hack Championships for Lady Teller, a classic mare. 'It was the best year of my life,' recalls David. 'My daughter, Lorraine, was born; I was champion point-to-point jockey for the fifth time, and I won the double at HOYS.' David is also the only person ever to have produced and ridden all three weight winners in one year, 1989 – Sea Lightwater, Skibereen and Mr Meade. He found them all as unbroken three-year-olds. Mr Meade claimed the Hunter Championship that year.

David's interest in racing continued alongside his showing career, and he recalls winning a hack title one morning at the Royal Lancashire Show (on Miss Betsy Profumo's Smooth Talk) and then driving 'hell for leather' to ride two winners in the afternoon at

► Mrs. B. Samwell's Lady Teller, ridden by David Tatlow, Champion Hack from 1968 to 1970.

continues ►

Chaddesley Corbett point-to-point. Even at HOYS, David would be keeping an eye on the races. One year, when he was riding a hack called Last Waltz, he decided to break with convention and show the horse in the preliminary judging wearing his top hat and tails. While most onlookers thought that this was just David displaying a touch of eccentricity, he did in fact have an ulterior motive – to disguise the fact that Last Waltz was a fraction long in the back.

David's eccentric behaviour escalated during the preliminary judging, for while he waited for his horse to be judged, he produced a chair and a newspaper and sat down to check the start times for the races at Fakenham, where he had four horses running. (In the early seventies he trained over eighty national hunt winners in under three years.) From time to time he could be seen dashing out of the ash arena at Wembley, across the car park and over the road to the nearest betting office to listen to the next race. 'The punters at the betting office must have thought I had come out of a theatre when they saw me appearing in my top hat and tails,' says David. All that dashing about in his finery was worth it when three of his four runners won their races and Last Waltz won his class.

▲ The late John Rawding with Jennifer Williams. It was Jennifer, widow of Dorian Williams, who put forward the idea for riding horse classes in 1986.

In 1986, riding horse classes were introduced at HOYS, and have subsequently become extremely popular. The idea, put forward by Mrs Jennifer Williams, widow of Dorian Williams, was to fill the gap between the hacks and hunters. Mrs Williams felt that there were few outlets in the showing world for slightly more substantial horses of around 16hh, a size that suited many people. Hacks had to be smaller, while the hunters were often about 17hh. The first riding horse classes at HOYS were judged by Judy Bradwell, who chose Mrs Suzy Rowe's five-year-old Meridian as her champion, ridden by Richard Ramsay. Mrs Rowe won the championship again in 1995 with Meridiana (no relation), but the most successful owner has been Mrs Carol Bardo, who has claimed the title five times with three different horses – Orlando, Soldier Brave and The Philanderer.

The in-hand classes, which had been introduced in 1965, had given much impetus to breeders. Few who saw him could forget the explosive trot of the aptly named Llanarth Flying Comet, one of the horses owned by the University College of Wales when it was left the Llanarth stud. This outstanding black Welsh cob stallion won the Lloyds Bank (as it was then) In-hand Championship at HOYS two years in a row (1979 and 1980). Another horse to achieve a multiple win in this class was the exquisite Hunting Eve. She first won in 1987, when John Rawding succeeded in qualifying four of the eight finalists in the championship. Hunting Eve, a chestnut mare by Three Wishes (a previous winner of this title), had originally qualified to compete under saddle at the 1986 show, but having already been covered she grew too quickly and could not be shown. So instead she came out the following year and swept the board as a brood mare, and she went on to win the in-hand championship at HOYS for the next two years, setting an unprecedented, and unlikely to be repeated, record.

AGAINST THE ODDS

Two of Robert Oliver's top horses survived bad accidents that could have brought an end to their show careers. Just two miles from home, on his way back from Horse of the Year Show after collecting his third championship win, hunter King's Warrior put his foot through the floor of Robert's lorry. Luckily, the driver stopped after hearing a bang, and went to investigate. There were other horses on the lorry, but it was the wooden floor under King's Warrior that had given way, and the fire brigade had to be called to extricate his trapped leg. 'His temperament saved him,' says Robert. 'He didn't try to fight or struggle; otherwise he would have done serious damage to himself.' Remarkably, his leg healed without scarring, and he twice more won his middleweight class at HOYS. Super Ted, another of Robert's stars in the show ring, also suffered a bad accident. This horse came from Ireland and was frequently seen in the hunting field, often being ridden by the whipper-in for the Ledbury hunt. While out hacking about a week before HOYS one year, he was hit by a car with such force that his rider ended up on the road with a broken leg. Super Ted escaped with superficial damage and went on to collect a total of six Cob Championships and one Champion of Champions title.

◀ Judy Bradwell riding Castlewellan, Working Hunter of the Year and winner of the Combined Training at HOYS in 1979, the same year that the pair won the three-day event in Punchestown.

ROY TRIGG

One of the greatest nagsmen of the twentieth century, Roy Trigg showed horses for a remarkable seventy seasons, starting as a young lad on ponies and ending 'in harness' when he died moments after winning reserve at the National Light Horse Championships at Malvern in 1994. He was eighty years old. As Trigg left the arena at Malvern after his success on five-year-old hunter Red Hand, he remarked to Jeff Osborne, rider of the champion, that he did not think he would be doing this job for much longer. Minutes later, in the stable area, still carrying his horse's bridle, he collapsed and died.[3]

In his younger days Roy Trigg had been a keen point-to-point rider, winning over a hundred races, and he also gained an outstanding reputation for breaking-in horses; the Queen Mother and leading trainers Ryan Price, Guy Harwood and John Dunlop all sent him valuable horses to be broken. It was through Roy Trigg that John Dunlop became involved in the showing world. He had seen Huggy Bear (Champion Cob at HOYS in 1981) at Roy's yard and was so taken by him that he asked Roy to look out for another nice cob. Roy, who had a good eye for a horse, spotted Just William 'in the rough', and produced him for John Dunlop to claim the Cob of the Year title at HOYS in 1988 and 1991, and to stand reserve to Super Ted on two other occasions.

Trigg produced several other outstanding cobs, including the grey heavyweight Jonathon, four times champion (1969, 1970, 1972 and 1973), and 1974 champion Justin Time (ridden by his daughter Sue and owned by Annette Landau). He also produced champion hunters Classic Tales and Aristocrat, but probably his best hunter was Admiral, one of the top heavyweights of his time and Hunter of Year at HOYS in both 1971 and 1972. Roy rode Champion Working Hunter Morning Glory in 1976. This horse, with the prefix Coral's, went on to win the Foxhunter Championship in 1980 with Derek Ricketts. When Roy died, his top horses were taken on with great success by his stepson Guy Landau.

► Roy Trigg on board Mr R.H. Bonnett's heavyweight Admiral, Champion Hunter in 1971 and 1972.

◄ Welsh cob Llanarth Flying Comet won the in-hand championship in 1979 and 1980. The handler is Len Bigley.

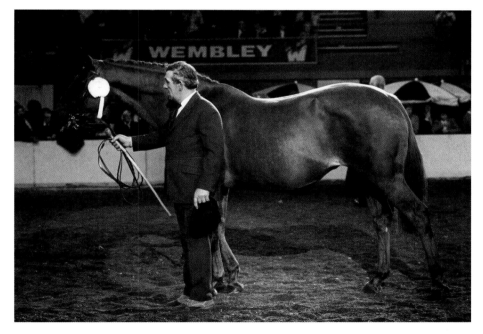

◄ Hunting Eve – led by John Rawding and owned by Miss A.J. Murray – the only horse to win the in-hand championship three years running, 1987–1989.

CHAPTER FOUR

A NEW ERA

Salvaged from the wreckage, reorganised and repackaged, Horse of the Year Show re-emerged in the twenty-first century as a very different beast from the one that struggled through the last decade of the twentieth. At root, it had the same basic format with the same prestigious and coveted titles, the same sense of achievement for riders who qualify to compete there, but there was a different, more up to date feel about it, with a new venue and many new showing classes.

The single most important change was the move to the National Exhibition Centre at Birmingham in 2002. While many people looked back to the old Wembley days with nostalgia, when winning your 'ticket to Wembley' was the catch phrase for qualification to HOYS, and travelling to London to compete was all part of the excitement, there is no doubt that the move to a more spacious, more attractive environment was the greatest catalyst to the show's revival and growth. 'We were nervous about people's reactions,' recalls Mike Gill, a former owner and director of Grandstand. 'But when the move was announced we received hundreds of letters and only one of them was negative.'

Tim Stockdale, a member of Britain's show-jumping team at the Beijing Olympics, believes that if the show had stayed at Wembley, it would not have survived. 'Gone are the days when people are happy to pay just to watch a couple of show-jumping classes, some showing and a display,' he says. 'Nowadays, they

◄ The 2009 Mountain and Moorland Champion Dunedin Marksman, ridden by Matthew Lawrence. The Mountain and Moorland Ridden Championships were introduced to HOYS in 1999.

want a day out; they want to do some shopping, to choose what they watch, and they also want a choice of good places to eat. We were strangled for space at Wembley. The trade stands were outside, and the way the show was being run was too old-fashioned.'

Exhibitors and spectators were not the only ones unhappy with Wembley. The show's organisers, Grandstand Media, were also struggling with the venue, which presented an endless stream of challenges and conflicts for the company to overcome. New structures would be put in without warning – one year Wembley plc rebuilt the stands with closed corners so there was nowhere to store the materials for the show-jumping courses – and concerts or football matches were often scheduled with no concessions to HOYS. When the Spice Girls were booked to play at Wembley on the Saturday before the show,

Grandstand Media were told that the stables could not be built in the car-park area until Sunday, three days before HOYS began. But having the stables put up in good time is one the top priorities for the show's organisers and, Spice Girls or not, the stables had to built. Concert-goers had to park their cars in between rows of half-built stables.

TIM STOCKDALE

The Mr Fix-it of show jumping, Tim has done much to raise the profile of the sport. He featured in a programme for the television series 'Faking It' (his task was to teach a lap-dancer how to show jump), and he was also a judge and trainer for the 2006 TV series 'Only Fools and Horses'. His first real taste of publicity came in 1989, when he and Michael Whitaker were the only two riders left in the Puissance at Horse of the Year Show. When the wall went up to just under 7 feet, they both had it down, at which point the organisers assumed they would share first prize and began dismantling the wall. But back in the collecting ring, the two protagonists got talking; it seemed that neither of them was prepared to give in so easily. Michael told Tim that his horse, Next Didi, would 'definitely jump the wall again' (he had cleared 7 foot 5 inches in Paris the previous year). Tim, riding Supermarket, was less certain about his horse's capabilities, but nonetheless replied, 'So will mine!' By now the spectators were beginning to leave their seats, but when it was announced that the two competitors were coming back in, they sat down again. The wall was rebuilt; both riders had another go, and both cleared it. The crowd were ecstatic, and the story made it on to 'Breakfast News' the next morning.

A natural sportsman, Tim's biggest decision as a youngster was whether to pursue a career in cricket or riding; in the end, he decided to concentrate on riding because at that time – in the early 1970s – show jumping had a higher profile than cricket. Tim made it to his first HOYS in 1982 at the age of eighteen, just after he had started working for Graham Fletcher. From the age of twenty-one, he has never missed a show. His best year was 2002 when he won the Grand Prix on Fresh Direct Parcival. In 2008, he rode for Britain in the Beijing Olympics.

▲ Tim Stockdale riding Supermarket in the Puissance in 1989, the year he shared first prize with Michael Whitaker and Next Didi. Both horses cleared the wall at their second attempt.

When work started on the new Wembley Stadium, it was clear the time had come to find HOYS a new home. By now, the show had started to increase its revenue (attendance figures had almost doubled since 1997), so it was possible to consider a more expensive site. London's ExCel and Earls Court were both considered, but in the end the NEC ticked all the boxes. It had a more rural setting, which is more in keeping with a horse show, plenty of space, hotels on site and a safer feel to it than Wembley – an important factor for a show that finishes late at night and attracts an audience that is 70 per cent female. But perhaps the most significant advantage was the NEC's proximity to a train station, an airport and a major road network, making it far more accessible to competitors and spectators than the other contenders.

It all looked good on paper, but would the gamble of wrenching HOYS from its spiritual home at Wembley actually pay off? Ticket sales soon proved that it had and the show had excellent viewing figures throughout the five days. 'A triumph' trilled the news page of *Horse and Hound*. There were, inevitably, a few teething problems; for example the scheduling was so tight that Katie Jerram had to miss

▼ Three winners from the Walker's yard in 2007: Broadstone Doulton (Robert Walker), So Smart (Sarah Walker) and Marshbrook St George (Vicky Hesford).

the ladies' hunter class, for which she was considered a favourite, to compete in the final judging of the lightweight hunters. Fortunately, she had a convincing win in this class and went on to claim the Show Hunter Championship with Rosenbright. Distances between horseboxes, stables and arenas were also greater at the NEC, putting more strain on already weary legs, but nonetheless the showing exhibitors endorsed the new venue with one of the best turnouts for many years, and it was clear that there would be no going back.

▶ Katie Jerram, one of the busiest and most successful riders on the showing circuit, riding the Supreme Champion at the 2010 show, dual winner of the Ladies' and Lightweight Hunter titles, Dunbeacon.

When Grandstand Media stepped in at the last minute to run HOYS 1997, the show had the lowest audience attendance it has ever known; the company therefore set about rebranding the show's image and targeting the core equestrian market. In previous years, Wembley plc had spent much of its advertising budget on displaying posters at railway and tube stations, and placing advertisements in national newspapers. The organisers had tried to broaden the show's appeal by putting more emphasis on the production and by increasing the entertainments and general razzmatazz. There was a sense that the show had lost its way, and the new organisers wanted to redress the balance and let the horses take centre stage again.

The show had been brought back from the brink just in time to celebrate its golden jubilee in 1998, and, as if by order, one of the golden oldies of the showing world, Bill Bryan, won twice – the Small Hunter title with Toy Boy and the lightweight cob class with Gay Gordon, both horses owned by Jill Ashmole. Richard Ramsay claimed the lions' share of the prizes that year by winning both the Hack and Riding Horse Championships, with Valentino and Orlando respectively, and also the inaugural Arab Championship on ten-year-old stallion Azraell. The horse's owner, Samantha Horwell, had handed over the ride to Richard after qualifying two stallions for the show.

▲ Judges John Chugg and Jo Bates leave the arena.

When Susan George became honorary president of Horse of the Year Show in 1998, her enthusiasm for Arabian horses provided a catalyst for the introduction of ridden classes for purebred Arabs, and their presence has added a new dimension to the show. There are separate classes for mares, geldings and stallions, with the top horses going through to compete for the championship.

One of the most successful riders of Arabs at HOYS has been Darren Crowe, who won the championship three times between 2001 and 2010, the first time with Katy Lake's Silvern Enchanter. In 2003, he won all three class divisions, riding Tiffani McCarthy's PHA Silvern Risalm to win the stallion class, Sue Hancock's Tawoos in the gelding class and Darren Ash's mare Jammilah. This mare took the championship, ridden by Joanne Woodward. Four years later, after a year off following serious illness, Darren Crowe claimed his second Arab Championship with thirteen-year-old PHA Silvern Risalm (by the very

SUSAN GEORGE

A busy acting career, a film production company, an equine therapy company, Susan George photography and a large Arabian Stud farm are all part of Susan George's busy life, and yet in 1998 she was prepared to take on another active role, that of honorary president of Horse of the Year Show. Every year since then, she has been an inspirational figurehead and ambassador.

At the height of her film career in the seventies, while living in Hollywood, Susan acquired her first horse, a partbred Arabian, and so began her passion for the breed. In 1995, she and her late husband, Simon MacCorkindale, having returned to England, set up her now world-recognised stud farm Georgian Arabians, which houses sixty home-breds. Many of her horses compete at the highest level in England, Europe and the Middle East throughout the showing season.

The success of Georgian Arabians is the culmination of years of tenacious hard work in pursuit of a vision, and in 2009, homebred Egatist became ridden Purebred Arabian Stallion of the Year at HOYS. He is now competing in dressage.

Having well and truly made her mark in the world of cinema and theatre (she is perhaps best known for her enigmatic portrayal of Amy, opposite Dustin Hoffman, in the classic hit movie 'Straw Dogs'), Susan George has now made an impressively positive contribution to the world of equestrianism, spreading the word of the horse wherever she travels. Last year she took on yet another new role, that of president of the Arabian Horse Society, and with her own brand of contagious enthusiasm and energy continues to promote the beauty, athleticism and versatility of the Arabian horse.

successful sire Silvern Sceptre), a horse that had won more than sixty titles in his career but had always just missed out on the HOYS crown, in spite of many attempts. Darren Crowe's third championship win, in 2010, was with Mrs Sussex's Silvern Prince.

(opposite page) Winner of the 2009 Purebred Arab stallion class, Susan George's Egatist, ridden by Abi Thorogood.

PONIES

By 1998, HOYS was hosting an extensive range of pony classes – lead rein (mini show ponies), first ridden, mountain and moorland working hunter, working hunter, riding, and show hunter. Since then, even more have been added, including classes for mountain and moorland riding ponies, mini mountain and moorland, coloured ponies and even miniature horses. In the early years of the show, the pony classes were traditionally held just on the Saturday; these days there are pony classes on every day of the show, and at the end of the afternoon classes an endless stream of small children and teenagers take their turn to exercise their charges in the showing arena. These young riders can be busy from 6 a.m. until 11 p.m.

▼ Darren Crowe claimed his third ridden Purebred Arab Championship when winning the title in 2010 on Caroline Sussex's Silvern Prince.

Native ponies have been a part of Horse of Year Show since the in-hand championships began in 1965, but ridden show classes for them were not introduced until 1999 (although there were already native working hunter pony classes) when the first Mountain and Moorland Pony of the Year was won by Heather Prescott with her Highland stallion Rannock of Trailtrow (bred by Gillian McMurray). It was a good year for the natives, as Pumphill Belladonna became the first Dartmoor ever to win the in-hand title. Eleven years later, her son, stallion Pumphill Buckthorn, pulled off a unique double to win both the flat and Working Hunter Mountain and Moorland titles. Before that, native ponies were in the spotlight in 2002 when Connemara stallion Castle Comet, ridden by Vanessa Compton, was selected by Liz Edgar and Jenny Pitman to take the Supreme ridden title. One of the top producers of mountain and moorland ponies to have emerged in recent years is Sam Roberts, who in 2009 qualified twelve ponies for HOYS, one in every section.

There have been some exceptional Welsh pony and cob winners in the in-hand classes at HOYS. In 1967, the Welsh cob Honyton Michael ap Braint, shown by Mostyn Isaac, became the first mountain and moorland winner of this championship, sponsored at the time by Fredericks, manufacturers of loose boxes. Treharne Tomboy, a Welsh mountain pony produced by David Reynolds, won in both 1968 and 1969, and Mr and Mrs Len Bigley, who have produced over forty qualifiers for the in-hand championship at HOYS, won with Llanarth Flying Comet in 1979 and 1980. Another dual winner was the roan stallion Pinewell Bucks Fizz, shown by one of the UK's leading producers, Colin Tibby, for Mrs A. Higgins. He took the Cuddy In-hand Championship in 2008 and 2009.

JULIE TEMPLETON

One of the most successful producers of show ponies on the circuit, Julie began her own career as an event rider, but soon switched to producing ponies. Her first major HOYS success came in 1986 when Gaylord of Keston won the Pony of the Year title. This was followed by two more pony championships in 1996 and 2004, with Trelawn Playboy and Colbeach Salaman respectively. Julie also produced the first Mini Show Pony champion, Roseisle Bridesmaid, when this class was introduced in 1992, and she had another first in the Mini Mountain and Moorland Championship, when these classes started in 1999, with Brierdene Llewelyn. In 2009, she qualified an impressive twenty-three horses and ponies for HOYS.

The riding pony classes have continued to go from strength to strength since 1997, and many riding pony producers have also had success in the plethora of other classes that now swell the pony ranks at HOYS. In 2005, Debbie Thomas had a remarkable year, producing the riding, intermediate, show hunter and mountain and moorland ridden champions, and she also fielded the top three ponies in the 138cm class. To cap an incredible week, the Supreme Pony title was awarded to the champion riding pony, Broadgrove Chatterbox. 'Beautifully ridden by Jemima Walker – who had a "good luck" autograph signed by her heroine, show jumping star Ellen Whitaker, in her pocket – … the pair gave a wonderful, mannerly display to wow both the sell-out crowd and judges Di Lampard and Michael Clayton.'[1]

Broadgrove Chatterbox (a former in-hand champion by Cusop Dimension out of Oldcourt Cantata) was home-bred by his owner Ann Fowler, who also bred the reserve on this occasion, Chatterbox's half sister Broadgrove Serenade. To add to Ann Fowler's already successful week, she watched her daughter, Alexandra, carry off the Intermediate Show Riding Type Championship with Alpine Diplomat.

It was the turn of a show hunter pony to take the Supreme Pony accolade in 2006, with Chloe Willett and Fairholme Rossetta's Rhapsody collecting the

▲ Pinewell Bucks Fizz, a Welsh Section A stallion owned by Mandy Higgins and shown by Colin Tibby, won the Cuddy Supreme In-hand title for two years in a row, 2008 and 2009.

top honours. This was not the first time a show hunter pony had claimed the top spot, though. In 2001, Gemma James gained a popular win on Debbie Thomas's Chiddock Spot On, bred by Gilly Davies from Chiddock Frankino out of Pendley Spotlight.

In the same year, the Hollings team claimed their third win in four years in the 138cm show pony class with Radway Flashdance (by Sandbourne Royal Ensign), and a young Laura Collett (now an international event rider) began her winning ways by taking the 128cm show pony class on Hamptonne Wild Orchard and going on to stand reserve to the Gilbert-Scotts' and Mrs J. Rucklidge's Jackets

► Broadgrove Chatterbox, owned by Mrs A. Fowler and ridden by Jemima Walker, winner of the 2005 Supreme Pony Championship.

Maybe (whose dam, Jackets Maysong, won the title in 1989). Two years later, Laura Collett won the Supreme Pony of the Year award with the Welsh Section A Penwayn Ryan.

One of the youngest riders to achieve serious stardom in the show classes was five-year-old Hannah Horton, who at her first HOYS appearance in 1999 took the overall Supreme title with her mini champion Greylands Little Gem, also aged five. Bred by Judith Thomas, and led by Jessica Pritchard, who broke her in, this delightful pony did not put a foot wrong, and his victory was a welcome tonic for Hannah's godparents, Majorie and Richard Ramsay, as the latter was sidelined at the time with a broken hip.

LADIES FIRST

During the seventies and eighties, lady riders had struggled to make their mark at HOYS in the hunter classes, but now the ladies were becoming an increasing threat to the men, although Guy Landau (who had taken on the rides from his late father-in-law, Roy Trigg) helped to keep them at bay by winning five Show Hunter Championships between 1997 and his retirement from the show ring in 2009. Katie Jerram broke through the male stranglehold during this period with her victory on Rosenbright in 2002, and two years later Sue Rawding was victorious with Reaction.

◄ Laura Collett riding her lap of honour after winning the Supreme Pony award in 2003 on the Welsh Section A pony Penwayn Ryan.

► Five-year-old Hannah Horton marks her HOYS debut by winning the Supreme Pony title with the mini pony Greylands Little Gem, also aged five.

▼ Guy Landau and John Dunlop's Finn McCool III in 2008, the year they won the Supreme Horse title. The following year the pair won the Hunter Championship for the second time, and Guy and Finn McCool retired from showing.

The 2005 showing classes at HOYS were dominated by women. Admittedly, Charles le Moignan and Robert Walker headed the hunters and small hunters respectively, but beyond that the men did not get much of a look in: Shelley Perham won the Supreme title with the ladies' hunter Bournebrook Golden Law; Louise Bell won the heavyweight hunter class and Reserve Hunter title with Rockstar; Christie Fairburn took the lightweight division with Second Quest; Kelly Lyons won the Working Hunter title with Barry Bug; Jo Jenkins won the Hack Championship with Daldorn State Melody; Natalie Lintott won the Riding Horse Championship with Gosh; Jane Beswick took top spot in the Coloured Horse and Pony Championship with Electric Storm; Frances Atkinson won the ridden Arabs with Muzonomy; and Jayne Webber rounded off an outstanding season by claiming the Cob Championship on Robocob.

GOING THE EXTRA MILE

In 2001, show classes around the country were severely disrupted by an outbreak of foot and mouth disease. Many shows that normally held qualifiers were cancelled, and, in a last-minute bid to get enough horses qualified for HOYS, extra classes were added to the calendar later in the season. In the end, there was a good turnout at the show. Elinor Steven made the 500-mile trip from Fife to compete in the Harness Pony of the Year, which she won convincingly with her mouse dun Highland gelding Murdoch of Creag Dhubh. The Harness Horse of the Year went to Tessa Reeve's Thank-you Ovation and Thank-you Oh Wow, an elegant pair of Morgan horses, two full brothers, ably driven by David Barker, repeating his success of 1997.

KATIE JERRAM

Katie's first experience of competing at Horse of the Year Show ended in tears when her much-treasured fourth-place rosette, won with great pride by the ten-year-old in the show pony class with the 13.2hh Pendley Wizzard, was chewed to bits by her puppy. Hastily stitched back together, the rosette still has pride of place in Katie's home, alongside hundreds of others that she has collected over the years, including awards for 22 class winners, 12 reserve champions and 11 champions at HOYS. One of the busiest riders on the showing circuit, Katie claimed the Supreme title in 2010 with Dunbeacon, a winner of both the Ladies' Hunter Championship and the lightweight hunter class that year.

Women have traditionally done well in the working hunter classes. The late Gilly Tatlow gained four HOYS championships. Louise Bell has been another prolific winner, and three-times champion, despite enduring a horrendous road accident in 2002 when she suffered multiple breaks to her leg. In the nine years between 2002 and 2010 (inclusive) only one man, Jack Cochrane, wrestled the Working

ROBERT WALKER

It was the thought of competing at HOYS in October 2010 that spurred Robert Walker to make the fastest possible recovery from a debilitating illness he had suffered four months earlier. A brain virus had left the thirty-five-year-old paralysed on one side and unable to speak, but as soon as Robert was able to start moving well enough, he was going for morning runs and lifting weights in the gym to build up his strength again, with one goal in mind: to ride the middleweight hunter Pride and Joy, his 'horse of a lifetime', at Horse of the Year Show. Still feeling weak, he was legged up on to Jill Day's six-year-old gelding (reserve champion for the past two years) only moments before the start of his class, and in a fairytale end to the day, he won the coveted Show Hunter Championship.

That achievement restored Robert's confidence and vitality, and by the end of the week, with another win under his belt (he took the heavyweight cob class with Starry Night), he was feeling much stronger. 'It's always a privilege to be at HOYS,' says Robert. 'Riding in the Cob Championship in front of a full house on a Saturday night can make the hairs on the back of your neck stand up. There is no place like it.'

Robert grew up with ponies and horses – his father, Tony, showed at HOYS – and he competed regularly at local shows in Yorkshire, in gymkhanas and show jumping, but the showing always fascinated him most. He was drawn to the idea of finding a good horse and bringing it as close to perfection as possible.

He first rode at HOYS at the age of sixteen, finishing well down the line in the small hunters, but he had been thrilled just to qualify. Twenty years later he can claim some twenty-five wins and numerous championships (three of them in 2007) with horses produced by him and his wife Sarah from their busy yard in Cheshire. Robert is also a keen hunting man, and is a Master of the Cheshire Hounds.

▲ An emotional moment for Robert Walker and his connections as he receives the Hunter Championship trophy in 2010 on Jill Day's Pride and Joy, four months after suffering a serious illness that left him paralysed on one side of his body.

Hunter title from the women, and in 2003, the working hunter Zin Zan, ridden by Justine Armstrong-Small, claimed the Supreme Horse Championship. It has to be said, however, that one of the most successful riders in working hunters since 1997 has been Tim Fairburn, despite a six month lay-off due to an injury shortly after the 1999 HOYS. Tim claimed the title three times between 1997 and 2001 with his consistent grey gelding Scotch The Rumours, but sadly this outstanding horse died of a heart attack on the eve of the 2002 show.

NEW CLASSES

In the 1980s and early nineties, it became increasingly difficult for amateur riders to make their mark on the showing world, and their chances of competing with any great success at HOYS were very low. So South Essex Insurance Brokers (SEIB) sponsored a series of classes that was to revolutionise the showing scene and open up the 'world's most famous horse show' to people who would never have thought it possible to win a prize there. The Search for a Star classes, first held in 1998, the same year that the popular classes for coloured horses were added, have been a resounding success, introducing hundreds of new riders to top-level showing and showcasing some outstanding new horses.

JAYNE WEBBER

In spite of her many successes at HOYS, the memory that stands out more than any other for Jayne is the day that, as a ten-year-old, she was legged up on to the legendary Arkle and allowed to sit on him for a few minutes. 'I just remember being totally in awe of him,' says Jayne.

It was a very special moment.' Arkle was taking part each day in the Parade of Personalities, and members of the public were sometimes allowed to visit the stable area where he was kept during the show. It was on one of these visits that Jayne was offered the chance to sit on this famous racehorse.

She has now produced plenty of famous horses herself. A former show pony rider and a member of Britain's pony eventing team, Jayne got back into showing after returning from a spell in South Africa by offering to help out the Ramsays when Richard Ramsay had broken his hip. This gave her the chance to ride Carol Bardo's Soldier Brave, with whom she won the Riding Horse Championship twice, claiming the Supreme Championship in 2004. Jayne's most successful year at HOYS was in 2009, when she won three championships – the Coloured title with The Humdinger, the Cob title with The Keystone Cob, and the Riding Horse title for the second year in a row with The Philanderer. The latter also collected the coveted Supreme Championship award. To round off an outstanding show, Jayne won the Racehorse to Riding Horse class with Mrs Amanda Bowlby's Ironman Muldoon.

▲ Jayne Webber and Carol Bardo's outstanding horse The Philanderer, winners of the Riding Horse Championship for two years in succession, and Supreme Horse in 2009.

Many of the amateur riders who have been encouraged to have a go at these classes have now become hooked on showing. Louise Bell, best known for producing working hunters, knows only too well what it is like to experience that special HOYS moment: 'Once you've won under the lights here, you want to do it again and again.'[2] New equine talent has also emerged from these novice classes: Almost Illegal, a horse placed third in its Search for a Star class in 2005, returned the following year to win the Hack Championship with Katie Jerram on board. According to Robert Oliver, one of the judges of Search for a Star, the standards of riding and of the condition and turnout of the horses in these classes has become so high that sometimes it is difficult to remember that it is an amateur competition.

The Search for a Star classes soon became the most talked about qualifiers for amateurs in the country. In essence, while they provide amateur riders and owners with the chance to compete at Horse of the Year Show, the standards imposed are identical to those applied to professionals. Thus, riders new to the show ring learn to produce their horses to a professional level. To help them achieve this, those riders who qualify horses at one of the five qualifying venues are invited to attend a training workshop to help them prepare for HOYS –

◄ The late Gilly Tatlow, well known for producing working hunters, competing on the 1998 Working Hunter Champion, Little Sister.

◄ Jack Cochrane receiving the Gilly Tatlow commemorative plate for winning the Working Hunter Championship on Mountain Ember. The horse won the championship in 2006 and 2007. Gilly Tatlow's father, John Blakeway, honorary show director in 1992, is presenting the plate.

producing horses to perform their best in the strange, artificial environment of the NEC is difficult enough even for the professionals.

Strict rules ensure that the participants are genuinely amateur riders, owners and horses. Thus no show judges, no professionals and no one who has ridden, exhibited or owned a horse in any show class at HOYS for the last fourteen years may enter. Similarly, horses and ponies produced in a professional showing yard and those shown by a professional are not eligible. There are now six separate Search for a Star classes at HOYS – working hunter, riding club show horse, show hunter, show and show hunter pony (combined), riding horse/hack and show cob

A PRINCE IN HARNESS

Glenshane Prince holds a remarkable record of qualifying for the Harness class at HOYS for nine years in succession, winning the championship on five occasions. His owner and driver Jean Clayden bought the Hackney gelding, by Ingfield Black Prince (winner of the Hackney of the Year title four times), as a two year old, and he soon became part of the family. During his outstanding career, in which he won 168 championships, Jean turned down many valuable offers for him, and he retired with his last performance at HOYS in 2010.

▼ Champion Harness Pony five times, Glenshane Prince is seen here with his owner and driver Jean Clayden, who retired him from competition at HOYS in 2010.

▲ Winners of the 2009 SEIB Search for a Star championship, Ciara McKibben and Welton Archer. The classes were introduced in 1988 and have become very popular.

– culminating in a championship held in the international arena, where riders are expected to wear a top hat and show jacket (black for men, blue for ladies – often borrowed on the day!). The classes are judged by Robert and Claire Oliver and Marjorie Ramsay, who provide added interest and information for spectators by giving their comments about each horse on a radio microphone.

Following the success of these classes, in 2006 SEIB backed the introduction of a show class for ex-racehorses, providing an excellent outlet for a group of horses the welfare of which had recently come under the spotlight. Six years earlier, the British Horseracing Board had launched the Retraining of Racehorses charity, a trust that aims to raise funds to support the rehoming of ex-racehorses. The aim of the classes at HOYS was to show that many racehorses (point-to-point, national hunt or flat) could be reschooled to become mannerly riding horses and could even become top-class show horses. Although it was nothing new for an ex-racehorse to do well in the show ring – Vin Toulson's first Hunter Champion, Prince's Street, had come off the racetrack – to have a class specifically for them at HOYS has provided another goal for these horses, and one that has helped ensure they are retrained to a high standard when their racing career is over.

SHOW JUMPING

While these new classes have provided a breath of fresh air in the showing rings, new faces in the show-jumping arena have given fresh impetus to the sport at HOYS. Among the most exciting new stars to emerge on the show-jumping scene in the last fourteen years are the Whitaker cousins, Ellen and Robert, together with Ben Maher, all of whom have become enormously popular with the HOYS spectators. Other talented riders, including Tina Fletcher (three times winner of the Queen Elizabeth II Cup) and Laura Renwick, add to the glamour and drama, and no one could now complain about 'the same old faces' – although it's still good to see a few of them around. One of the most remarkable aspects of show jumping at HOYS in recent years has been the chance to watch two generations of the famous Whitaker family battle it out for honours in the international arena at Birmingham. Their presence provides an extraordinary opportunity (and one that is almost unique to Britain) to see father compete against son, and uncles compete against nieces and nephews, and it creates a reassuring sense of continuity as well as intense but friendly rivalry. And, of

BEN MAHER

One of the most successful of Britain's younger generation of riders, Ben first competed at HOYS in 1993 when he was ten years old, coming second in the 128cm finals on Beau's Springbox. However, he really shot to fame eleven years later when he won the Puissance at HOYS, his first entry in any Puissance event. Riding Mrs Moore's Eperlaan de Fouquet, known as Blue, both Ben and his horse were suffering from nerves on the night of the class.

Ben takes up the story: 'The crowd was getting very excited, cheering and clapping loudly. You could feel the sheer energy generating from the arena, but I think they noticed that Blue was unsettled, so they started shushing each other when we entered the arena. By the later rounds, you could hear a pin drop they were all so quiet. It was lovely that they were all so supportive and I could feel them willing us over the great wall. Before I knew it we were in the final round along with John Whitaker

and Keith Shore, and the wall was at 2.23m [7 feet 2 inches]. I was the last to go and I knew that all I had to do to win was to go clear. I was thinking: "Oh my God! I have never jumped this high. I hope Blue can do it!" Even before we had landed, I knew we had done it because the sound of the crowd was deafening.'[1]

Two years later, Ben and Blue were winning at HOYS again, this time sharing their Puissance victory with Cian O'Connor and Robert Whitaker. The previous year, Ben had gone into the record books at Hickstead by winning both the Speed Derby and Hickstead Derby in the same week and, at the age of twenty-two, becoming the youngest rider to win the Derby since twenty-year-old Michael Whitaker twenty-five years earlier. Ben was selected to compete on the British team in the Bejiing Olympics in 2008, and the following year collected $100,000 when he came third in the Calgary Grand Prix on Robin Hood W.

course, there is always the consolation for the family that if one Whitaker fails, there is likely to be another who succeeds.

This era has been marked by the return to form of two great riders who had both suffered a devastating illness or injury. At the age of forty-six, John Whitaker had a brief brush with death in November 2000 when he had a cerebral haemorrhage while competing in Sweden. Despite the seriousness of his illness, he was back on a Nations Cup team in June the following year, when the team for the competition in Drammen, Norway, was made up entirely of Whitakers – John, his son Robert, daughter Louise and brother Michael. But for the next year John struggled to regain his status in the upper echelons of the sport, and in particular to get back into the World Cup shows. It was 'a long climb back towards the top ten',[3] but any doubts that he would give up the fight were dispelled at the 2002 Horse of the Year Show when he won the Daewoo National Championship on the Thursday night and received a standing ovation from the packed arena. It was the only class for which he had managed to qualify, and he won it in convincing style. In the jump-off, Tim Stockdale with Fresh Direct Parcival had jumped a competitive clear round against the clock, only to have his time shaved by 1.5 seconds by Keith Shore on It's Magic Max; but John, last to go on Lord Z, gave an outstanding performance to finish an incredible 2.5 seconds under Keith Shore's time.

'In thirty years of competition, I've never seen you ride a better round,' said the text message sent to John by Nick Skelton immediately after the class. That year Nick was also making a welcome return to the HOYS arena, after a three-year gap. In September 2000 he had broken his top vertebra in two places and, in spite of spending two months in a metal neck brace, had trouble getting his injury to heal. So in February 2001 he decided to announce his retirement from international show jumping. He was forty-two. Before his injury, though, Nick had already found John and Lisa Hales' outstanding stallion Arko, and when he eventually started to ride again, it was this horse that gave him the inspiration to return to the top of the sport. HOYS 2002 was his first international show in more than two years.

While Nick Skelton was nursing his broken neck, Robert Smith was flying high at the 2000 HOYS, winning a remarkable seven classes – three national and five international competitions. He began the week by showcasing two outstanding young horses that were to bring him much future success; six-year-old stallion

▲ Ben Maher and Eperlaan de Fouquet on their way to winning their first-ever Puissance in 2004. The pair won again in 2006, this time sharing first prize with Cian O'Connor and Robert Whitaker.

Marius Claudius won the AON five-and-six-year-old class and the Foxhunter Championship, and seven-year-old Senator Mr Springfield, which had come to Robert from Jimmy McCloskey in Ireland the previous spring, won the Daewoo Championship. This talented horse went on to win the Grand Prix at the end of a week in which Robert also won the Speed Horse of the Year, the Woodpecker Trophy and the Xerox Business Services Cup.

The junior and young rider classes in this period were a hotbed of good talent. In 1999, Grace Barton gained her second successive Young Rider title, and Alice Beaumont won the junior rider title – Leading Pony Show Jumper of the Year – on the legendary pony Colton Maelstrom. This pony won again, with Alice's sister Martha, in 2001, the year that Robert Whitaker secured the first of his two Young Rider Championships. The Pavitt sisters, Louise and Nicole, were also making a name for themselves, and for the three years from 2005 to 2007, the Leading Pony Show Jumper of the Year class was dominated by young Whitakers, William, Thomas and George each claiming the title in succession.

► Demolition job – things not going quite to plan for Keith Shore and Anderson's Free Spirit in the 2004 Puissance.

◀ Another Whitaker win – William Whitaker, son of Ian and Alison, celebrates winning the Junior Foxhunter title in 2003 on Devlin.

ROBERT WHITAKER

Between 2001 – the year he won the first of his two successive Young Rider Championships – and 2010, Robert has won or come second in at least one class at HOYS every year, and he is likely to improve upon this record, given that he has clearly inherited the show-jumping talents of his father, John. One of those talents is the ability to remain calm and focused under pressure, which, combined with his own steely determination, has helped him to secure some brilliant results. He honed his skills at junior and young rider level, winning five team gold medals between 1999 and 2004, and his record at HOYS over the last ten years has been outstanding. It includes two Puissance wins, and two HOYS Cup victories. His best year so far is 2008, when he won four classes and came third in two others.

► One of the most
consistent riders
at HOYS is Robert
Whitaker, seen here
in 2010 on his way
to winning the Zinc
Management Trophy
with Omelli.

COLTON MAELSTROM

Sometimes referred to as the mini Milton, this spirited pony resembled Milton only in her remarkable jumping ability not, alas, in her looks. Saved from the abattoir by her first owner, Pat Morris, 'Apey' proved a little too enthusiastic for Pat's daughter and was sold on to Ian Knobbs, who lived in the village of Colton – hence the pony's name. Her breeding is unknown, but her performance record is a part of show-jumping history: from 1994 to 2005 she competed in twelve European Pony Championships ridden by seven different riders, and was the only pony to win the individual title two years in succession (1995 and 1996 with Ireland's Emma Wilson). She was on the victorious British team for eight years in a row, winning the individual title for a third time with Martha Beaumont in 2002.

At HOYS this remarkable pony won the Leading Pony Show Jumper of the Year title three times – in 1997 with Sammy Pharo, in 1999 with Alice Beaumont and in 2001 with Martha Beaumont. William Whitaker was the last rider to compete at a European championships with Colton Maelstrom, winning a team silver medal in 2005, and he also rode her into second place in the Leading Pony Show Jumper of the Year at HOYS. He won the competition with his other ride, the Sewell's French-bred stallion Indien de Here.

◄ The remarkable pony Colton Maelstrom pictured with William Whitaker on board. The pony took three different riders to the Junior Rider of the Year title, and competed at twelve European Pony Championships with seven different riders.

▶ (opposite page) Ellen Whitaker riding Kanselier at the 2010 show, the year she won three competitions on the opening day of the international classes.

▼ Laura Renwick and Oz de Breve, an outstanding partnership. They were runners up in the 2009 Foxhunter Championship and won the 2010 Leading Show Jumper of the Year title.

In the late 1980s and nineties, it was quite rare for a woman to win one of the major senior show-jumping classes at HOYS, but since the start of the twenty-first century more women have been getting into the frame, in particular Laura Renwick, Tina Fletcher and Ellen Whitaker. At the 2010 show, they dominated proceedings with Laura Renwick claiming three classes, including the Foxhunter Championship (her second win in five years) and the coveted Leading Show Jumper of the Year competition. Ellen Whitaker won three classes on the opening night of the international show jumping, and followed this up with a dramatic win in the Puissance, which she shared with Tina Fletcher. Further-

more, in the national competitions, Louise Pavitt won the six-year-old championship, Nicky Boulter won the Grade C championship, Di Fairclough won the Amateur Classic, and four of the six junior classes were won by girls. Could this be a future trend, or was it just an exceptional year? Perhaps by the time the show celebrates its seventy-fifth anniversary in 2023 we shall know the answer.

ELLEN WHITAKER

Ellen Whitaker has competed at every Horse of the Year Show since she first qualified for the 128cm class at the age of eight. At her first show, she managed to jump clear in the first round, but her pony ran off with her against the clock in the jump-off and hit the last fence, putting them in seventh place.

As the daughter of Steven Whitaker, Ellen had watched her uncles, Michael and John, compete at HOYS, and from a very early age she knew that this was what she wanted to do. 'My parents never pushed me,' she says. These days, in spite of all her experience at international level (she won a team silver in the Junior European championships in 2003; she first rode for a senior British Nations Cup team in 2004 at the age of eighteen; and she won a team bronze medal at the 2007 European championships), the golden girl of show jumping still gets nervous at HOYS. 'There is nothing like jumping in front of a home crowd. This is the show I always want to do well in.'

Ellen's enthusiasm and love for the sport is infectious, and there is always a stream of young admirers queuing up for her autograph. In both 2009 and 2010, she had outstanding results at the show: in 2009, she won the Puissance outright on Ladina B, and also won the Speed Horse of the Year and the Leading Show Jumper title. The following year she won three classes on the opening day of the international show jumping, and then battled it out for joint honours in the Puissance with Tina Fletcher; they were the only two riders to clear the wall at 7 feet 2 inches and were treated to a full Mexican wave from the capacity crowd.

CHAPTER FIVE

TELEVISION

'Ten minutes to air; ten minutes.' The production assistant sitting in front of the bank of television screens in Sky Sports' main production truck starts the countdown for the evening's live transmission from Birmingham's NEC. 'Stand by Alex; roll orange camera; cue Alex,' says the director, Mike Allen, but there is a problem. Alex Hammond's auto-cue is not showing up properly and she is having trouble reading it. Luckily, this is just the run through and the matter is soon put right.

'Five minutes to air; five minutes.' The countdown continues, relentlessly. 'Can you just tidy Andy's collar a bit,' says Mike. Andy Austin and James Fisher are waiting at the edge of the collecting ring with Alex, ready to take part in the introduction to the show.

'Two minutes to air; two minutes.' Mike is not happy. 'We need to sort these guys out. Get James out of the way of the cables and bring Andy forward a bit. They should be standing on the bits of tape we put on the floor. Okay, Pony Club teams on Red camera. Standby Red; standby guys.'

'Five, four, three, two, one,' the final countdown begins. 'Roll Orange [camera]; roll 2010 [the pre-recorded music and film that starts the show's coverage]; standby Alex; role Brown; cue Alex.' The introductions begin; Alex Hammond, the unflappable and charming front woman for Sky Sports coverage of Horse of the Year Show welcomes viewers to the show and chats with Andy Austin and

ALEX HAMMOND

Horses have long featured in Alex Hammond's life – she was a junior show jumper and then an amateur flat jockey – so she has first-hand knowledge of equestrian sport. She is also an accomplished musician, playing bass guitar and tuba. Her media career began when she became a founding presenter of the Racing Channel, and she joined Sky Sports in 2003 as a racing expert, presenting the 'Good Morning Sports Fans' programme. Alex is now familiar to equestrian viewers as the presenter of Horse of the Year Show, usually accompanied by Andy Austin in the glass 'bubble' above the arena at the NEC.

▲ Sky Sports presenter Alex Hammond takes instructions from a cameraman.

James Fisher, while behind them, in a somewhat surreal take, the Knights of Middle England pass by on their way to give their display in the main arena.

At 8.12 p.m. exactly the cameras will go live in the international arena to film the Prince Philip Cup competition, so if the sixteen Pony Club children and their ponies are expected to be even just thirty seconds late in starting, the Sky Sports production team, headed by executive producer Trisha Tolchard, must decide how best to fill that thirty seconds. They may go back to Alex Hammond (sometimes in these situations she must ad lib to fill the gap) or they may run some pre-recorded film.

Throughout the three hours of live coverage, the programme is interspersed with pre-recorded features and live interviews. Suzanne Dando, Sky Sports' glamorous roving reporter, is constantly on standby to provide these interviews. She will do a course walk of the main class with one of the top riders, pre-record interviews with grooms and riders in the stables, and talk to riders in the collecting ring after they have jumped their rounds. Other features and behind-the-scenes stories will have been prepared during the day (some are done weeks before the show), and can be slotted into the programme as required, but the main show-jumping class of the night always goes out live.

For four nights in succession, Sky Sports transmits a three-hour programme from Horse of the Year Show. This may not seem like a lot of air time, but the amount of equipment, technical staff, planning and preparation required to provide the high standard of transmission is staggering. Planning begins six

◄ Ringside view: Sky Sports presenter Alex Hammond in the 'bubble' overlooking the international arena at the NEC.

▼ Choosing the best camera shot – the view from inside one of the three production trucks used by Sky Sports at HOYS.

▲ Suzanne Dando interviews
Horse and Hound columnist
Graham Fletcher.

months before the show when site visits are made to check camera positions, lights and commentators' seating and to sort out any changes to the organisation and to the NEC itself that might affect Sky Sports' coverage. In 2009, for example, when the arena entrance had to be moved because of the development of a new restaurant at the NEC, the commentators were seated so high up in the stands that they could not get a full view of the arena.

To grasp the scale of the operation it is worth noting a few statistics: the 90 strong TV crew consists of 30 production staff and 60 technicians for cameras, videos, lights, sound and electricity. For the technically inclined, there are 16 cameras including two radio cameras, one of which is a Steadicam (a counter-balanced camera that enables pictures to remain steady while the operator is walking around); two jibs (cameras mounted on a long arm allowing the head to move through an arc to follow the action); a superslo camera for slow-motion replays (three times slower than normal); an Arri Hi-Motion camera (10 times slower than normal); an I-Movix camera (40 times slower than normal); a remote control camera and a fixed radio mini camera placed in the fences for close-up views of the jumping. In addition to the cameras, there are 16 general microphones around the main arena, radio microphones for interviews and two special microphones suspended from the roof gantry for the 5.1 surround sound. To supply all of this equipment and to connect it to the three massive production trucks, over 12.5 kilometres (nearly 8 miles) of cables are installed before the show gets under way. Sky Sports even brings its own catering unit to feed its army of workers for the duration of the show.

In charge of the entire set-up is Trisha Tolchard, who is responsible for planning and coordinating both the pre-recorded and live output, and for liaising with the show controller, Val Turner, to ensure that commercial breaks and interviews can be allocated sufficient space within the timetable. If there are

SUZANNE DANDO

A regular television presenter, Suzanne joined the Sky Sports team in 2005 when the company started live broadcasts from Horse of the Year Show. Now she enjoys riding for pleasure, but as a youngster she was 'not allowed near a horse' because she was pursuing a successful career in gymnastics – Suzanne competed in the 1979 world championships, and in 1980 was British national champion and also captain of the British Olympic team in Moscow.

last-minute gaps to fill, Trisha will take snap decisions on what to use, while the director, Mike Allen, will put those decisions into practice. 'It is nerve-wracking sometimes,' says Trisha. 'The first time we broadcast live from here, in 2005, the Pony Club Games were seven minutes late starting, so I had quickly to find a feature to fill the gap and then change the auto-cue to introduce the feature.'

Trisha also liaises with Sky Sports headquarters, particularly if the show is running a few minutes late and is likely to finish after the 11 p.m. cut-off time, so that scheduled programmes can be rearranged to allow for the overrun. 'We would never go off air before a class has finished,' explains Trisha. 'Live sports coverage takes precedence over pre-recorded events.'

It is indeed the 'live' element that makes the job so exciting. Although much of the preparation, filming and editing goes on in advance, putting it all together during a live, three-hour transmission is a major undertaking. In one of the three production trucks parked outside the NEC stadium sits Phil Murphy, the director of show-jumping production, who watches all the live coverage of each class from twelve different cameras and is continuously choosing which particular camera shot to use at any given moment. These are then relayed through to the main production truck, where Mike Allen is in charge of what goes out on air. In the third production lorry is Tim Brown, the video-tape coordinator, who will send through pre-recorded and edited tapes to Mike whenever they are required for transmission. This truck also has five EVS (disc-based recorder) machines and three tape machines recording all the show jumping for slow-motion replays at the end of each round. These are cued in by Mike when needed.

Nine people are based in the main production truck, including an auto-cue operator, who is constantly checking and updating the auto-cue, and two operators working on an EVS hard-disk recorder to produce the montages that lead into the advertisement breaks and also close the show each day – a collection of the best moments of the day cut to music. It is relentless and intensive work.

▲ Interview time – Laura Renwick at the 2010 show, when she won the Leading Show Jumper of the Year title and claimed her second Foxhunter Championship.

There are so many different facets to Horse of the Year Show, and so much going on, that the live transmission is a constant juggling act. Sky Sports prides itself on providing full, all-encompassing coverage of the show, bringing in background information, explanations, good stories and interviews to add to the excitement and interest of the show-jumping classes and other competitions and displays. These are all included in the programme before live coverage begins on the main show-jumping class of the night. And live, means live. There is no built-in time delay to the programme.

All this goes out to viewers in high definition with 5.1 surround sound. It is up-to-the-minute technology and a far cry from the days when Dorian Williams made his first broadcasts for the BBC from Harringay in 1950. At that time, Dorian handled both the public-address system and the television commentary in what was basically a one-man show. 'I can remember a number of occasions,' he wrote,[1] 'when in the short break between the first round and the jump-off,

► Jessica Mendoza, Leading Pony Show Jumper of 2010, with her trainer Andy Austin, who is one of the Sky Sports' presenters.

DORIAN WILLIAMS

Known as the voice of show jumping, Dorian Williams' contribution to Horse of the Year Show, and to the equestrian world in general, was immense. Television commentator, journalist, author and a Master of Foxhounds, he was instrumental in promoting show jumping to the height of its popularity during the 1950s and sixties, and continued to champion its cause until he died from cancer in July 1985.

Although he played a major role in the production and organisation of Horse of the Year Show, he is probably best remembered for his brilliant commentaries; he had a great knowledge of the sport and a voice that was easy on the ear, but above all he was a master of timing and delivery, knowing when to remain silent and how to build up the tension and excitement in a competition. He was also a keen amateur actor, something that undoubtedly helped him to create drama in his commentaries, and in 1949 he established an annual Shakespeare festival at his family home, Pendley Manor, near Tring.

Michael Clayton, editor of *Horse and Hound* from 1974 to 1997, writes this about him: 'Dorian Williams' contribution as a commentator was perhaps under appreciated by some in the show world who did not at the time understand the real need for a bridge between their specialist interests and the wider public. He was an actor and natural communicator, and created interest in equestrianism among people who had absolutely no experience of horses. In those days a Horse of the Year Show class was done live with no more than two cameras, and Dorian Williams' sighs and hisses were about the only sound effects. He was a master of long silent pauses and dramatic moments – a skill that seems utterly lost among today's sports commentators, who chatter ceaselessly.'

Dorian's first career was as a schoolmaster, and after the Second World War his interest in education prompted him to set up a centre of education, mostly for adults, at Pendley. Throughout his life he suffered bouts of ill-health (he survived three operations for cancer), and all efforts to join the army during the war were thwarted because he failed the medicals. However, he was able to return to his first great love in life, hunting, in 1950, and by the end of his first season with the Grafton was asked to take on the joint Mastership with Colonel Neil Foster. In 1954 he became Master of the Whaddon Chase, a post he held until 1980.

Dorian was involved with Horse of the Year Show from the start. In 1946, his father, Colonel V.D.S. Williams, had been asked to help organise the National Horse Show, the first big show to be held after the war, and he realised only a week before the show was due to start that he did not have anyone to do the public-address announcements. He immediately contacted his son to tell him he had a job for him. When Dorian was somewhat taken aback by the news that he was to be the announcer at the National Show in a week's time, his father said, 'Well, you're supposed to be educated and know how to speak; and you've been brought up with horses. You'll love it.'

His father was right. Dorian took on the job for the three-day show; three years later he was in charge of the public address for the first Horse of the Year Show at Harringay, and three years after that he became the BBC's first official equestrian commentator, a role he retained for the next thirty years.

Dorian's involvement with HOYS went well beyond his role as commentator. He acted as adviser and supporter to Mike Ansell, he devised and wrote some of the best displays, and his natural talent for theatre influenced the music and much of the general 'production' of the show. His commentary box was the

continues ▶

control centre of the show, and in the early days his job included commentating for the BBC while also doing the ringside commentary and being at the hub of the minute by minute running of the show.

In addition to his commitments to HOYS and the BBC, Dorian was a prolific author and journalist. He founded the 'Off the Bit' column in *Horse and Hound* in 1961, writing under the pseudonym 'Loriner', and he continued to write every Loriner contribution without missing a single issue until his death. Few knew the real identity of Loriner, and Dorian's enormous knowledge in all areas of equestrianism, and the scope and versatility of his articles, led many readers to assume that the column was the work of a group of writers.

Dorian wrote twenty-five books, many of them on show jumping but including two autobiographies, a collection of fictional stories for children, known as the Wendy series, and two other books – *Pancho* and *Kingdom for a Horse* – aimed at adults. His wife Jennifer was a successful producer and breeder of show ponies and hacks, and Dorian was chairman of the British Horse Society for nine years, from 1973 to 1982, and president for the next two years. In 1978 he was awarded the OBE in recognition of his services to the world of the horse.

while the fences were being raised, having given out the clear rounds and the height of the new fences, I would then leap out of my commentary position, double down the back to interview one of the finalists, then race back, just in time to announce the start of the jump-off. Very occasionally, I would pick up the wrong microphone, but no one ever seemed to worry unduly.'

▼ Dorian Williams, the voice of show jumping, carrying out his role as commentator. Dorian was also a Master of Foxhounds, journalist and amateur actor and was involved with the running of the show from the start.

When Horse of the Year Show first started, the BBC had little interest in show jumping, and it took all of Mike Ansell's persuasive powers to get them to cover the show. Television had only just begun to re-establish its sports coverage after the war. No one at the BBC knew much about show jumping, and, as far as the British public was concerned, the sport was still a novelty. But in 1950, one competition in particular caught the attention of the viewing public and brought home to the BBC just how entertaining show jumping could be. The compelling dual between Pat Smythe on Finality and Harry Llewellyn on Foxhunter in the Puissance probably sealed the fate of show jumping's television coverage for the next thirty years.

The participants in the Puissance that year had been whittled down to two riders after the first two rounds: a twenty-year-old girl riding a 15hh mare bred from a horse that had spent most of her life pulling a milk cart, and an ex-jockey (Harry Llewellyn twice rode in the Grand National) with a large and already famous horse, the pair having won the prestigious King George V Gold Cup as well as an Olympic team bronze medal.

In the third round they both jumped clear but, going first in the next round, Finality lowered a pole on the triple bar, even though she managed to clear the wall. It appeared that the door was now open for Harry Llewellyn and the incomparable Foxhunter to win the competition, but the big gelding just tapped a brick out of the wall, so they were still equal, on four faults apiece.

Dorian Williams takes up the story:[2]

> The fences were raised. There was an absolute hush as the diminutive Finality and the youthful Pat Smythe rode into the ring. They galloped down to the triple bar, screwed over it, landing well to the left-hand side, but she was clear. Then Pat Smythe did a truly remarkable thing. She pulled up Finality altogether, and there were many people who thought that she had decided that the big, red wall was too much and that she was therefore going to retire. But not at all. In fact, she was just giving the little mare a brief opportunity to get properly balanced. She turned at the end of the arena to face the wall, gathered the reins, applied the pressure of her legs to Finality's sides and set off towards this great wall. She only cleared it by an inch or two, just rapping it with the hind hooves, but she was clear. And so, to keep in the competition, the great Foxhunter had to go clear again as well.
>
> He came in looking every inch the greatest show jumper in the world – as undoubtedly he then was. He jumped the triple bar safely, and this time Colonel Harry Llewellyn was allowing no careless mistake at the wall. He collected himself, measured his stride, drove forward and cleared the wall.
>
> And so both were clear yet again. There was a pause. The atmosphere in the stadium was by this time as tense as only these great occasions can inspire. Some eight thousand people awaited the appearance of Finality for yet another jump-off.
>
> At this moment the telephone at my commentary position (which is also the control point at Horse of the Year Show) rang. My assistant picked up the telephone and then whispered something to me. I was asked to make an announcement. But I did nothing. There was a few moments' pause and then my assistant whispered to me, 'You were told to give it out.' But

I declined. I felt that what I was asked to announce could, in fact, be made public in a far more dramatic way. Instead, therefore, I gave the signal to open the gates from the collecting ring into the arena.

The gates were opened and into the arena rode the mighty Foxhunter, and by his side the little Finality – the David and Goliath that had been thrilling the crowd for the last half hour. When they reached the centre of the arena I gave another signal and the 'boxing lights' were switched on, bathing the whole of the centre of that famous arena in a bright amber light. At that moment Harry Llewellyn leant down and offered his hand to Pat Smythe, who took it. Before that vast crowd they shook hands and Harry Llewellyn took off his hat to Pat.

That gesture made it quite clear that they had decided to divide … I do not think I have ever heard a cheer the likes of the one which went up in the Harringay Stadium at that second Horse of the Year Show …

Already it was nearly midnight. As far as television was concerned we had overrun by more than an hour, but I very much doubt if more than a handful of viewers had switched off, for during the last two hours, they had had something that had turned out to be absolutely compulsive viewing – perhaps for the very first time as far as show jumping was concerned.

For more than two hours the telephone was ringing. Viewers were telephoning the Harringay Stadium, Horse of the Year Show Office, the BBC, even my own home, to say what fantastic viewing they had enjoyed. I have little doubt that it was this great competition, which had so caught the imagination not only of the spectators present but of the millions of viewers watching at home, that was to make the BBC appreciate to the full the possibility of show jumping as a television sport.

Two years later that appreciation was consolidated when Britain's show-jumping team won the gold medal at the Helsinki Olympics. It was the only gold medal won by Britain at these games, and it was won in the eleventh hour (show jumping was traditionally the final event in the main stadium before the closing ceremony), so the riders gained enormous publicity and the sport's popularity was propelled into the stratosphere. Thousands flocked to watch the show at Harringay a few weeks later, and even more tuned in on television to view the evening performances.

In those days, Horse of the Year Show had the advantage of being broadcast just after the 9 o'clock news on BBC, so the programme went out live on prime-time television, giving it a huge advantage over other sports. Furthermore, in the first ten years of the show the BBC was the only television channel available, so whatever was put on was likely to be watched. Once ITV came on air in 1959, viewers had more choice, but by then Horse of the Year Show was so firmly established that it held on to most of its audience. In fact when HOYS was on, ITV discovered to its chagrin that it could lose as many as one and a half million viewers in an evening, creating a serious slump in its advertising sales.

However, once the BBC found itself facing a rival channel, a greater emphasis was immediately placed on technology, on the basis that the channel that produced the cleverest pictures and developed the best techniques would win acclaim. Their efforts to outdo each other in technical expertise were probably largely lost on the general public, who basically just wanted to be entertained, but the battle for viewers had, in Dorian Williams' view, a detrimental effect on standards, a levelling down rather than up. 'I soon became conscious of a subtle change in the BBC's attitude, even in my sport,' he wrote.[3] 'It was becoming apparent that the BBC now required what they would describe as a more "professional" performance from their commentators, but what I would describe as a more "journalistic" approach, punchy, brash, attacking, the emphasis on the sensational … My whisper-over-the-shoulder technique was no longer what was wanted.'

ITV had tried to poach Dorian from the BBC soon after its channel was founded, but as he was under an 'exclusive' contract, Dorian instead recommended Raymond Brooks-Ward, whom he had met some years earlier at his future wife Jennifer's twenty-first birthday party (Jennifer and Dorian had married two years later). Raymond, keen to get into commentating, began assisting Dorian at shows, and when the opportunity came up to work for ITV his career took off.

By the early 1970s, Horse of the Year Show was attracting some 65–70 million viewers during the week, and a survey published in *The Field* found that show jumping was the second most popular television sport to football. But within twenty years the BBC had reduced its coverage of the show to a single, canned programme on the Sunday afternoon. Where did it all go wrong? The BBC blamed the show jumpers, and the show jumpers blamed the BBC.

On the riders' part, the top show jumpers had been failing to make much impression on the international scene at this time – a few championship medals might have given the sport a much needed boost. But the BBC had not helped matters by over-exposing the sport. In the early eighties it was televising every day of the Hickstead Derby, the Royal International, Horse of the Year Show and Olympia. Relying too much on the past success of show jumping's television appeal, it had not updated its presentation format, which was often lacklustre, predictable and unimaginative. Often, to please sponsors, the BBC would broadcast up to three competitions, showing little more than the jump-off of each, which generally featured the same top riders. David Broome had predicted problems for television coverage as early as 1983, when he commented that six days of undiluted show jumping at HOYS was too much, and that there might need to be changes.

RAYMOND BROOKS-WARD

Raymond Brooks-Ward, a familiar voice on BBC television broadcasts, was well known for his lively and informed commentaries, but he was also a man of enormous influence and control behind the scenes. As managing director and one-third shareholder (the other shareholders being the BSJA and the BHS) of British Equestrian Promotions, a company he set up with Bob Dean in 1974, he combined the careers of commentator, sponsorship negotiator and show director, ultimately becoming the 'most powerful individual in the competitive equestrian scene'.[1]

'At Horse of the Year Show, the Royal International and the Olympia Christmas Show, which he founded in 1972, he performed an amazing multi-role: he directed or part directed the shows, he organised the sponsorships on which BEP took commissions, negotiated the TV contracts, performed much of the public-address commentaries, and could be seen in his odd few spare moments checking the seating in the VIP restaurant.'[2]

Raymond was born in 1930 and briefly followed his father into the catering business before dabbling in farming in Hertfordshire. It was his love of hunting that brought him directly into contact with the equestrian world, and from the age of nine, when his uncle bought him his first pony, Raymond was a regular follower of the Enfield Chase. By the time he was fifteen he was whipping-in for the hunt, and in 1972 he became a Master, a post he held for seventeen years.

In 1951, he offered to provide a commentary at the Enfield Chase point-to-point, and soon he was commentating on point-to-points all around the country. His attempts to get into flat racing with the BBC were less successful, but by the late fifties he was assisting Dorian Williams at many of the big shows. So when ITV started up in 1959, Raymond secured a job with them and his career as a commentator took off. Soon he was covering Hickstead and the Royal International for ITV, as well as on radio for the BBC. When Dorian retired in 1981, Raymond stepped into his shoes as the BBC's senior equestrian commentator.

When the changes came, instead of reducing the number of days that were broadcast from the show, or updating their approach to the sport, the BBC took the decision to cut out live coverage altogether, with the exception of an occasional live slot on Saturday's 'Grandstand', shunting HOYS into a canned programme that was transmitted after midnight. Harvey Smith was enraged: 'The BBC must know that the kids, parents, grandmas and farmers are not going to stay up half the night to watch it!'[4]

Once the decision was made to cease live coverage, the show's decline seemed inevitable. Without the live, prime-time slot, viewing figures dropped further; newspaper editors started to give less space to show-jumping reports and instead filled their pages with features about the sorry state of Horse of the Year Show; sponsors became disenchanted because the show was no longer such good value for promotion and publicity, so prize money decreased, which meant that fewer top foreign riders bothered attending HOYS, and thus the show's prestige declined. The BBC's withdrawal had left the show floundering.

The HOYS management teams did, of course, learn to live without live television, and even survived (just) the complete withdrawal of BBC coverage after the

▲ Raymond Brooks-Ward talking to Paddy McMahon in Baltimore, USA (1980). Commentator and organiser of many shows, Raymond had enormous influence on the equestrian world.

◄ Stephen Hadley and Flying Wild, winners of the Foxhunter Championship in 1968.
▲ Stephen joined the BBC in 1980 and commentated alongside Raymond Brooks-Ward at HOYS.

▲ Mike Tucker commentating at the 2010 show. A former event rider, Mike joined the Sky Sports team when live coverage began in 2005.

1991 show at Wembley. The BBC itself had been suffering from lack of funding, which limited the scope of its transmissions from HOYS. It also meant that there was a failure to invest in new technology, and some its best producers left for greener pastures. For example, only four cameras were in use in the main arena at Wembley in 1989, and forty on-site members of staff were required to produce the programmes. Compare that with Sky Sports' ten cameras in the main arena, and ninety-strong crew working with the best technology available. 'Sky Sports does a fantastic job,' says John Whitaker. 'The coverage is excellent.'

Mike Tucker, show-jumping commentator, joined the Sky Sports team when it first began live coverage from the NEC in 2005. Mike had honed his commentating skills on the county show circuit in the 1970s after expressing an interest in commentating to Raymond Brooks-Ward. His television debut came after a chance encounter with some BBC crew at a party, after which he was invited to have a go at commentating during the Midland Bank Horse Trials Championships. The following year, when competing at Badminton, producer Fred Viner asked him to join the BBC commentary team after completing his cross-country round. A successful rider and cross-country course designer, most of Mike's initial work for the BBC was at horse trials. When Dorian Williams died in 1985, Mike took over some of his work in show jumping, but Raymond Brooks-Ward still did most of the BBC commentaries at the big shows. It was not until Raymond died in 1992 that Mike took over his role, by which time the BBC had pretty well turned its back on live show-jumping coverage.

► The technical stuff.

◀ Famous face in the crowd – Martin Clunes.

When Sky Sports began its live coverage, initially at Hickstead and then at HOYS, Mike was well placed to help them, and he now works for both the BBC and Sky Sports. 'Going out live can be nerve-wracking, but you get used to it,' he says. 'You don't get many opportunities now to do live broadcasts, but they are the best part of my job. I get a real kick out of it.' Whereas once Mike's adrenalin rush would have come from riding around a tough cross-country course, now it comes from doing live commentary.

CHAPTER SIX

BACKSTAGE

For most of the year the Grandstand Media office in Harpenden is the hub of the show's organisation. From there, each show is meticulously planned and the myriad different jobs dealt with – choosing the judges, booking displays, securing sponsorships, dealing with entries, sending out press releases, preparing the programme, finding accommodation for officials and booking contractors are just some of the tasks undertaken. The office produces a 'Staff Handbook', 110 pages long, giving every detail about the show from accreditation and ticketing to shuttle buses and lost children. Grandstand Media also analyse qualifiers, manage/sell tradestands and merchandising, and do all their marketing in-house.

The final build-up begins on site at the NEC Arena two weeks before the show starts, and follows a detailed programme of instructions, which sets out exactly when and where things should be delivered, when certain work should be undertaken and by whom. The whole process runs with military precision, although as with anything of this size and complexity, a certain amount of flexibility is required. One year, within three days of the show commencing, the organisers discovered that the barriers for the sides of the international arena were still in Belgium when they should have been in Birmingham. The supplier had misread the delivery date on his contract.

There is no shortage of buildings at the NEC, but external ground space is at a premium. Every spare inch of tarmac on the 50-acre site is used either for contractors' vehicles, officials' caravans, stabling or car parking. The stables, over 800 of them, take up almost the entire area of the south car park, allowing also for the stable manager's office, vet's office, declarations office and isolation stables. Setting up the stables with their surrounding 3km of security fencing is the first major task to be carried out, as they must be ready in time to receive the display horses, which arrive two days early in order to rehearse their performances in the main arena. More horses arrive the following day, and by the first day of the show, the stable blocks are a hive of activity.

Inside the stadium buildings, about five days before lift-off, the extensive lighting system is rigged up, a job that can take up to eight hours to complete; the public-address system goes in, the arena seating goes in, and the all-weather surfaces are laid, both in the international arena and the showing arena. Sky Television erects its 'bubble' above the main arena from where the commentators watch the show and transmit their live commentary, the hospitality boxes are constructed (a bespoke, four-tier VIP suite that will host more than 1,500

▼ A complex system of lighting has to be put in place five days before the show begins.

guests throughout the show), the carpets are laid (12,500 square metres of them) and the drapes are put in place. The show offices and press facilities are also partitioned off along with all the necessary telephone and broadband connections and office furniture. On most days there are well over a hundred people working on site to create an international showground out of two empty buildings and a large expanse of tarmac.

On the two days before the show starts, the main arena is in full use with a busy schedule of rehearsals, including practices for lighting and sound, the arena party assisting with course building, the scurry driving and the Pony Club mounted games. The day before the show starts, the trade-stand holders arrive to set up their stands, and in the evening there are full dress rehearsals for all the displays in the international arena, while in the showing arena the showing fraternity have the chance to exercise their horses in strict rotation up until 11 p.m. The scheduling remains tight for the rest of week, with exercise sessions in both arenas taking place from 5 a.m. each day and, in the case of the showing arena, continuing after the end of the day's classes until late each night. There is not much time for sleep.

It is the showing people who have the most antisocial hours. Classes begin at 7 a.m. each day, or even earlier, which means being up well before daylight to start the long process of cleaning, plaiting, tacking up and adding the finishing touches to the horses or ponies in time for the long walk from the stables to the showing arena at the far end of the NEC buildings. Some of the classes – the hunters, hacks and cobs for example – are held in the international arena early in the morning before the show jumping gets under way, but most of the pony classes take place in the showing arena, which has its own special atmosphere and identity. It operates almost independently, with its own bars and restaurants, but it is connected to the main arena by a vast retail area – all under one roof.

▲ Dressing the fences is all a part of the job. The 'Silk and Stem' team supplies silk flowers for the show.

Frances Youngs is the arena controller for the showing ring, and it is her task to ensure that all the classes run smoothly and, most importantly, run to time, from first thing in the morning until 6 p.m. every day. Frances, who has been involved with the show from nearly every angle – as a spectator, groom, exhibitor and steward – is constantly watching the clock and keeping everyone up to the mark. If classes do run late, it can have a knock-on effect in the inter national as well as the showing ring, because many of the showing championships take place in the international arena. Riders can also have tight schedules, and if the classes do not run to time, they might find that they need to be in two places at once.

Today's showing arena is a different world from the original showing environment at Horse of the Year Show. In the early days, there was an outdoor ash surface, which could be either too dusty or hock deep, depending on the weather. If it did rain, showing conditions were miserable, and the horses were certainly not seen at their best; nor was it much fun for spectators. The arena surface was improved over time, and in the last few years at Wembley a large tent was erected, which, although protecting riders and horses from the elements, was barely big enough to cope with the classes. 'The ceiling was so low that you almost had to duck if you were wearing a top hat,' recalls David Tatlow. The shortage of space meant that classes were split into two sections for the

▼ Exercise time in the showing arena. Classes begin at 7 a.m. and finish around 6 p.m. each day, followed by five hours of exercise time for competitiors.

preliminary judging. One year, the steward, Nick Brooks-Ward, told David Tatlow in jest that he was in the third hack section. Not realising it was a joke, David waited until the first two sections had been judged before discovering that there was no third section.

When the show moved to the NEC in 2002, the showing classes got their own indoor arena, which was a vast improvement. In fact, the new Horse and Hound arena, as it was initially called, became so popular that the noise of cheers and clapping when a winner was announced could be heard from the international arena, which was separated from the showing only by a large curtain. In an attempt to improve things further for the showing audience, the organisers put in extra seating in 2007, so that the entire arena was surrounded by stands. While the idea was well meant, there were not enough seats for all the spectators and, with no standing room available for the overflow, security were having to deny people access to watch the show. 'It was the worst decision we could have made,' recalls Mark Wein, the show director at that time. 'On the first day, we ran out of capacity and I nearly had a lynch mob on me. We decided to pull out the new seats that night and put it back to how it had been in previous years.'

That debacle was the catalyst for an early move of the showing arena to its new site in Hall 1, which, although farther from the stables – riders now have to walk their horses for about ten minutes around the NEC buildings to the arena – has much more space. There is a large collecting ring, with enough room to exercise horses, and a generous main arena with seating stands down the two long sides. At one end there is a bar for sponsors, and at the other a champagne bar and food outlet, with VIP seating. There is also a large restaurant beside the collecting ring. In fact, the arena is so well served that it is easy to forget that a big international show is taking place on the other side of the trade stands. When the new showing arena first opened, Nick Brooks-Ward had to ask Frances Youngs to make an announcement each day to tell visitors that this was not the main show; many spectators arriving at the NEC had found themselves at the showing arena and, thinking this was where all the action took place, stayed there.

'I think HOYS is the only show where people will pay to come and watch show classes. The interest is enormous,' says Frances Youngs. The arena has its own unique atmosphere and has become an increasingly important part of the show, particularly as the number of show classes has continued to increase. Much effort has been made to upgrade the area, and these days music accompanies the

► John Dunlop's Little Alice in the Cuddy Supreme In-hand Horse class, doing a lap of honour in front of a packed audience in the showing arena.

IN THE PINK

Lynn Russell, who has been showing at HOYS since she began her sponsorship with Bailey Horse Feeds about twenty-five years ago, once produced a pink horse at the show. Each year Snuggy Hoods create an outfit for her HOYS horses and in 2006 the company decided to design a fluorescent pink suit for her coloured horse Ascoteer. During the night it rained heavily and unfortunately Ascoteer's stable had a leaky roof. When Lynn removed Ascoteer's rug the next morning, she found that the dye had run and she had a pink horse. 'I was standing in the car park under the floodlights in the pouring rain at 4 a.m. trying to clip him,' recalls Lynn. When that did not work, she tried washing and scrubbing, but all to no avail, and later that morning in her show class quite a few caustic comments were heard about her 'coloured' horse. To add insult to injury, just as she was waiting for the stewards to call the horses forward for the final line-up, Ascoteer kicked out, hitting the boards on the edge of the showing arena and sending alarmed spectators scattering in all directions. There was nothing else for it but to leave the ring. Not only had she suffered the indignity of exhibiting a pink horse but she did not even manage to finish her class. It all came right the following year, however, when she stood reserve in the Coloured Horse Championship with a correctly coloured Ascoteer.

▲ Lynn Russell with Ascoteer, reserve Coloured Horse Champion in 2008. The previous year he had been dyed pink by mistake.

▲ The ground jury and appeals committee at work.

classes (providing music that is modern enough for the youngsters is a challenge, according to Frances). Class winners do their lap of honour to the same music that is used in the international arena.

One of the major changes resulting from showing classes moving entirely indoors at the NEC is that the horses are no longer judged on concrete for their conformation. Some people consider this a pity, because on concrete there is no chance of disguising a minor conformation fault or any slight unsoundness, whereas on a softer surface these problems are sometime less apparent. Other people are only too glad to see an end to the unforgiving concrete, on which many a show horse's prospects were ruined.

Long hours are the order of the day for all the officials at HOYS. Frank Grunnill, the FEI chief steward at the show, and his team of three assistants are on duty from 5 a.m. to midnight each day. Frank's task is to ensure that all the international rules and regulations on stabling, veterinary inspections, collecting-ring procedure and anything else that impacts on the welfare of the horses are strictly adhered to. He also oversees the exercising timetable in both arenas, where a steward is always on hand to make sure there are no accidents. In the international arena, more than forty horses may be being exercised at the same time, so the steward sends them all round on one rein for about ten minutes, and then asks everyone to change the rein. Woe betides anyone who makes a bid for independent action.

▶ Overseeing the horse inspection for the international show jumpers, FEI chief steward Frank Grunnill with vet James Sutton, checking the horse.

Frank's own equestrian experience, besides working as a steward for some twenty years, goes back to the days when he was a mounted police officer with the Merseyside Police Force. He competed at HOYS a few times for Police Horse of the Year but, alas, never succeeded in winning. In those days, many more police forces had a mounted branch and so there were plenty of contestants for the title, but as the number of mounted officers decreased, the competition was eventually phased out. However, HOYS still sometimes features the popular Metropolitan Police Activity Ride as one of its displays.

Another of Frank's responsibilities is to ensure that the show-jumping competitors are ready on time, so that the class can proceed without any gaps between each horse's round. The only exception is when Sky Sports takes a commercial break, which then allows a three-minute pause before the next competitor. As one rider goes into the main arena to jump, another comes into the tunnel from the collecting ring to stand poised for action. The collecting-ring stewards must make sure that this procedure runs like clockwork, to keep the show on time.

Now that the show has live television coverage, keeping to time has never been more important, but even without the pressure of television, timing is important. Hefty fines have to be paid to the NEC if the evening performance runs past 11 p.m. – a prospect that keeps Val Turner, the international arena controller, constantly on her toes. Each day, before the 9.30 a.m. meeting with the production team, commentators and stewards, Val puts together the orders for the day, an extensive list covering every aspect of the show down to the last detail – how many prizes will be presented in each class; who will present them; which stewards are in charge of particular jobs; how long each display will take.

'In the last ten years the show has become more like a theatrical production, rather than just a horse show,' says Val. One corner of the stadium seating area is

▲ The show's chief veterinary officer, James Sutton, whose father was also a veterinary official at HOYS.

▲ Frank Grunnill, the FEI chief steward, keeps an eye on things in the outdoor area.

SORE SHINS

As chief FEI steward, one of Frank Grunnill's many tasks is to look underneath the exercise boots of horses in the collecting ring to check their legs. Although it is all part of the routine for him, it is perhaps not such an obvious request for some of the less experienced show jumpers. One year, Frank pointed to a young rider and said, 'Boots please,' only to turn round a minute later and find the boy sitting on the ground removing his own riding boots.

► Keeping an eye on the competition. Show jumpers watch the closed-circuit television in the collecting ring.

▼ Part of the production team – commentators Steve Wilde and Nick Brooks-Ward.

taken up with the production side of the show. This is the base for the team in charge of sound, light and even smoke, and their 'show caller' (stage manager), Ben Fox, who cues them in; for the public-address system and Sky Sports commentators; and for Sky Sports graphics team, who also do the graphics for the central screen in the arena. Below them, near the entrance to the arena, is the bubble where the Sky Sports presentation team sits – in the days when David Vine was the anchor man for the BBC, he spent most of the evening huddled up in a thick coat standing out in the collecting ring. The three members of the ground jury (the show-jumping judges) also sit in the production corner, as does Val who, from her position at the hub of the control centre, keeps her finger on the pulse of show. She communicates with the Sky Sports production lorry, which is parked on the tarmac outside the NEC building and from where the images and commentaries go out live; with the show-jumping course designers; and also with the equestrian coordinator, Betty Peacock, who is in charge of the presentations and displays.

Betty and her husband John, a former driver of a team of heavy horses who used to perform in the musical drive each year at Wembley, provide the link between the main arena and the production team, and because Betty is usually in the arena during presentations, Val can contact her to let her know if things need

PURPLE AND GOLD

The coveted HOYS rugs, with their vibrant colours and beautiful embroidery, are awarded to every champion at the show, and no fewer than seventy-two of these special rugs are supplied to the show organisers every year by Masta. The rugs are bound and piped in the HOYS gold and purple colours, ready for presentation.

speeding up or slowing down. The showing championship classes do provide Val with a 'buffer zone' – she can ask for the horses to be brought into the final line-up as quickly as possible when time is tight (the horses have already been pre-judged), or she can tell the stewards to keep the horses going around the arena for longer on the rare occasions when there is time to spare.

'My role is to pull everything together,' explains Val. 'I have to keep everyone up to scratch. Sometimes it feels as if we are squeezing a quart into a pint pot.' But a busy programme means more entertainment for spectators. Val must also keep in contact with the Sky Sports team, whose live programme goes out on air at 8 p.m. each evening for four nights of the show. Following the usual introductions and interviews, the cameras will show live coverage of the Pony Club mounted games, which must start promptly at 8.12 p.m. If they are going to be late, Val has to warn the Sky Sports production team so that they can fill in the air time with a small feature or interview. It is all down to split-second timing.

It is a tough call for someone whose first job at HOYS ended in disgrace. When Val came to help at Wembley in the 1990s, Jon Doney, the show director at the time, told her she could assist the rosette girls. So on the first night she appeared in her 'posh frock' and was told by Tissie Reason (now the Senior Rosette Steward and a joint organiser of the Chatsworth Horse Trials with Val Turner) that she could have a basket of carrots and go to the bottom of the line-up to give a carrot to each horse. Standing in last place was Geoff Billington, and Val cheekily asked him if *he* would like a carrot. In return, Geoff thought it would be entertaining to grab her by the scruff of her neck and lift her off her feet. Carrots scattered in all directions.

Once Val had got her feet back on the ground and had hastily picked up her carrots from the arena floor, she attempted to regain her composure and continue her task, but the damage was done. On leaving the arena, she was severely

► Val Turner, international arena controller, keeping an eye on her watch. It is her job to make sure everything comes together on time.

reprimanded for making an exhibition of herself and was told she would not be allowed back into the arena again. Instead, she ended up sitting in an office answering the phone for Patrick Daniel, the arena controller. She progressed to doing the cards for the show-jumping classes – putting each horse's card in order so that the commentator could see at a glance who was in the lead, who was lying second, and so on. Then she became Patrick's assistant, and from him learnt the finer details and military precision required to carry out the controller's job. 'Patrick was a stickler for detail, and would spend hours getting the daily orders exactly right. He was also a traditionalist and he didn't like all the new production – the lights and the music and the razzmatazz. He preferred the old military band.'

Val took over his role in 2003, the year after the show moved to the NEC. It is certainly a job with plenty of pressure, but it has its lighter moments. On the last day of the show in 2009, Sky Sports had asked Val if they could film a pre-record of the audience from the middle of the arena, so she gave the presenter and cameras a slot just before one of the championship showing classes got under way. Unfortunately, she had forgotten to inform Colin Brooks, the senior showing steward (now retired), of this arrangement and, as the Sky Sports crew came into the international arena, Colin was already there calling in the horses for the championship. A message came through on his radio telling him to stop the championship horses from coming in, but he still did not know what was going on. Meanwhile, Val had a frantic call from the Sky Sports production manager telling her to get Colin out of the way, as he kept appearing in the picture. So Colin received the message that he was to stand directly behind the camera. The problem for him was that the camera was being moved around in a circle, panning the audience, so Colin had to keep running around behind it to stay out of the picture. The production team were crying with laughter as they watched this comical scene.

▲ Bob Ellis, course designer at HOYS, says, 'I worry if I get too many clears, and I worry if I don't get enough.'

It was no laughing matter for HOYS course designer Bob Ellis in 2005, the first year of live television coverage from the NEC, when it seemed that he had made a serious miscalculation in the standard of the Grand Prix track. 'There was a production meeting in the morning,' recalls Bob, 'and timing was a big issue because Sky Sports wanted to wrap up their programme with a shot of everyone singing 'Auld Lang Syne' at the end. I was told that there would not be time for any more than seven clear rounds in the last class, the Grand Prix – so, no pressure then! When the class started, five of the first six horses went clear. I was so worried; I thought I had better have my car waiting outside with the engine running, ready for a quick getaway ...'

As it turned out, there were no more clears in the rest of the first round, so the timing was perfect. But achieving such precision is one of the biggest headaches for a course designer, who is always under pressure to keep the show running to time. 'I am constantly looking at my watch,' says Bob. 'I am a born worrier. I worry if I get too many clears, and I worry if I don't get enough.' Bob is now assisted by Kelvin Bywater, a master of colour schemes and decorations as well as course designing, and the two of them begin planning their courses about a month before the show begins. Once these plans have been coordinated, Kelvin puts together a comprehensive 'shopping list' of all the materials needed from

► Pony Club steward Rowley Boulton – looking a little sheepish.

the British Showjumping store in Aldershot – flags, trailers, fillers, about 200 poles and 60 pairs of wings, all in specified colours and all freshly painted. When they go back at the end of the show, they are usually in need of another coat of paint, having been thrown on and off trailers and storage racks, often at great speed, in between competitions.

The plans for each show-jumping class are meticulously drawn. In the very early years of HOYS, Colonel Ansell used to design courses with a few model jumps on his desk; now Bob and Kelvin produce design drawings of architectural accuracy. The arena is split into four sections, and each of these sections is the responsibility of one course builder. The course builders and their crews operate out of each of the four corners of the arena, where they have a supply of materials ready to build the fences in their section. Thus Bob and Kelvin's plans are drawn to show which fences will be built by which crew; they also show the size of each fence, the relative distances, what materials are to be used and how each fence should be constructed. Around the bottom edge of the international arena are markers with numbers on them, providing a sort of grid reference to indicate where a fence should be located; string lines are run out, so that the fences can be placed accurately in straight lines.

During the twenty-five minute interval, the construction process goes something like this: ten minutes to harrow the arena; seven or eight minutes to put out the string lines and build the course; another minute to remove the string lines and complete the finishing touches. If time is tight, Kelvin can often be seen walking around the fences making final adjustments, followed by Bob with the judges, who need to inspect the course. After them come the riders, who have come into the arena to walk the course. Another five minutes of interval time is allowed for the first rider to get back to his horse, mount and prepare for the competition. Then the show gets under way again. Such is the interest and fascination of this whole process that many spectators choose to stay in their seats during the interval to watch it, rather than dashing out for some food and drink, or a spot of shopping.

If the first half of the show has overrun, Val Turner will try to bring it back on schedule by reducing the interval slightly, which puts even greater pressure on the course builders. Fortunately, Bob, a former show jumper who used to ride for Stephen Hadley before setting up his own yard, runs a slick operation. He begins training the arena crew, a group of young student volunteers, two days before the show starts. The students are familiarised with the materials, and during the day practise two or three course builds in which they learn how to measure and build the fences. There is one more rehearsal before the show begins. After each evening performance, all the materials needed for the next day's courses – there are normally at least four show-jumping classes each day – must be put ready in their respective corners before everyone finishes work at around midnight. If spectators ever see students dashing frantically from one corner of the arena to another during a course build, there is a good chance they have mislaid a set of poles or some crucial fillers, and somebody will be in trouble.

The course-building team involves an arena party of 36 students, 12 course builders (including assistants), two tractor men and 12 florists, the latter organised by Angie Murray from Silk and Stem. In the 1970s, the course building was carried out by just a handful of army men in each corner, who could carry a show-jump wing in each hand. These days the wings are so substantial and so ornate that it can take two or three people to carry them. The courses are also more technical and varied than they used to be. 'If the courses had been like this in 1975, we'd have had a riot,' says Bob. The whole style of course designing has changed in the last twenty-five years, with more complex layouts, angles and turns; the materials have become lighter, and the cups shallower. These changes were needed to provide a greater challenge for horses and riders, whose standards have improved enormously.

Another person who spends the week at HOYS trying to squeeze a quart into a pint pot is the stable manager Pete Harnett. Finding enough space to park all the horseboxes is one of his biggest headaches, and it is not unknown for a small queue of lorries to develop while waiting for other vehicles to leave the premises and free up some space. Unlike the international show jumpers, who have their own high-security stable area, many of the show horses stay at HOYS for one or two nights only, so there is a constant coming and going of equine visitors, rather like guests checking in and out of a hotel.

▼ Inside the international stables at the NEC during HOYS week.

Not everything is quite up to scratch in this particular hotel. For one thing, when it rains the water runs down the tarmac and underneath the stables, soaking the stable beds. Experienced exhibitors now arrive at Birmingham with plastic sheeting, which they fit across the stable floor and attach to the sides of the stables before they put down their bedding. It is bit like remembering to take a plug for your hotel sink when you travel to India.

ESCAPE ARTISTS

There have been plenty of these, but one of the most alarming incidents occurred during the early days at Wembley when two horses belonging to Italian rider Vittorio Orlandi got out of their stables and were discovered galloping along the North Circular. Luckily, they were caught without major incident. These days, any escaping equines are contained within the fenced perimeter of the stables, but that does not stop some of them from taking a midnight stroll around the stable blocks. In 2005, Edward Young had some sleepless nights when he had to keep responding to phone calls from the stable security staff telling him that his horse, Goodwill Hunting, had escaped yet again. In spite of every effort to keep him on the right side of his stable door, including tying string around the door bolts, he managed to undo most of the knots with little difficulty. 'Things could have been worse,' said his owner. 'At home, he has a habit of letting out everything else as well.'[1]

▼ Scurry driver Chris Orchard prepares dinner …

► … So where is our dinner?

▼ Stable manager Peter Harnett, who is charge of providing accommodation for some 1,500 horses during HOYS week.

JET-SETTING JOB

Daley Fisher knows all about working behind the scenes with the show jumpers. He has been Ben Maher's groom for the last five years, and has travelled all over the world with Ben's top horses in his care. 'You do tend to give your life to this job because you are always away, or always in the truck going somewhere, but it's fun and I do have a good social life at the shows because I meet up with many of the same people,' explains Daley. At least the NEC is only a two-hour journey from Ben's yard in Essex, which makes things a little more relaxed when it comes to competing at Horse of the Year Show. Daley arrives the day before the start of the international show jumping. He sorts out the bedding, gets the horses off the lorry and then presents them for the trot up that evening. All the international show jumpers have to pass a veterinary inspection before they compete. Sometimes Daley will exercise horses for Ben, and this has to be done in strict adherence to the show's busy exercise timetable, often involving early starts, but otherwise it is his job to make sure Ben's horses are ready on time for all their competitions. Accommodation is in the lorry, but with sole charge of four horses, and classes not finishing until 11 p.m., there is not much time for sleeping.

From his temporary office, Pete keeps track of which horses are in which stables on a large plan of the area, carefully marked out with stable numbers and length of occupancy of each stable. The changeover rate can be up to 300 horses a day, and the owners of each new arrival must report to the equine office to have passports checked by a vet before entering the stable complex. A former member of the King's Troop Royal Horse Artillery, Pete oversees a team of 23 people dealing with some 1,500 horses during the week.

► Final preparations
– Daley Fisher, groom
to Ben Maher, adjusts
a back boot in the
collecting ring.

There is never much rest in the stable area. Horses are competing or being exercised until 11 p.m. each night. By the time they have been fed and rugged for the night, it will be be just two or three hours before an alarm clock goes off in a horsebox somewhere on site to wake a groom or rider with a horse in one of the early show classes, and then the preparations will begin for the day's busy schedule of competitions. Along the perimeter track around the stadium, there is a constant stream of horses and ponies on their way to or back from the arenas. Everyone has their place and their time in an endless succession of preparations and performances.

▶ Exercising in the outdoor arena in the stable area.

CHAPTER SEVEN

DONE FOR FUN

The Pony Club mounted games and the scurry driving have become two of the most popular competitions at Horse of the Year Show – intense, competitive, full of drama and hugely entertaining, each team desperate to win their coveted title but everyone having fun in the process.

PONY CLUB MOUNTED GAMES

For the Pony Club children lucky enough to qualify for the show, the fun begins early with a party near the international arena, where rehearsals are still taking place for the show's opening. Plenty of dressing-up, entertainment and general larking about are the order of the evening – a little light relief at the start of an intense week for the children and their parents.

Competitions begin the next day under the spotlights of the international arena and in front of a large, vociferous audience. It can be a daunting moment for both riders and ponies, especially the first time. Then there is the pressure of the competition itself – your team's success and honour rests on your shoulders as you hurtle down the length of the arena to pick up a flag, or leap off your pony to step smartly along a row of upturned buckets. On Thursday evening that pressure intensifies, because now the competition to qualify for the final on Sunday evening starts in earnest and, furthermore, live television coverage begins. Children and ponies must be ready to start racing on the dot of 8.12 p.m. each

◄ Athleticism, accuracy and speed – a member of the Oakley Hunt West team taking part in the Pony Club Mounted Games for the Prince Philip Cup at HOYS in 2008. Oakley Hunt West won the competition five times between 1989 and 2010.

Concentration

Contemplation

Jubilation

Synchronisation

night, for it is at this moment that the Sky Sports' cameras in the main arena start to roll. If you fall off now, or knock over your team's carefully constructed pile of foam bricks, it will not just be the 9,250 spectators at the NEC who laugh at your blunder; it will be millions of television viewers as well.

Back at the stables, the sense of team commitment and pride continues. The stable area is decked out with ribbons, rosettes, sashes, photographs and even pot plants, and on Saturday morning the normally well-kept stable lines are in immaculate order. Not a speck of shavings or hay is to be seen anywhere along Pony Club Row; tack is clean and neatly organised in spotless tack rooms, and children in polished jodhpur boots, wearing their team colours, are lined up outside their ponies' stables, waiting for the celebrity inspection to begin. In the hurly burly and general chaos of the stable area, this is an oasis of cleanliness and order. Here, the ethos of the Pony Club is seen at its best – discipline, knowledge, team spirit and, above all, fun. This is a time for friendships to be made and renewed, and even romances kindled. Stephen Lovell and Beverley Clayton, members of the Oakley Hunt West team in 1976, are now married with two children.

▼ Pony Club tackroom – kept in immaculate order.

The Pony Club mounted games have been a part of Horse of the Year Show since 1957. Before then, some Pony Club activity rides had been featured, but there were no competitions for the youngsters unless they had a smart show pony or a good show-jumping pony. It was HRH Prince Philip who had the idea of introducing a competition for 'ordinary children on ordinary ponies'. As Mike Ansell recalls in his autobiography:[1]

> We'd always been concerned to ring the changes on entertainments other than jumping at Horse of the Year Show … So in 1955 I was delighted when, at Badminton, Prince Philip told me he was tired of watching the young 'trotting and cantering around the ring on their Show ponies and obviously getting into trouble from the parents if they did not win'. Surely I could arrange races for them, to make it more exciting, and the ponies needn't necessarily be 'Show' ponies. I was delighted: that was just what we wanted. Colonel Guy Cubitt [chairman of the Pony Club] encouraged us, and with Charles Adderley and Raymond Brooks-Ward's help we set about preparing Games: these were always for teams of four, no prize money, only rosettes. I sent my suggestions to His Royal Highness, and wasn't the least surprised to receive a letter containing many amendments and improvements.

The first Prince Philip Cup competitions were given an experimental trial at Harringay in 1957, when teams from the London area only were invited to participate – the Enfield Chase, the Garth, the North West Kent and the South Oxfordshire Hunt. The following year the competition was opened to all Pony Club branches around the country, and by 1959 no fewer than 164 branches entered the regional qualifiers. These days, about 250 branches participate every year in the qualifying competitions – regional qualifiers followed by zone finals. Six teams make it through to Horse of the Year Show. Each of these teams is made up of five riders and ponies, and four compete at any one time. There are competitions at every performance of the show, and the teams collect points depending on how well they do during the week. On the last night, the four teams with the highest scores in accumulated points battle it out for the honour of claiming the Prince Philip Cup.

For 13 of the last 33 years (up to 2010) that winning team has been the Eglinton branch of the Pony Club, from Ayrshire in Scotland, and they have qualified 26 times. Their team's extraordinary record is due to a very large extent to the dedication of one man, Robert Noble, who trained the Eglinton team from 1974 until early in 2007 when, at the age of eighty-two, he decided he was 'due a wee rest' and handed over the reins to Francis Pearson. The following year he was awarded an MBE for his work, and when his daughter, Enice Vennard, asked ex-Pony Club members to write recommending him for the award, she received some seventy letters from as far afield as New Zealand and Australia, where some of his former pupils now live.

THE PRINCE PHILIP CUP

The following extract is taken from the 1957 HOYS programme, the year the first experimental Pony Club games were held: 'The objects of the Mounted Games are to provide the members of the Pony Club with an opportunity to compete on good and well trained ponies that do not necessarily require to be of high quality or great value. They will encourage the young riders to train their ponies to be obedient and themselves to become active and practical horsemen, who will compete with enthusiasm and determination. At the same time they will bring to the notice of Show Organisers the value of these competitions, not only for the encouragement of riders, but also for the enjoyment of the spectators.' The winners of the first mounted games were North West Kent, and each team member received a medal commissioned by Buckingham Palace and struck by the Royal Mint – a tradition that has continued to this day.

► Prince Philip, who had the initial idea of holding Pony Club games at HOYS, talks to members of the winning Enfield Chase team in 1961. Games were held for the first time in 1957.

Philip meets the teams at the 1961 Horse of the year show.

SELINA

At twenty-two years of age (although possibly nearer thirty) the dark bay, 12hh Welsh Section B mare Selina was one of the most experienced ponies competing at HOYS in 2010. She was making her eighth appearance at the NEC, and has been on the winning team twice. She competed once with the Ammond Valley team, three times with the Clydach, ridden by Natasha Hopkins, and three times with the Atherstone Hunt, ridden once by Chloe Golding and twice by Katy King. In 2010, she was ridden by Molly Hughes for the Berwyn and Dee. Gail Golding still owns this remarkable pony. After her fourth season with the Atherstone (she qualified one year but did not go to HOYS), the Goldings decided to retire her, but two years later they realised that she would be better off leading a more active life, so she came back into the sport. 'Looking at her in the arena, you could see she still loves it,' says Gail. 'A lot of ponies are good, but there are only a few who really love it, and they are ones you see coming back again and again.'

▲ Selina competing at HOYS in 2010 with Molly Hughes for the Berwyn and Dee branch of the Pony Club.

◀ Ready for inspection. Members of the Berwyn and Dee branch of the Pony Club lined up outside their stables.

► Members of the Eglinton Pony Club gallop along the Ayrshire beach where they train during the winter. The Eglinton branch won the Prince Philip Cup thirteen times between 1978 and 2005.

A retired farmer and keen breeder of Clydesdales, Robert Noble became involved with training the Eglinton teams when Enice began participating in the mounted games. In those early days, there was little support for the games in the area and Robert struggled to raise a team, but two years later the Eglinton missed qualifying for HOYS by just half a point. Spurred on by coming so close to their target, the following year they did qualify, and finished a creditable third; and in 1978 they took the show by storm, winning every performance. From then on, there was no stopping them. For the next eighteen years the team failed to qualify just once; they set a new record by winning at HOYS three years in succession (1982 to 1984), and then broke their own record when they won for five years in a row between 1991 and 1996. The only teams to have come anywhere near the Eglinton's supremacy are the Oakley Hunt West, who, up until 2010, had won the Cup five times, and the Atherstone Hunt, also winners on five occasions, the first in 1964.

Of the many victories, Robert found that first one, in 1978, the sweetest. It was all the more rewarding because most of the ponies had been bought locally, from Stirling horse sales, for around 200 guineas, and had been trained by the Pony Club children themselves. One of these ponies, Olly, a little grey ridden initially by Enice, became the backbone of the Eglinton team for six years in a row. He died prematurely from a ruptured blood vessel in 1983, and was much missed.

MR SHIFTER

This remarkable 12.1hh Welsh pony competed at HOYS eleven times, starting as a four year old in 1976, ridden by Stephen Lovell with Oakley Hunt West. Julie Roff (now Barrett) bought him in 1979 and she competed on him at HOYS in 1981, 1983 and 1984. After Wembley in 1984, he moved to his new home in Ayrshire, with the Barr family, but after one year Jane Barr outgrew him and he was sold to Maureen Borland, whose son Scott rode him at HOYS in 1986 and 1987 (when he was a winner). Mr Shifter was then taken on by Maureen Borland's daughter, Julie, who competed on him at Wembley for the next three years, winning in 1988 and coming second in 1989. He did one more year at HOYS, in 1991, with Derek Loy of the Eglinton branch, before being loaned by Maureen Borland to the younger children, and he became the backbone of the junior A team for the next nine years. He died aged twenty-seven.

▲ Mr Shifter competed at HOYS eleven times, starting with Oakley Hunt West and finishing with the Eglinton. He is seen here competing at the 1988 show.

Careful planning goes into any trip to HOYS, but Robert was caught off his guard one year as he left the arena at Wembley to find Cilla Black and a TV crew waiting for him in a 'Surprise Surprise' stunt. Robert and his team of riders were later filmed with Cilla, who was sporting a bright pink tracksuit, as they trained on the beach in Ayr on a freezing windswept day, and the film was broadcast on Cilla's television programme.

The objective of the Pony Club games – to motivate and encourage young riders and to improve their riding skills – has certainly been fulfilled by this competition at HOYS. Many good riders, including show jumper Louise Whitaker, who competed with the Rockford Harriers' team, have honed their early equestrian skills from their initial training for the mounted games. Others, including Charlotte Castle from the Oakley West team, have gone on to do well in eventing. The Pony Club children, often from many varied backgrounds, learn to work together as a team, and gain agility and self-confidence from the training. They must be dedicated and prepared to put in long hours of practice, and they

► Robert Noble, trainer of the mounted games team of the Eglinton branch of the Pony Club for thirty-two years, is greeted by Cilla Black in a 'Surprise, Surprise' stunt at HOYS.

must learn to control an excitable pony and to stay focused in front of 9,000+ screaming people. It is not easy, but a good sense of humour and a strong team spirit do much to help.

'The children remember it all their lives,' says Gail Golding, whose daughter, Chloe, competed on the Atherstone team in 2005 and 2006. 'And when they are older, they want their children to do it, because they had such a good time themselves.'

SCURRY DRIVING

Another fast and furious sport, this one is strictly for adults – or at least for those over fourteen, the minimum age for drivers and grooms. This exciting competition has been thrilling the crowds at HOYS for over thirty years. Jeff Osborne, who had been involved in scurry driving as a sponsor and competitor for many years, describes what it takes to be a part of this sport:

Drivers come in all shapes and sizes – tall ones, short ones, fat ones, thin ones, some with hair some without, male or female, all can succeed. Vehicles, too, come in a variety of shapes and designs, but all must have four wheels and a brake and the front wheels must measure over 130cm wide. Wheels with wire spokes and pneumatic tyres are not allowed. As in Formula 1, wheels are continuously being developed, and at Horse of the Year Show, where the surface is more holding than grass, the set-up is adjusted for the different terrain.

The competition is decided on time from start to finish, but drivers incur a five-second penalty if they dislodge one of the balls that sit on top of each cone. Subsequent balls dislodged incur a ten-second penalty. Missing a set of cones altogether adds time because the driver has to return and go through them before going through another set of cones.

The forerunner to scurry driving as we know it today was the obstacle driving competition, which took place at HOYS in the 1960s, and which had developed from the cone driving phase of driving trials. The first people to take part were therefore those with coaching teams, such as the renowned whip John Parker, but it was difficult to manoeuvre a four-in-hand team in an indoor arena with sufficient speed to create a really exciting competition. Thus, classes for pairs of horses, using beer barrels instead of cones (the competitions were sponsored

▼ Kicking up the sand – Drayton Eeyore and Piglet race around the scurry driving course with Jemma Millman at the controls.

by Watney Mann), were introduced to make things easier and faster, but the horses still wore full harness and pulled traditional driving vehicles, so it was more a test of accuracy than speed.

Information from the 1968 programme for HOYS explains that drivers would compete around a maximum of six barrels, and there was a given time for the course. No points were gained for completing the course faster than the time allowed, but competitors would incur one fault for every second over the time allowed. The course was 'to be driven at least at a sharp trot'. A piebald gelding and mare, known as Whisky and Splash, owned and driven by Mrs P. Stewart-Smith won the competition in 1968.

As the pair driving competitions gained momentum, the driving fraternity turned their attention to finding horses that were handy enough to do well in barrel racing, as well as compete successfully in driving trials. At this time, Pat Cooke, one of the most successful scurry drivers in the history of the sport at HOYS, had a pair of Hungarian horses, called Pride and Prejudice, that were particularly adept at the cone phase of driving trials, so Pat drove them with great success in the pair obstacle driving classes as well. However, once pair driving classes for ponies had been introduced, the horses' days were numbered. The ponies were so much faster, so much more entertaining to watch, that the horses were soon faded out of the pair driving contests and the ponies were then divided into two height levels, under 12hh and over 12hh.

▲ Jeff Osborne receiving the Equestrian of the Year Trophy from the show's honorary president, Susan George.

JEFF OSBORNE

One of the greatest supporters of Horse of the Year Show, and a winner of the HOYS Equestrian of the Year in 2007, Jeff Osborne is known to his friends and followers as 'The Scurry King'. His company, Osborne Refrigerators, with its distinctive triangular logo, has been associated with HOYS for over thirty-five years, sponsoring show jumping and show classes (hacks, cobs and riding horses), but it is scurry driving for which Jeff is now best known, both as a sponsor and competitor.

Although he had little interest in horses until he took up hunting, when he was in his late thirties,

Jeff's subsequent involvement in the equestrian world has been full on, whether in show jumping (his initial sport), showing, judging or scurry driving. His enthusiasm for driving took off after he was stabled next to John Marson one year at HOYS, and John let him have a go at driving his ponies down Wembley High Street. Having decided that he 'didn't like falling off horses any more', Jeff took to this new sport with his usual verve and determination, and within his first year of driving had qualified a team of ponies, Caption and Logo, for the HOYS championship.

▲ Whisky and Splash, driven by Mrs P. Stewart-Smith, were winners of the first pairs driving competition, forerunner of scurry driving, in 1968.

◀ Pat Cooke taking part in horses pairs driving in the early 1970s, when barrels instead of cones were used, and the horses still wore full harness.

PAT AND SARAH COOKE

Mother and daughter, both hugely successful scurry drivers at HOYS, have been immersed in driving all their lives. Pat's father was George Mossman, of driving trials fame, and her sister is well-known whip Christine Dick. Pat honed her driving skills at an early age. Soon after the pony scurry driving had begun to take off at HOYS, George Mossman bought each of his four grandchildren a pony. As Pat's two girls were very young and did not ride the ponies much to start with, Pat decided to break them to harness and enter them in the pony section of the pair horse driving (now called the double harness scurry). The ponies were called

Punch and Judy, and at that time they pulled a four-wheel rally cart that had been built in the late 1800s, and wore a full collar harness. They won at HOYS in 1975.

Sarah also began driving as a youngster, and at the age of twelve (at a time when junior whips were allowed to compete in scurry driving against the seniors) she qualified for her first HOYS championships. From then on, Sarah never failed to qualify and has not missed Horse of Year Show for thirty-one years. In 2010, she claimed her sixth title, giving a faultless display with her mother's Section A ponies Bow and Arrow. They did not touch a cone all week.

Once this happened, the sport opened up to more people, because ponies were so much cheaper to keep than horses. Often a good scurry pony could be picked up for a song at a local sale, and perhaps paired up with a child's outgrown first pony in need of another job. Ponies and carriages could all fit into one horsebox, and at the shows the two ponies could even share a stable. Here was the driving equivalent of the Pony Club mounted games.

As the sport expanded, a couple of enterprising drivers developed specialist vehicles for the job. Neil Swanson, an engineer who, at one time, competed with five pairs of ponies, built the prototype for today's modern scurry vehicles – lightweight, metal carts with more manoeuvrability than the traditional vehicles. John Marson, another successful driver, also began building vehicles specifically for scurry driving, allowing the ponies to go even faster without such a danger of tipping up the carriage, although it does still happen from time to time. It is largely the responsibility of the groom, sitting on the back of the vehicle, to move his or her weight around to keep the vehicle from turning over as the ponies hurtle round a sharp bend, but the whip (i.e. driver) must also take some responsibility – a sudden surge of power from the ponies at the wrong moment can have disastrous consequences.

Ponies with names such as Pooh Bear and Piglet (winners with Jemma Millman in 2008 and 2009) and Whistle and Flute (driven by Sally Mawer to win in 2004

and 2005) add to the charm of this much-loved competition. The ponies, sweet as they are, need to be sharp and focused, and keen on the racing. They have to want to do it, and they have to be confident enough to cope with the bright lights and the cheering crowd. Before the competitions begin in earnest, the teams have only one chance to practise in the big arena at the NEC, and on that occasion there are no spectators, and therefore no noise. Pinky and Perky, an outstanding pair driven by Sarah Cooke, took three years to learn to cope with the bright lights and the noise. They would enter the arena, stick their heads up in the air to look at the lights and the audience, and refuse to listen to their driver. 'When they did that, they were useless,' explained Sarah Cooke. 'But I'm glad we persevered, because when they eventually settled they were unbeatable.'

Jeff Osborne provides an excellent description of what it is like to drive scurry ponies:

> They may be smaller than the modern racing car, but ponies have minds of their own – and in double harness scurry there are two of them! Ponies do not have to be 'posh' with breeding histories that go back generations. What is important is that they run together, almost as one. Unlike the ridden animal, the driver has no physical contact with the ponies; they

▲ On her way to winning her sixth Double Harness Scurry Racing Championship – Sarah Cooke with Bow and Arrow in 2010.

► Getting ready for action – Jeff Osborne waits in the collecting ring for another round of the double-harness scurry racing.

must learn to respond to the driver's voice. 'Left' and 'right' are quickly learnt but it takes longer to learn the tones of voice requiring a change of pace. This is what determines the speed, not the whip, which is used only as a reminder and a guide. Experience is gained through long hours of practice, but [you must] appreciate that it is difficult to practise appearing under the spotlight and in the intense atmosphere of the international arena. When the commentator calls upon the crowd to encourage the ponies, the effect is quite dramatic. They really rise to the occasion. They are great little show-offs.

FORMER FUN AND GAMES

Other popular competitions that used to be held at HOYS were Police Horse of the Year, Riding Club Quadrilles, the Jockeys' Championships and Horseball.

Police Horse of the Year

Started in 1962, this was worth a not inconsiderable £75 to the winner. The competition was judged in two phases, the first for equitation (worth 40 marks) and the second for street nuisances (30 marks). A maximum of 20 marks were awarded for turnout, and another 10 for condition.

According to the programme for the first year, in phase 1 the 'judges may require competitors to carry out any of the following tests riding with one hand: walk, trot, canter, figure of eight, halt, half pass (left and right), rein back, dismount and mount either side.' The street nuisances could consist of people waving flags, sounding rattles, opening umbrellas, firing revolvers and sounding fire-bells; other distractions could be hanging dummies, fluttering washing, a band of itinerant musicians and a barrel falling as the horse walked past. While some or all of this was going on, the rider, remaining on the horse, could be asked to open and close a gate, or step over fallen bodies.

The first competition attracted sixteen entries and two of them – Robin ridden by Constable Marment from Bristol, and Angus IV ridden by Constable Miller from Yorkshire – were well used to the atmosphere at Wembley, since they had been in charge of the parade of personalities in 1959 and 1961 respectively. However, the class was won by Grey Sky, a 16.1hh gelding exhibited by the Birmingham City police force, and the same force also claimed second place with another grey gelding, Graydon. Horses had been entered by forces from Yorkshire, Stafford, London, Liverpool, Manchester, Bristol and Birmingham.

Now the competition has been replaced by occasional displays in the form of Metropolitan Police Activity Rides.

Riding Club Quadrilles

From the mid-1960s, when they began, the riding club quadrilles became increasingly competitive, and also increasingly well presented as riders dressed up in costumes to give their quadrille a theme. These classes were the highlight of the year for many riding clubs, and members would spend hours preparing and practising for their moment under the spotlight. Only four teams could qualify each year, and they were judged throughout the week. Then the winning team performed again on the last night of the show. In 1968, a young Princess Anne represented the Battle and District Riding Club in their quadrille, and her team came second.

The Jockeys' Championships

The format of this competition, sponsored by Schroder Life, changed several times during the seventies, although it usually took place on the opening night

► Princess Anne on Man Friday (*centre*) waits to be presented with her award after competing in the Riding Clubs Quadrille with the Battle and District Riding Club in 1968. The team finished second.

of the show. Basically a show-jumping competition open to national hunt riders, the contest was won for two years in succession (1974 and 1975) by David Turner. In 1977, champion jockey John Francome, displaying his experience as a former junior international show jumper, won the competition from another champion jockey, Bob Davies. In 1981, the event became a jumpers' and jockeys' relay, for which jockeys teamed up with a top show jumper, and in 1983 it was modified to run as the Olympic show-jumping relay – this time including an Olympic rider with a jockey and a show jumper. It was won by Jennie Loriston-Clarke, Steven Smith and Bill Smith, but the competition seemed to be losing its way, and when Monday's gala nights were dropped, so was the jockeys' jumping.

Horseball

In 1990, a series of exhibition matches were played at Horse of the Year Show by visiting French teams, with the aim of introducing the sport into Britain. Within three years, this had developed into a full European Horseball championship with teams from England, Belgium, Portugal, France, Italy and Germany taking part. Heats took place during the week, and the two finalists battled it out for the title on the final day of the show.

The game, played between two teams of four riders, resembles basketball on horseback. The players must pass the ball – specially adapted with leather handles – from one to another with the objective of scoring goals by throwing it through a raised net (similar to a basketball net). If the ball is dropped or knocked to the ground, it is retrieved by a rider swooping down and picking it up in his hand, and then pulling himself back into the saddle. A strap linking the stirrups together under the horse's girth helps the rider to regain his position after making the pick-up. High-speed tackles and skirmishes are common, and the horses must be trained to respond quickly to their riders' aids, often without the use of reins. The sport's great advantage over polo is that it is designed to be played within the confines of a 60 by 20 metre school, and since its introduction at Horse of the Year Show (it is no longer played there), a British Horseball Association has been formed and many Pony Club branches have also taken up the sport.

CHAPTER EIGHT

THE ENTERTAINERS

Amusing, inspiring, dramatic or nostalgic, the displays have always been an integral and important part of Horse of the Year Show. Even at Harringay, at the very first show, the organisers realised that something was needed to add variety to the showing and show-jumping classes, so a dressage display and a Pony Club activity ride were put on to fulfil that role. Unfortunately, these were not enough to prevent the audience starting up a slow hand-clap as they waited for the show-jumping courses to be built – a lengthy process in those early days. So by the following year Colonel Ansell had put his former Rough Riding Sergeant-Major, Mr Lee, on to the case, and in no time at all the ex-army rider had produced a delightful musical ride with thirty-one members of the Cattistock Pony Club – five of them belonging to the Bullen family.

As Jennie Loriston-Clarke recalls, 'We were all in the ride, including my older brother Michael and my three-year-old sister Sarah, who rode a lovely grey Welsh pony called Flurry. Jane [now Holderness-Roddam], aged five, rode Coed Coch Pryderi, Charlie rode the Dartmoor pony champion New Moon and I rode a show pony called Rosalind. Mr Lee soon got us all licked into shape. There was no messing about!'

Three years later, there was a display by Lis Hartel, the Danish dressage rider who had courageously fought back from a severe polio attack to win the individual silver medal at the 1952 Helsinki Olympics, the first year that women had been

◀ (opposite page) Drum horse from the Household Cavalry display, part of the HOYS diamond jubilee celebrations in 2008.

permitted to take part in Olympic dressage. By all accounts, her displays at Harringay with her mare Jubilee were outstanding, and they certainly had a very strong impact on eleven-year-old Jennie Bullen. It was watching Lis Hartel at Harringay that inspired her to take up dressage, and twenty-six years later she gained an individual bronze medal at the World Championship, the highest placing ever achieved by a British dressage rider until Laura Bechtolsheimer

THE FIRST PONY CLUB ACTIVITY RIDE

Eight members of the Crawley and Horsham branch of the Pony Club were invited to provide an activity ride to be performed each day at the first Horse of the Year Show in 1949. The riders, who trained hard for weeks before the show, were Nigel Rawlings, Ann Blake, Carol McLennan, Pat Taylor, Diana Webley, Valerie Gooda, Gay Tregoning and Ann Wisdom. The display included jumping the ponies on and off a small square stand, and down a series of fences, with the riders putting on their coats and powdering their noses as they went. The activity ride was well received, and in subsequent years different branches of the Pony Club were given the honour of performing similar displays.

▼ Rehearsing at Catherston Manor for the Cattistock Pony Club Musical Ride, which included five members of the Bullen family.

won individual silver in 2010. During Jennie's hugely successful dressage career, she also competed in five Olympic Games.

'Lis Hartel was totally before her time,' according to David Broome, whose memory of her display is also still vivid. 'She did dressage to music some forty years before others cottoned on to it, and it brought the house down every night. Her performances were perfection, and all the more incredible because she was invalided and had to be helped on to her horse.'

Davina Whiteman, who was riding show ponies at the time, was also deeply affected by the display. 'We had never seen anything like it before. Being indoors, under those lights and with the audience so close to the horse, it made the whole thing totally captivating.'

The following year, the Bullen family were once again involved in the entertainments, this time taking part in the 'best Pony Club display we have ever seen at this show', according to the Town and Country page of *Horse and Hound*. The enormous cast, under the direction of Colonel Jack Bullen, included riders from the Cattistock and other West Country Pony Clubs, a harness contingent from

▼ Saddling up time at Harringay for the Cattistock Pony Club Musical Ride.

POOL OF LIGHT

As a child, Jane Holderness-Roddam (née Bullen) regularly attended the show at Harringay with her family, and took part in some of the displays. 'The main light had a large canopy over it so that the light was channelled down into the centre of the arena. There was something magical about that pool of light in a dark arena. In those days, the winners really did do their final round under the spotlight, while the remainder of the arena was completely blacked out. Watching it used to bring a lump to my throat.'

the Wimbledon Pony Club and a party on foot from the Old Berks. The whole display was made up of some forty children under the age of sixteen, the only exception being Mrs 'Pug' Whitehead, an international show jumper who was small enough to ride a pony and act as the famous huntsman James Pig.

Entitled 'The Meet at the Cat and Custard Pot', the display was scripted by Dorian Williams with characters based on the R.S. Surtees books. As the children taking part were all mounted on ponies, it was a complete hunt in miniature. After the meet, the 'field' left the pub and, to the sound of hounds in full cry, were supposed to race around the arena over some small brush fences, but at the rehearsal the ponies were so star struck by their surroundings that hardly any of them could be persuaded to jump. At that point, Mr Lee came to the rescue by standing in the centre of the arena and cracking a hunting crop to great effect – the ponies were soon galloping over the fences.

The display was revived and revised in 1964 to coincide with the centenary of R.S. Surtees' death, and on this occasion the cast was made up of well-known riders, 'many of whom displayed a hitherto untapped histrionic talent'.[1] It was all the more entertaining because most of the riders could be easily recognised underneath their early Victorian costumes – even those who were sporting additional whiskers and top hats. Popular show jumper George Hobbs took centre stage as John Jorrocks; hunt secretary, Mrs Fleeceall, was played by Raymond Brooks-Ward, and other members of the cast included Douglas Bunn and David Barker.

'But perhaps,' wrote Pamela Macgregor-Morris, 'the biggest ovation greeted Fred Welch as Soapey Sponge, Alan Oliver as Facey Romford and Sarah Legard as Lucy Glitters, a noisy trio who entered into the spirit of the thing with enormous enthusiasm.' Jennie Bullen was the elegant and captivating Miss de Glancey, riding side-saddle on the former hack champion, Desert Storm, and Cynthia Haydon was the 'raffish and dashing' Lady Scattercash, puffing an enormous cigar as she drove a pair of Hackneys with her usual expertise. The display, entitled 'Jorrocks Rides Again', was clearly as much fun for the participants as it was for the audience.

Perhaps the most enduring and nostalgic display at HOYS was one that was born out of necessity. After the first show in 1949, it was clear to the organisers that they needed to be much more efficient at reducing the delays between classes. On top of the task of erecting and dismantling show jumps, the arena needed to be regularly harrowed – a tedious time waster as far as the audience was concerned. Colonel Mike Ansell solved this last problem by using heavy horses, instead of tractors, to pull the harrows, thus making it more entertaining for spectators.

▼ Heavy horses performing their famous cartwheel manoeuvre at HOYS in 1972. The musical drive was introduced originally to entertain spectators while, at the same time, harrowing the arena for the next jumping class.

He had drawn his idea from a visit to the Toronto Winter Fair before the Second World War, where he had seen the ice rink being swept by an arena party on skates, who carried out the job in formation. Applying this to heavy horses pulling harrows, the famous Musical Ride of the Heavy Horses came into being.

Initially, when the horses were introduced to the Harringay arena, the four teams simply paraded around with their harrows, carrying out the task of preparing the arena for the next class, but soon this developed into a musical drive – the music was specially chosen by Sir Malcolm Sargent – with complicated patterns, including a cartwheel movement, and ending with a final surge down the arena of all twelve of these magnificent horses lined up abreast.

John Peacock, who is now an official at HOYS, was one of the men who drove a team of Shires, which he did nearly every year from 1968 until their last regular performance in 1977. Although a musical drive of heavy horses has been revived on occasion, simply as a display, the arena is now harrowed at great speed by a couple of tractors.

The parade of champions was another regular feature of the show, and one which many people still remember with awe and affection. It started in 1950 with a parade of just one horse at each performance. This was the grand old show jumper Silver Mint. Five years earlier, he had won the BSJA high jump event at the age of twenty-seven, and his appearance was so well received that a bigger parade, known as the horse personalities parade, was organised for subsequent shows. Over the years, many great names from all walks of the equestrian world have appeared. Racehorses, including Grand National winners Nickel Coin and Nicolas Silver, have paraded, and in 1963 Mandarin was there after he had won the Hennessy Gold Cup, the Cheltenham Gold Cup and the Grand Steeplechase de Paris (the race in which Fred Winter piloted him home without a bridle). Pit ponies, show ponies and horses, Shire horses and event horses have been included – Pretty Polly, Bubbly, the Hackney mare Holywell Florette and Sheila Wilcox's High and Mighty for example. Dorian Williams, with his keen sense of entertainment, would help the bandmaster decide on tunes to accompany each horse as it entered the ring – 'I Did It My Way' for the back-kicking Vibart; 'Knees Up Mother Brown' for the Hackney pony Highstone Nicholas; 'Smoke Gets In Your Eyes' for Peter Robeson's show jumper Craven A, to name a few.

Arkle was a huge favourite with the crowds, ridden by his jockey Pat Taaffe in the famous yellow and black colours. Each evening, when his owner, Anne, Duchess of Westminster, went into the arena to give him a lump of sugar, the applause from the spectators 'all but brought down the stadium'.[2] One year the great Thoroughbred stallion Hyperion disgraced himself in the arena after taking a shine to Pat Smythe's mare Tosca during his first parade of the show. When evidence of his state of mind became obvious, orders were quickly given to dim the lights, while he was hastily led from the arena. In 1980, the parade of champions was replaced by 'London Pride', a display that included the Household Cavalry and the royal carriage, which was put on in celebration of the Queen Mother's eightieth birthday. Although the parade of personalities returned in 1983, its days were numbered and it is no longer a regular feature of the show.

David Tatlow recalls being enormously impressed by a demonstration given in 1966 by Spanish rider Senor Don Angel Peralta, who showed how his Andalusian horses were trained to avoid a bull by using a contraption consisting of a one-wheeled bike with an artificial bull's head, including the all important horns, attached to the top of the handlebars. Members of the audience were invited to come into the arena and have a go at pushing the 'bull' towards the horse, and Peralta offered £5 (a lot of money in those days) to anyone who could touch his horses with the horns. 'The horse was so good at getting out of the way; it was unbelievable,' recalls David. 'It would leap sideways, jump over the horns, gallop backwards. You could approach the horse from any direction at any speed, but you couldn't touch it. I don't think anyone got the money.'

The demonstration from the Spaniard did not meet with everyone's approval, however; those opposed to bull fighting felt that Peralta should not have been invited to the show. Mrs Glenda Spooner, founder of Ponies of Britain and a champion of equine welfare, was one of those who were unhappy with the display, and she wrote to Colonel Ansell to indicate, politely, that she felt he was wrong to have included it in the show. At the same time, she also wrote to a friend in much stronger terms, saying that she thought Colonel Ansell was a tyrant and a bully, who would never listen to anyone else's opinion.

Unfortunately, the two letters went in the wrong envelopes, and Colonel Ansell received the latter. He invited Glenda Spooner to his show office in Bedford Square, offered her a drink and thanked her for her letter, which he then passed across the table to her. On realising her error, she was momentarily silenced, but ultimately they were able to laugh about it. 'It was a case of Greek meets Greek,' wrote Dorian Williams.[3]

Dressage of a more classical nature was provided by members of the Spanish Riding School of Vienna in 1969, on their first trip to Wembley. They gave two outstanding performances, offering many people the only chance they would ever have to see these magnificent and beautifully trained horses. Dressage

► The Spanish Riding School performing at Horse of the Year Show in 1969.

displays and quadrilles have nearly always been well received at the show. The Swiss Cavalry School and the French Cadre Noir have also given performances, and in 1997 Britain's young dressage riders began giving regular displays (as part of the BYRDS scheme). In 1984, after the Los Angeles Olympics, Reiner Klimke and his gold-medal partner Ahlerich, were given a warm welcome when they performed at Wembley, and Britain's top dressage rider at the time, Christopher Bartle (who was sixth in LA), also gave a display.

The Musical Ride of the Household Cavalry holds a special place at HOYS, and is always a much-loved addition to the programme. Performing in full state ceremonial uniform, some twenty-six members of the Household Cavalry carry out a fast-moving, sometimes daring, but always well-executed ride that never fails to impress. The soldiers are well drilled and well rehearsed, and are in demand for their displays all over the world.

Initially, those enlisting in the Household Cavalry receive basic training at Pirbright, where riding is one of a number of skills taught to the new recruits. Those who show an aptitude for riding will be selected for mounted duty and undergo a further sixteen weeks of gruelling training at Windsor, taking responsibility for their own horse. A final four weeks are spent in ceremonial uniform before the passing-out parade in front of the commanding officer. Enrolment is then made into either the Life Guards or the Blues and Royals Squadron of the Household Cavalry Mounted Regiment at Hyde Park Barracks in London.

◄ A dramatic entry – the Household Cavalry performing at HOYS in 2004.

Their ceremonial duties, which date back to the regiment's formation in 1961, include providing escorts for state occasions, such as the opening of parliament, royal jubilees, state visits to London, Windsor or Edinburgh, and of course the Queen's birthday parade. Better known as trooping the colour, this involves nearly 200 horses, including the massed bands of the Household Cavalry with their distinctive drum horses. Squadrons from the Household Cavalry have also been deployed in Bosnia and Afghanistan.

▲ The Household Cavalry line up for the salute at the end of their display at the 2008 show. The Musical Ride of the Household Cavalry is one of the most popular displays at HOYS.

The Metropolitan Police provide their own unique display of horsemanship with their popular activity ride. Spectators can marvel at the bravery of the horses and the skills of the riders as they perform stunts ranging from jumping through hoops of fire to removing saddles while jumping down a line of small fences. Although these displays show horses and riders at the height of their training and ability, it nonetheless gives an indication of the long hours of work and dedication that are put in to training a police horse and its rider.

A police officer must serve in the force for at least two years before becoming eligible to join the mounted branch, and only one in five applicants is accepted. Recruits undergo a sixteen-week intensive training course before qualifying, after which they are expected to ride all the horses at the stables before being allocated their own mount. Compulsory refresher courses for the riders take place every year.

The horses, too, are carefully selected. They should combine the spirit of a thoroughbred with the strength of a draught horse. It usually takes around six months to train each horse, familiarising them with all the hazards, sights

◄ Playing with fire! The Metropolitan branch of the mounted police giving one of their spectacular displays at the show.

and sounds they will experience on duty in London. A mounted officer's job includes high-visibility patrols, designed to deter wrong-doers by their presence, and public-order duties, which usually means crowd control at public events, such as football matches. From a vantage point eight feet above the ground, a mounted officer's view can be invaluable at a crowded venue.

A mounted police officer may be able to remove his saddle while jumping fences, but the French trick rider Lorenzo, who appeared at the show in 2004, could jump over a fence on two horses at once while standing with a foot on each horse's back. Daniel Naprous, 'the Masked Caballero', was another trick rider who brought drama to the show, and the Knights of Middle England have provided a noisy but brilliantly executed display. In contrast to these, the magical displays by Jean François Pignon have been quiet and calm. His horses, initially two beautiful grey mares, performed without any form of tack or other

► Frédéric Pignon and one of his stallions at the 2010 show; an extraordinary display of mutual trust and respect.

equipment. Pignon could ride them, stand on their backs (one foot on each horse), lie down with them, send them away, bring them back and change their pace, all by the use of his voice and his body language. He first performed at HOYS in 2002, and returned in 2005, on this occasion with five horses. Other riders recall seeing Jean François leave the stable area before his performances with all five of his horses – none of them wearing any tack. The horses followed him, without wavering or stopping to talk to other horses, all the way through the stable lines and along the track to the main arena.

In 2010, Jean François' brother, Frédéric, gave an outstanding performance with six stallions that also performed at liberty. It was almost as if the whole thing was a game for the horses, and although Frédéric carried a whip, it was only ever used for directional purposes. The horses carried out half-passes, pirouettes, changes of pace, standing on blocks and, of course, the all-important bow to the audience. It was an extraordinary display of mutual trust and respect.

Even in Dorian Williams' day there was often debate about the displays – should they simply be frivolous entertainment or should they showcase excellence in equestrian expertise? Striking the right balance is not easy, but there is no doubt that the displays at HOYS provide an opportunity to experience equestrianism outside the boundaries of every day competitive riding, and to see some remarkable talents.

CHAPTER NINE

THE SHOW GOES ON

Throughout its long history, Horse of the Year Show has had a far-reaching influence on the equestrian world. From its early days, when it brought show jumping to the attention of the British public, it has provided a focal point for riders from all parts of the equestrian spectrum, and, in spite of its many changes and upheavals over the years, it has, remarkably, held true to Tony Collings' original vision of a show to find the champion of champions.

For more than sixty years, HOYS has remained the most prestigious show in Britain; it is the one at which showing people and show jumpers alike all aspire to compete, and as such it has played a major role in promoting the breeding and production of some of the best horses in the world. HOYS is the target; only the best qualify and only the very best have a chance of winning, and so standards continue to improve as riders strive to achieve their dream. This is the show's legacy to equestrianism. It has enhanced the kudos and value of producing top horses, it has raised standards, it has boosted the equestrian industry and it has provided thousands of riders with the opportunity to showcase their horses to a growing equestrian audience.

The show continues to fulfil this vital role, and its future is therefore immensely important. Only fifteen years ago the show was in danger of being lost. The dwindling interest in show jumping from the mid-1970s onwards had had a detrimental effect on its appeal for sponsorship and television, and support from

▲ Bringing on the next generation. Peter Charles walks a show-jumping course in the international arena with his son Harry.

those sources had given the show so much impetus in its first twenty-five years. Furthermore, the show had faltered in finding the right management during the 1990s. As a result, it had been left in a precarious financial state by 1997.

That was the year HOYS reached its lowest point ever; immense financial difficulties and spiralling costs had taken their toll and the show was struggling to survive, but no one wanted to see the world's most famous horse show go under. HOYS was saved with just weeks to spare by the dedication, energy and willpower exhibited not only by the new event management team headed by Mark Wein and Mike Gill, but also by sponsors, judges, officials, stewards, volunteers and enthusiasts. Thanks to their efforts, the show went ahead, riding on a wave of goodwill and gratitude from the equestrian community, who were prepared to put up with high entry fees and low prize money if this is what it took to secure the future of their show. Against all odds, the show came back from the brink and was actually deemed a success.

This renewed vigour and faith in the show has continued to build momentum ever since; HOYS is constantly moving forwards, staying up to date with new classes and formats, as well as reviewing and understanding what competitors and societies need from the show. And it has managed to do this without losing sight of its roots and traditions. While aiming to entertain a full house of spectators, the show also has to function as the home of the BSJA national championships and of the supreme championships for the various showing and breeding societies, not to mention the Pony Club mounted games finals and the scurry driving finals. A great many individuals and organisations, all with different interests and priorities, have to be accommodated. In 2011 the show will run over six days, starting on the Tuesday.

Much research and discussion takes place to ensure that HOYS stays in tune with trends and changes in the equestrian world. To host such prestigious finals and maintain the show's reputation as being the gold standard, constant measures are taken to review every detail. Whether this is the surface the horses exercise and compete on, the position of the stables in the car parks to reduce flooding, changes to qualifying rounds to encourage a better geographical representation or reassessment of qualifying classes to improve native breed participation, no stone is left unturned to ensure that each autumn Horse of the Year Show is a worthy host to over 56,000 spectators, over 175 judges, stewards and officials and 1,500 horses and riders.

Support for the show comes from all sources, and an indication of the scale of this support can be gleaned from the huge amount of related traffic on internet and social media platforms. At the time of writing, nearly 70,000 fans regularly log on to the HOYS' Facebook page, for example, taking an interest and making their views known. These internet fans are staunch supporters of the classes, the history, the displays, the qualifying rounds and the famous riders, and they even support each other through the page by answering queries and offering advice to newcomers. Throughout the year, the build-up for the next HOYS provides a focal point for all enthusiasts, be they competitors or keen spectators, and this is the perfect platform for them to feel in the thick of it all the time. They want to know who has qualified, to discuss results, comment on pictures, ask questions and source behind-the-scenes information. As HOYS gets bigger and better, its following increases, and fans find it hugely rewarding to be involved in this way.

In 2003, Grandstand Media extended its contract with the BSJA (now British Showjumping) to continue running HOYS until 2036, which has proved beneficial to both sides. The BSJA can rest assured that the organisers are fully committed to running this show for many years to come, thus providing continuity, security and the knowledge that plans for the future can be made with confidence. The management team know that their ideas and developments can be seen through in the long term no matter what challenges are thrown up in the wake of such a large and long-running event.

Following the show's 60th anniversary in 2008, Grandstand Media entered a new era with a fresh team at the helm. Mike Gill and Mark Wein had poured heart and soul into the show since 1997 and when Mike left in 2007 and Mark at the end of 2008, Sandy Anderson, a loyal supporter of the show, who had been a silent partner alongside Mike and Mark for some time, bought the group in its entirety and became chairman. On Mark's departure Helena Pettit became managing director. Sandy and Helena are keen to maintain the momentum created by Mike and Mark, and also to take the show to the next level of equestrian sporting entertainment. Their view is that while the show must always remain true to its roots and continue to be the finale of the equestrian season, it is paramount to keep the show fresh and relevant.

Helena, with a diverse sporting background herself, is dedicated to ensuring that the era over which she and her team preside will be remembered not only for guarding the show's values but also for stretching its horizons as it continues to evolve and grow. She is supported by a small, permanent staff at the head offices in Harpenden, consisting of Keith Field as the finance manager; Samantha Anderson heading up Natalie Luckins, Emma Wardell, Catrina Wootton and Laura Hardwick in the commercial team; Kate Lawrence and Kate Macdonald in the operations team; Gemma Hall and Kelli Thomas in the equestrian team and Sarah Briscoe, Charlotte Read and Gregg Taylor in the marketing and PR team. Grandstand Media together with its band of tireless officials are true enthusiasts of the show and passionate guardians of its future.

Eager to connect with competitors and visitors to Horse of the Year Show and to further develop relationships with the associated societies, Grandstand Media is continually venturing into new territory. In 2011 the show trialled running for six days to incorporate the Express Eventing Final, and several other new classes were added to enhance the show timetable. In house, it recently launched a bespoke on-line entry system; it is now creating and managing a new range of merchandise, and it is rolling out a new marketing and PR strategy. Grandstand Media continues to trial new initiatives as it endeavours to ensure the show delivers beyond everyone's expectations and remains the household name that so many people have fought so hard to maintain.

Horse of the Year Show not only survives but flourishes, enjoying support from both its die-hard fans and the cluster of newcomers that appear every year. Any team that manages a show of this scale and popularity understands that they are privileged to do so and are merely the guardians of something very special. The success of Horse of the Year Show depends on its many supporters – the competitors, spectators, owners, breeders, officials and volunteers. The hard work, dedication and enthusiasm of many of these people kept the show alive when it was floundering in the mid-1990s, and they continue to make HOYS what it is today. It is for them, and for future generations, that the show must go on.

▲ Helena Pettit (left), managing director of Grandstand Media, presents Mary Allison with her ten-year pin, awarded to all officials who have worked for the show for ten years.

▼ Caught up in the excitement of the occasion, spectators in the hospitality boxes join in the Mexican wave that swept around the arena moments before the final round of the 2010 Puissance in which Tina Fletcher and Ellen Whitaker tied for first place.

SOURCES

INTRODUCTION
1 *Porlock Vale Riding School* 1946–1961 Jacqueline Peck

CHAPTER ONE: A PROMISING START
1 *Horse of the Year, The Story of a Unique Horse Show* Dorian Williams, 1976
2 *Soldier On, An Autobiography* Colonel Sir Mike Ansell
3 *Horse of the Year, The Story of a Unique Horse Show* Dorian Williams, 1976
4 *Horse of the Year, The Story of a Unique Horse Show* Dorian Williams, 1976
5 Alan Smith in the *Daily Telegraph*
6 *Soldier On, An Autobiography* Colonel Sir Mike Ansell
7 *Soldier On, An Autobiography* Colonel Sir Mike Ansell
8 *Soldier On, An Autobiography* Colonel Sir Mike Ansell
9 1949/1950 *Horsemans' Year*, from an article by Tony Collings
10 *Champion Horses and Ponies* Pamela Macgregor-Morris
11 *Champion Horses and Ponies* Pamela Macgregor-Morris
12 Pamela Macgregor-Morris in *Horse and Hound*
13 *Horse of the Year, The Story of a Unique Horse Show* Dorian Williams, 1976

Boxed pen portraits and stories
1 *Horse of the Year, The Story of a Unique Horse Show* Dorian Williams, 1976
2 *Foxhunter Champions* Sue Clarke
3 *Champion Horses and Ponies* Pamela Macgregor-Morris

CHAPTER TWO: HALCYON DAYS
1 Pamela Macgregor-Morris in *Horse and Hound*
2 Pamela Macgregor-Morris in *Horse and Hound*
3 'Town and Country', *Horse and Hound*, 13 October 1967
4 Pamela Macgregor-Morris in *Horse and Hound*
5 Pamela Macgregor-Morris in *Horse and Hound*

Boxed pen portraits and stories
1 *Horse of the Year, The Story of a Unique Horse Show* Dorian Williams, 1976
2 *Soldier On, An Autobiography* Colonel Sir Mike Ansell
3 *Horse of the Year, The Story of a Unique Horse Show* Dorian Williams, 1976
4 *Women and Horses* Gillian Newsum
5 *Horse and Hound*
6 *Shear Gold, An Autobiography* Leslie Law

CHAPTER THREE: CHANGING FORTUNES
1 *Country Life* magazine, 15 October 1987
2 'Town and Country', *Horse and Hound*, 1981

3 *Horse and Hound*
4 The *Daily Telegraph*, 7 October 1992
5 The *Daily Telegraph*, 28 September 1993
6 *Horse and Hound*
7 *Horse and Hound*
8 *Champion Horses and Ponies* Pamela Macgregor-Morris

Boxed pen portraits and stories
1 'Town and Country', *Horse and Hound*, 1953
2 The *Daily Telegraph*
3 Obituary by Elizabeth Polling, the *Independent*

CHAPTER FOUR: A NEW ERA
1 *Horse and Hound*
2 2002 Horse of the Year Show programme
3 The *Times*, 12 October 1992

Boxed pen portraits and stories
1 Horse of the Year Show programme, 2007

CHAPTER FIVE: TELEVISION
1 *Horse of the Year, The Story of a Unique Horse Show* Dorian Williams, 1976
2 *Great Sporting Moments: Show Jumping* Dorian Williams
3 *Between the Lines* Dorian Williams
4 *Horse and Hound*, 12 October 1989

Boxed pen portraits and stories
1 *Horse and Hound*, 27 August 1992
2 *Horse and Hound*, 27 August 1992

CHAPTER SIX: BACKSTAGE
Boxed pen portraits and stories
1 *Horse and Hound*

CHAPTER SEVEN: DONE FOR FUN
1 *Soldier On, An Autobiography* Colonel Sir Mike Ansell

CHAPTER EIGHT: THE ENTERTAINERS
1 Pamela Macgregor-Morris in *Horse and Hound*
2 *Horse of the Year, The Story of a Unique Horse Show* Dorian Williams, 1976
3 *Horse of the Year, The Story of a Unique Horse Show* Dorian Williams, 1976

HOYS RESULTS

SHOW JUMPING

Junior and Young Riders National Classes

128cm Championship
NB This class was not run in 1995 or between 1997 and 2000

Year	Horse	Rider
2010	Pendini	Jessica Hewitt
2009	Grianagh Harley	Christie Pritchard
2008	Matthew's Girl	Millie Allen
2007	Charley's Angel	Jessica Mendoza
2006	Get Ready Freddie	Rosie Gunn
2005	Silver Wonder	Pippa Allen
2004	Magic Shadow	Charlie Evans
2003	My Little Tinker	Danika Plumley
2002	Proud Flyer	Jordan Whitaker
2001	Corralass	Coral Mowbray
1996	Air Wolf	Gemma Fletcher
1994	Little Chopper	Sarah Stokes
1993	Metric	Stacy Willsone
1992	Little Chopper	Sarah Stokes

138cm Championship
NB This class was not run between 1997 and 2000

Year	Horse	Rider
2010	My Bugsy Malone	Darby Ward
2009	More than Milton	Darby Ward
2008	Fountain Ranger	Jessica Crosby
2007	More than Milton	Olivia Wells
2006	Sakama Chezni	Pippa Allen
2005	Fountain Ranger	James Smith
2004	Grey Palace	Jordan Whitaker
2003	Strawberry Fair III	Matthew Sampson
2002	Silverlea Rozencavalier	Emma Jane Moore
2001	Mystic Starlight Express	William Whitaker
1996	Allwood Lad	Gemma Kay
1995	Window Glow Beaker	Lee Williams
1994	Forever Katie	Louise Whitaker
1993	Ferrybound	Nicola Western
1992	Barley Corn V	Vicky Ashworth

◄ Ben Maher fixes the winning rosette to My Bugsy Malone after Derby Ward's win in the 138cm championships in 2010. She also won the same class in 2009 with More than Milton.

Leading Pony Show Jumper of the Year (formerly Leading Junior Jumper of the Year)

Year	Horse	Rider
2010	Tixylix	Jessica Mendoza
2009	Paddy Power	Laura Robinson
2008	New York Spritzer	Roberta Roe
2007	Miami Bound	George Whitaker
2006	Miami Bound	Thomas Whitaker
2005	Indien de Here	William Whitaker
2004	CJ's Kemosabi	Louise Saywell
2003	Spottie Dot Com	Sophie Broome
2002	CJ's Kemosabi	Andrew Mizon
2001	Colton Maelstrom	Martha Beaumont
2000	Phearless Phantom	Anton Owens
1999	Colton Maelstrom	Alice Beaumont
1998	Gold Harvest	Laura Stephenson
1997	Colton Maelstrom	Sammy Pharo
1996	Easy Gold	Janie Loveday
1995	Current Ruella	Sally-Ann How
1994	Maltstreet Mystic	Paul Barker
1993	Ballymoss	Lucy Henderson
1992	Strawberry Mojo	Nicky Bingham
1991	St Ives Orient Express	Scott Smith
1990	Sandy 'B'	Guy Goosen
1989	Silver King	Miss S. Bowen
1988	Goresbridge	Z. Brooks
1987	Rogerio	Nigel Coupe
1986	Goresbridge	Z. Brooks
1985	The Welshman	Peter Murphy
1984	Woodnymph III	C. Crow
1983	Double L	N. Emery
1982	Dane Castle	P. Sutton
1981	Dragonhill Rushlight	R. Bevis
1980	The Welshman III	M. Wilson
1979	Rival II	C. Thomas
1978	Telstar XXI	K. Fuller
1977	Dunglenn VII	Michael Mac
1976	Tamarisk II	Michael Whitaker
1975	Stardust XXX	Jane Nicol
1974	Rockwood Cedric	D. Saffell
1973	Starlight XLII	Graham Gillespie
1972	Pim III	P. Pitcher
1971	Court Colando	P. Wilson
1970	Jenny Wren IX	J. Tempest
1969	Ki-Ming	John Simms
1968	Pablo	M. Hall
1967	Kangaroo	Nicola Loffett
1966	Kangaroo	Nicola Loffett

Year	Horse	Rider
1965	Pierrot	Miss L. Raper
1964	Pierrot	Miss L. Raper
1963	Little Robert	Miss G. Cambridge
1962	Grey Mist VIII	Miss C. Inskip
1961	Mister Robin	Miss P. Langton
	Carreg Guest	D. Hughes
1960	Carreg Guest	Miss J. Goodwin
	Lulu II	Miss A. Westwood
1959	Blue Flake	D. Hughes
1958	Baccarat	Miss S. Barnes
	Paul V	Miss D. Anholm
1957	Lulu II	Miss B. Vincent
1956	Cherry	J. James
1955	Carreg Guest	Valerie Wood
1954	Ballydoyle Prince	A. Makin
	Munden Magpie	Miss M. Barnes
1953	Lucky Strike	John Howle
	Springbok	E. Makin
1952	Munden Magpie	T. Barnes
1951	Tony	A. Watkins
1950	Brandy of White Cloud	Miss P. Moss
1949	Vintage	Yvonne Fossey

▲ Lap of honour for Roberta Roe and New York Spritzer, winners of the 2008 Leading Pony Show Jumper.

Pony Foxhunter Championship (Formerly Junior Foxhunter)

Year	Horse	Rider
2010	Amili Jr Z	Thomas Plaster
2009	Wicked II	Pippa Allen
2008	Funfair	Steph Gunn
2007	Scharonie	Emily West
2006	Stainsby Style	Matthew Sampson
2005	Who's Bob	Claire Bailey
2004	Flame of Tara	James Reveley
2003	Devlin	William Whitaker
2002	Blue Amber	Hanna Penny
2001	New York Blues	Louise Pavitt
2000	Loobeen Shamrock	Emma Shaw
1999	Ballykissangel III	Louise Renwick
1998	Classic Henna	Claudia Jordan
1997	Bobby Bracken	Sarah Marshall
1996	Miami Blaze	Sarah Marshall
1995	Gray Spartan	Grace Barton
1994	Mr Checkmate	George Horne
1993	Ultra Gold	Stephanie Scott
1992	Dovecote Holly	Amanda Cowan
1991	Tom Cobbley	Paul Barker
1990	Classical Hero	Andrew Davies
1989	April Star	Sarah Winterbottom
1988	Top Rhos Tango	Jane Gregory
1987	Arapaho	Miss R. Edmunds
1986	Southwell News	M. Williams
1985	Pacer	P. Carline

Pony Newcomers Championship

Year	Horse	Rider
2010	Rumworth Taylors Twilight	Chantelle Duggan
2009	Tireve Midnight Express	Jasmin Cain
2008	Scharonie	Emily West
2007	Fermali's Silke	Jessie Drea
2006	Tinka's Pearl	Matthew Sampson
2005	Stainsby Style	Matthew Sampson
2004	Tick Tock Two Tone	Emma Stoker
2003	Custom Cruiser	Laura Mantel
2002	Blue Amber	Hanna Penny
2001	Weaves Legacy	Tara Shearer
2000	Miami Bound	Lauley Squibb
1999	Greenfields Pride	Gregory Dodd
1998	Edenside Sunshine	Asha Narsapur
1997	Murphy's Girl III	Christinal Hall
1996	Portsunlight	Dominic Moss
1995	Landown 3's Are Wild	L. Penny
1994	Cool Mule	Oliver Townend
1993	Ultra Gold	Stephanie Scott
1992	LA Flashback	L. Yeoman
1991	Mowtown Magic	A. McLaughlin
1990	Classical Hero	Andrew Davies
1989	Sunset Dream	J. Ratcliffe
1988	A Chance Encounter	T. Partridge
1987	La Campensina	John Renwick
1986	Cherrington Serenade	Guy Goosen
1985	Wellhouse Warrior	S. Thomas

Young Riders Championship

NB This class was not run in 1969

Year	Horse	Rider	Year	Horse	Rider
2010	Chauvanist	Daniel Neilson	1997	Masterly	Caroline Webley
2009	Chianti Classico	Matthew Sampson	1996	Cowboy Magic Deep Heat	Louise Whitaker
2008	Saffier van de Kreek	Hannah Paul	1995	Gemstone	Miss M. Baryard
2007	Maestro de Rend Peine	Nicole Pavitt	1994	Highflyer	Miss J. Dennis
2006	Vahagn de Lozanna	Ryan Prater	1993	Miniature Quickstep	Andrew Davies
2005	Henri de Here	Ellen Whitaker	1992	TWT Suntory	Nigel Coupe
2004	Make Haste	Louise Pavitt	1991	Welham	Miss K. Durham
2003	Landini	Tors Millin	1990	The Mint	M. McCourt
2002	Lord Liberty	Robert Whitaker	1989	Invincible Lad	Nigel Coupe
2001	Virtual Village Randi	Robert Whitaker	1988	Everest Surething	Marie Edgar
2000	Azimuth	Stuart Needs	1987	Wessex Ballyflash	Paul Sutton
1999	Mace Park Valhallah	Grace Barton	1986	Fallon	J. Fry
1998	Valhallam	Grace Barton	1985	My Lucky Maywood	L. Bradley

Young Riders Championship *continued*

Year	Horse	Rider
1984	Viewpoint	Philip Heffer
1983	Diamond T	Paul Sutton
1982	Penny Farthing	Matthew Lanni
1981	Soloman Sandpiper	J. Yardley
1980	Cantaberry	Marcus Chambers
1979	Tauna Dora	M. Mac
1978	McGinty	Miss V. Gascoine
1977	Berricote Cappachino	Michael Whitaker
1976	Berricote Cappachino	Michael Whitaker
1975	Paddy Connelly	J. Brown
1974	Everest Maybe	Nick Skelton
1973	Speculator	Miss D. Johnsey
1972	Oyster	Miss P. Wilson
1971	Garnet	C. Whitney
1970	Relincho	R. Richardson
1968	Psalm	Ann Moore
1967	North Riding	C. Barker
1966	Dominic IV	J. Baillie
1965	Foxtrott XII	Miss S. Roger Smith
1964	Paddies Pride	Miss G. Clarke
1963	Sherree	R. Woodward
1962	Dunbell	J. Bradnock

► A jubilant Matt Sampson after winning the 2009 Young Rider Championship on Chianti Classico.

◄ The 2010 Young Riders Champion Daniel Neilson and Chauvanist. The pair also won the Speed Horse of the Year class.

Senior National Classes

6 Year Old Championship

NB This class was not run in 2008

Year	Horse	Rider
2010	Don VHP Z	Louise Pavitt
2009	Big Star	Nick Skelton
2007	Beluga II	Laura Renwick
2006	Caritiar Z	Philip Miller
2005	Senette	Scott Brash
2004	Radetzky S	Robert Bevis
2003	Hollywood	Carron Nicol
2002	Oakhill Supreme	Robert Smith
2001	Macepark Velsk	Grace Barton
2000	Senator Marius Claudius	Robert Smith
1999	Grannus Lady	John Renwick

7 Year Old Championship

Year	Horse	Rider
2010	Waterstone II	Robert Whitaker
2009	Super Trooper de Ness	Nicky Boulter
2008	Beaujolais	Scott Brash
2007	Lara Joy II	Geoff Luckett
2006	Limelight de Breve	Laura Renwick
2005	Carisco	Christian Weier
2004	Fresh Direct Corlato	Tim Stockdale
2003	Pamone	Louise Whitaker
2002	Midtime	Robert Bevis
2001	Its Magic Max	Keith Shore
2000	Tornedo FC	Billy Twomey
1999	Temple Voyager	John Renwick
1998	Junior II	Michael Whitaker
1997	Virtual Village Carte Gene	Nick Skelton

British Showjumping Amateur Classic

Year	Horse	Rider
2010	Limerick	Di Fairclough
2009	Don Douglas	Ian Wynne
2008	Wake Up	Gemma Hallett

Foxhunter Championship

Year	Horse	Rider
2010	Parvatti de Breve	Laura Renwick
2009	Sultan V	Bruce Menzies
2008	Sauron ML	Scott Brash
2007	Marcolas G	Simon Nicholson
2006	Limelight De Breve	Laura Renwick
2005	Romanov II	Philip Spivey
2004	Lwoen Herz	David McPherson
2003	Opportunity B	Helen Tredwell
2002	Unbelievable Darco	Jo Clee
2001	Mondriaan	William Funnell
2000	Senator Marius Claudius	Robert Smith
1999	Luidam	John Popely
1998	Carnival Spirit II	Damien Charles
1997	Temple What a Flash	John Renwick
1996	Honnie	Duncan Inglis
1995	Everest Ashley	Michael Whitaker
1994	Valentino R	Peter Murphy

▲ Sultan V, winner of the 2009 Foxhunter Championship, ridden by Bruce Menzies.

Foxhunter Championship *continued*

Year	Horse	Rider	Year	Horse	Rider
1993	Fleurance	John Popely	1973	Hold Hard	Graham Fletcher
1992	Itziweeni	Malcolm Pyrah	1972	Miss Tina	Liz Clower
1991	Henderson O'Flynn	Michael Whitaker	1971	Mannering	Harvey Smith
1990	Balou	Nigel Coupe	1970	Pennywort	Paula Graham
1989	Cut Loose	Nick Skelton	1969	Walkie Talkie	Caroline Bradley
1988	Don Kelly	Nick Skelton	1968	Flying Wild	Stephen Hadley
1987	Everest Oyster	Emma Jane Mac	1967	Miranda XIV	Derek Ricketts
1986	Edisford Bridge	Geoff Billington	1966	Top of the Morning	David Broome
1985	Everest Asher	Liz Edgar	1965	Topaz III	Aileen Ross
1984	Once More	William Funnell	1964	Lights Out	Julie Nash
1983	Charlie Brummel	Mennell Watson	1963	Rockwell	Althea Roger Smith
1982	Cafe Noir	Geoff Goodwin	1962	Beethoven	Douglas Bunn
1981	Hopscotch	John Whitaker	1961	The Barrhead Builder	Dougie Iggulden
1980	Coral's Morning Glory	Derek Ricketts	1960	Bawbee of Edinbarnet	Dougie Iggulden
1979	Saucy Brown	Malcolm Pyrah	1959	Savernake	Pat Holland
1978	L.B.F.	Stuart Davidson	1958	Rambler IV	Arwyn John
1977	Port Paddy	Mallowry Spens	1957	Lucky Sam	Anne Barker
1976	Ryehill	Peter Richardson	1956	Andrew Cobb Esq MFH	John Weaver
1975	St Corry	Willie Sheret	1955	Royal Lord	Miss B.P. Rose
1974	Olympic Star	Harvey Smith	1954	Dreamboat	Frances Stanbury

◄ David McPherson receiving the Foxhunter trophy in 2004 from Lucy Higginson, Editor of *Horse and Hound*.

► Nicky Boulter and Super Trooper de Ness, winners of the Grade C Championship in 2010. They also won the 2009 7-year old Championship, and were second in the Senior Newcomers in 2008.

Grade C Championship

Year	Horse	Rider
2010	Super Trooper de Ness	Nicky Boulter
2009	Sultan V	Bruce Menzies
2008	Univeau	Phillip Miller
2007	Halida du Rouet	Mennel Watson
2006	Amaryllis VD Heffink	Nicole Pavitt
2005	Cassius Clay II	Geoff Billington
2004	Pircolando M	Tim Stockdale
2003	Market Force	Billy Twomey
2002	Saffier	Billy Twomey
2001	Tropicana	Veronique Whitaker
2000	Laughtons Dreams	Keith Doyle
1999	Temple Guess What	John Renwick
1998	Aniapollo	William Funnell
1997	McCoist	Tina Fletcher
1996	Sparticus	Tina Cassan
1995	Tinka's Boy	Alison Bradley
1994	Sagase	Paul Barker
1993	Moneymore	Carl Edwards
1992	Union du Taillon	Andrew Saywell
1991	Sportsfield	Andrew Saywell
1990	Alan Paul Florida	Sarah Skelton
1989	Everest Unique	Marie Edgar
1988	Laurentide	Geoff Glazzard
1987	Paradise Peppermill	John Harris
1986	Edisford Bridge	Geoff Billington
1985	PPD	Peter Murphy
1984	Halo	Nick Skelton
1983	Take Your Pick	Steven Whitaker
1982	Trimoco Brington	Caroline Bradley
1981	Remember Me	Geoff Goodwin
1980	Courtway	John Roberts
1979	Newton Green	Derek Ricketts
1978	Atomic Light	P. Miles
1977	Star Gay Time	J. Brown
1976	Tigre	Caroline Bradley
1975	Tabbal	Ann Backhouse
1974	Sally Ann	Geoff Goodwin
1973	Inter City	Mrs M. Dawes

Newcomers Championship

Year	Horse	Rider
2010	Molly Malone V	Anthony Condon
2009	V Anubertha	Matthew Sampson
2008	Chauvanist	Daniel Nielson
2007	Beluga II	Laura Renwick
2006	Toscane R	Billy Twomey
2005	Angelina	Warren Clarke
2004	Baretto	Fredrick Bergendorff
2003	Tiran	Mennell Watson
2002	Aicina	Michael Whitaker
2001	Lakeland Gold Diamond	Simon Buckley
2000	Ashdale Quest	Dave Quigley
1999	Peloma	Peter Murphy
1998	Divine Des Cabanes	Simon Crippen
1997	Carneville	Matthew Lanni
1996	Upton's Iranda	Andrew Saywell
1995	Scarlet Samsara	Tina Youngman
1994	Upton's LB	Mennell Watson
1993	Pennwood Fleetway	Geoff Glazzard
1992	Chinka	Michael Wynne
1991	Maybe this Time	Rhona Simpson
1990	Just Jazz	Helen Evans
1989	Smart Move	W.J. Halliday
1988	Temple What Now	Alan Clutterbuck
1987	Polishman	Miss H. Rees
1986	Lexy	Matthew Lanni
1985	Quarto	A. Marsh

Senior International Classes

Dick Turpin Stakes

NB This class was not run in 2000 or between 1985 and 1995

Year	Horse	Rider
2010	Valention VII	Sam Hutton
2009	Phaline K	Dirk Demeersman
2008	Fantasia	Billy Twomey
2007	Cortaflex Amber du Montois	William Funnell
2006	Compliment 2	Geoff Luckett
2005	Capriola VD Helle	Kristof Cleeren
2004	Kalusha	Robert Smith
2003	Lutte P	Leon Thjissen
2002	Mr Springfield	Robert Smith
2001	Phin Phin	Roelof Bril
1999	Truman	Roelof Bril
1998	Traxdata Dolli	Peter Charles
1997	Dolli	Peter Charles
1996	Radni	John Whitaker
1984	Everest Radius	Nick Skelton
1983	Sea Pearl	Malcolm Pyrah
1982	Paddy Connelly	Campbell Graham
1981	Vista	Robert Smith
1980	Wallaby	Nick Skelton
1979	Rossantico	E. Wauters
1978	Golden Gate	L. Merkel
1977	Marshall	G. Myberg
1976	Ballymacaw	R.W. Summer
1975	Maconda	Eddie Macken
1974	Middle Road	Caroline Bradley
1973	Everest Boomerang	Liz Edgar
1972	Chane Link	Lionel Dunning
1971	Meridan	M. Spens
1970	The Whip	Graham Fletcher
1969	Brandy Jim	Mrs C. Barker
1968	Uncle Max	Ted Edgar
1967	Laramie II	Miss S. Edwards
1966	Redskin II	Miss J. Passey
1965	St Justin	Fred Welch
1964	St Justin	Fred Welch
1963	Jubilant	Miss M. Makin
1962	Donner	P. Harrison
1961	Pegasus XIII	Ted Williams
1960	Lucky Sam	David Barker
1959	Smokey Bob	T.M. Charlesworth
1958	Rambler IV	A. John
1957	Topper VI	Fred Welch
1956	Danny Boy	Pat Moss

Year	Horse	Rider
1955	Costa	D. Beard
1954	Tosca	Pat Smythe
1953	John Gilpin	Alan Oliver
1952	Dusty Miller	Miss F. Spink
1951	Eforegit	Carley Beard

▲ Alan Smith, former equestrian correspondent of the *Daily Telegraph*, attempting to present Billy Twomey on Fantasia with their trophy for winning the Dick Turpin Stakes in 2008.

Leading Show Jumper of the Year

Year	Horse	Rider
2010	Oz de Breve	Laura Renwick
2009	Equimax Ocolado	Ellen Whitaker
2008	Je T'aime Flamenco	Billy Twomey
2007	Katchina Mail	Patrice Delaveau
2006	Anthem	Laura Kraut
2005	Two Mills Showtime	Robert Maguire
2004	Portofino 63	Michael Whitaker
	Leading Show Jumper combines with Grand Prix	
2003	Lavaletto	Duncan Inglis
2002	Handell II	Michael Whitaker
2001	Abbervail Dream	Di Lampard
2000	Heartbreaker	Peter Geerink
1999	Virtual Village Welham	John Whitaker
1998	Barry Bug	William Funnell
1997	Virtual Village Heyman	John Whitaker
1996	Carnival Bouncer	M. Hughes
1995	Everest Midnight Madness	Michael Whitaker
1994	Everest Midnight Madness	Michael Whitaker
1993	Everest Grannusch	John Whitaker
1992	Henderson Gammon	John Whitaker
1991	Alan Paul Phoenix Park	Nick Skelton
1990	Lannegan	David Broome
1989	Brook Street Picnic	Scott Smith
1988	Next Milton	John Whitaker
1987	Towerlands Anglezarke	Malcolm Pyrah
1986	Ned Kelly	Sue Pountain
1985	Everest St James	Nick Skelton
1984	Furst Z	Jeff McVean
1983	Apollo II	Geoff Glazzard
1982	St James	Nick Skelton
1981	Mr Ross	David Broome
1980	Towerlands Anglezarke	Malcolm Pyrah
1979	Video	Robert Smith
1978	Maybe	Nick Skelton
1977	Marius	Caroline Bradley
1976	Speculator	Debbie Johnsey
1975	Sportsman	David Broome
1974	Tauna Dora	Graham Fletcher
1973	Sportsman	David Broome
1972	Psalm	Ann Moore
1971	Pitz Palu	Alan Oliver
1970	Stroller	Marion Mould
1969	Uncle Max	Ted Edgar
1968	Vibart	Andrew Fielder
1967	Harvester VI	Harvey Smith
1966	Vibart	Andrew Fielder

Year	Horse	Rider
1965	Warpaint	Harvey Smith
1964	Atlanta	Mrs C.D. Barker
1963	Vibart	Andrew Fielder
1962	Flanagan	Pat Smythe
1961	Mayfly	Miss C. Beard
	Lucky Sam	David Barker
1960	Pegasus XIII	Ted Williams
1959	Farmer's Boy	Harvey Smith
1958	Mr Pollard	Pat Smythe
	Jane Summers	Ted Edgar
1957	Pegasus XIII	Ted Williams
1956	Nizefella	Wilf White
1955	Sunday Morning	Ted Williams
1954	Earlsrath Rambler	Dawn Palethorpe
1953	Red Admiral	Alan Oliver
1952	Snowstorm	William Hanson
1951	Eforegiot	Carley Beard
1950	Sheila	Tommy Makin Esq
1949	Finality	Pat Smythe

Puissance

Year	Horse	Rider
2010	Ladina B	Ellen Whitaker
	Promised Land	Tina Fletcher
2009	Ladina B	Ellen Whitaker
2008	Finbarr V	Robert Whitaker
2007	Una II	Guy Williams
2006	Eperlaan de Fouquet	Ben Maher
	Casper	Cian O'Connor
	Finbarr V	Robert Whitaker
2005	Lactic II	John Whitaker
	Exploit de Roulard	John Whitaker
2004	Eperlaan de Fouquet	Ben Maher
2003	Sarah's Pride	Carl Curtis
	Giacomo	Robert Maguire
2002	Steps Helskinki	John Whitaker
	Giacomo	Robert Maguire
	Vert de Gris	Keith Shore
2001	Wiston Bridge	Tim Stockdale
2000	Shearwater Baghera	David McPherson
1999	Lionel II	Rob Hoekstra
1998	Valiska Forever	Philip Le Jeune
	Calero	Roelof Bril
	Lionel II	Rob Hoekstra
1997	Sagrat	Guy Goosen

Puissance *continued*

Year	Horse	Rider	Year	Horse	Rider
1996	Manusco	Geoff Billington	1966	Sweep III	Alan Oliver
	Elanville	John Whitaker		Goodbye III	Seamus Hayes
	Elton	Michael Whitaker	1965	Goodbye III	Seamus Hayes
1995	Gold	Robert Smith		Lucky Sam	David Boston Barker
	Sagrat	Guy Goosen	1964	Scholli	Miss U. Richter
1994	Gold	Robert Smith	1963	Dundrum	Tommy Wade
1993	Benjumin	Warren Clarke	1962	O'Malley	Harvey Smith
1992	Henderson Gammon	John Whitaker		Warpaint	Harvey Smith
1991	Optiebeurs Golo	Franke Sloothaak		Dundrum	Tommy Wade
1990	Next Didi	Michael Whitaker	1961	Tamara	A. Ebben
	Alan Paul Apollo	Nick Skelton		Rockette	G.M. Ancinelli
	Optiebeurs Lausbub	Otto Becker	1960	Sunsalve	David Broome
1989	Supermarket	Tim Stockdale	1959	The Rock	Capt. Piero d'Inzeo
	Next Didi	Michael Whitaker	1958	Red Admiral	Alan Oliver
1988	Brook Street City Tycoon	Robert Smith	1957	Halla	Hans Winkler
1987	Brook Street Vista	Steven Smith		Red Admiral	Alan Oliver
	Whisper Grey	Jeff McVean	1956	Craven A	Peter Robeson
	Alwins Ass	Franke Sloothaak		Sudden	Mr T. Barnes
1986	Rebound	Alan Fazakerley		Sunsalve	Elizabeth Anderson
	Wabbs	Wabbs Mehlkopf	1955	Red Admiral	Alan Oliver
1985	Furst Z	Jeff McVean	1954	Nizefella	Wilf White
1984	Miss Moet	Nelson Pessoa	1953	Leicester Lad	Mr E. Makin
1983	Carroll's Royal Lion	Eddie Macken	1952	Craven A	Mr Peter Robeson
1982	Sanyo Technology	Harvey Smith	1951	Foxhunter	Lt. Col. Harry Llewellyn
	Whato	Lesley McNaught	1950	Foxhunter	Lt. Col. Harry Llewellyn
1981	Ransome	F. Tyteca		Finality	Pat Smythe
1980	Goldfink	Gary Gillespie	1949	Tankard	Brian Butler
1979	Bouncer	Rowland Fernyhough			
1978	Rossmore II	Fred Welsh			
1977	Graf	Harvey Smith			
1976	Warwick Rex	Alwyn Schockemohle			
	Snaffles	Tony Newbery			
1975	Ramiro	Fritz Ligges			
	Genius	Fritz Ligges			
1974	New Yorker	Caroline Bradley			
1973	Warwickshire Lad	F. Tyteca			
1972	Kalkallo Prince	Ray Howe			
1971	Lucky Strike	Malcolm Pyrah			
	Believe	Capt. Piero d'Inzeo			
1970	Mattie Brown	Harvey Smith			
1969	Rival	Ted Williams			
	War Lord	George Hobbs			
1968	Uncle Max	Ted Edgar			
1967	Harvester	Harvey Smith			
	O'Malley	Harvey Smith			
	Weisel	Fritz Ligges			

◄ Clearing the wall to claim joint first place in the 2010 Puissance: Tina Fletcher and Promised Land.

Speed Horse of the Year

NB This class was not run in 1994

Year	Horse	Rider
2010	Chauvanist	Daniel Nielson
2009	Kanselier	Ellen Whitaker
2008	Kanselier	Ellen Whitaker
2007	Rex	Mark Armstrong
2006	Henri de Here	Ellen Whitaker
2005	Intermission	Billy Twomey
2004	Cortaflex Machiavelli	William Funnell
2003	Quinten II	Ellen Whitaker
2002	Ivoor	Francois Mathy
2001	Brookend Fuehrer	John Renwick
2000	Senator Calouvet du Rouhert	Robert Smith
1999	RGB Nikias	Ludo Philippaerts
1998	Virtual Village Two Step	Michael Whitaker
1997	Helada	Stefan Coften
1996	Shurlands Governer	Francois Mathy
1995	Everest Mr Mesieur	Michael Whitaker
1993	Monterry II	James Fisher
1992	Panachee du Thot	Alexandra Lederman
1991	Alan Paul Major Wager	Nick Skelton
1990	Alan Paul Fiorella	Nick Skelton
1989	Everest Gringo	Emma-Jane Mac
1988	Invincible Lad	Nigel Coupe
1987	Tutein	Annette Lewis
1986	Tutein	Annette Lewis

▲ A regular competitor at HOYS, William Funnell has won the Speed Horse of the Year (2004) and the Dick Turpin Stakes (2007). He is seen here competing at the 2010 show on Billy Congo.

Grand Prix

NB This was the Victor Ludorum from 1950–75; the Radio Rentals Championship 1976–84; and the Grand Prix from 1985–2003. In 2004, the Grand Prix and Leading Showjumper merged to become one class.

Year	Horse	Rider	Year	Horse	Rider
2003	Loro Piana Hamlet	Guy Williams	1989	Argonaut	Franke Sloothaak
2002	Fresh Direct Parcival	Tim Stockdale	1988	Aramis	Franke Sloothaak
2001	Caresino	Hauke Luther	1987	Next Warren Point	Michael Whitaker
2000	Senator Mr Springfield	Robert Smith	1986	Towerlands Anglezarke	Malcolm Pyrah
1999	Burgravvin	Roelof Bril	1985	Boysie	David Bowen
1998	Gino	Bruce Goodwin	1984	Towerlands Anglezarke	Malcolm Pyrah
1997	Virtual Village Showtime	Nick Skelton	1983	Shining Example	Robert Smith
1996	Bowriver Queen	James Fisher	1982	FMS Barbarella	Lesley McNaught
1995	Everest Showtime	Nick Skelton	1981	Mr Ross	David Broome
1994	Everest Grannusch	John Whitaker	1980	Maybe	Nick Skelton
1993	Everest Grannusch	John Whitaker	1979	Carroll's Boomerang	Eddie Macken
1992	Henderson my Mesieur	Michael Whitaker	1978	Sanya San Mar	Harvey Smith
1991	Almox Classic Touch	Ludgar Beerbaum	1977	Boomerang	Eddie Macken
1990	Alan Paul Grandslam	Nick Skelton	1976	Boomerang	Eddie Macken

Grand Prix *continued*

Year	Horse	Rider	Year	Horse	Rider
1975	Boomerang	Eddie Macken	1962	Trigger Hill	Julie Nash
1974	Philco	David Broome	1961	Dundrum	Tommy Wade
1973	Flipper	Hugo Simon	1960	Sunsalve	David Broome
1972	Pennwood Forge Mill	Paddy McMahon	1959	Bandit IV	Anne Townsend
1971	Hideaway	Mike Saywell	1958	Nugget	J. Walmsley
1970	Pitz Palu	Alan Oliver	1957	Nizefella	Wilf White
1969	Pitz Palu	Alan Oliver	1956	Celebration	Capt. Piero d'Inzeo
1968	Pitz Palu	Alan Oliver	1955	Earlsrath Rambler	Dawn Palethorpe
1967	Harvester VI	Harvey Smith	1954	Prince Hal	Pat Smythe
1966	Mister Softie	David Broome	1953	Tosca	Pat Smythe
1965	North Flight	W. Barker	1952	Craven A	Peter Robeson
1964	Royal Lord	George Hobbs	1951	Hack On	Col. J. Lewis
1963	Firecrest	Peter Robeson	1950	Foxhunter	Lt. Col. Harry Llewellyn

► Eddie Macken and Boomerang. As a combination, they won the the Grand Prix four times.

SHOWING

HORSES
Arab Horse of the Year

Year	Horse	Owner	Rider
2010	Silvern Prince	Mrs Caroline Sussex	Darren Crowe
2009	Elustarius	Miss Caroline Trigg	Frances Atkinson
2008	Majestic Cavalier	Hayley Hyde-Andrews	Wendy Gibson
2007	PHA Silvern Risalm	Tiffani McCarthy	Darren Crowe
2006	Toman	Mrs Judith Evans	Ann Hooley
2005	Muzonomy	The Hon. Mrs M. A. Wragg	Frances Atkinson
2004	Shadow Blue	Mr & Mrs Titterington	Liz Needham
2003	Jammilah	Darren Ash	Joanne Woodward
2002	Johara El Kheil	Mrs & Ms E. Marsh	Vicky Marsh
2001	Silvern Enchanter	Katy Lake	Darren Crowe
2000	Imad	Mrs Diana Whittome	Jane M. Harries
1999	Rusleem	Stephen McMorrow	Stephen McMorrow
1998	Azraell	Miss S. L. Horwell	Richard Ramsay

Cob of the Year

NB This class was not run between 1955 and 1959

Year	Horse	Owner	Rider
2010	Hallmark IX	Sculpture to Wear	Jack Cochrane
2009	The Keystone Cob	Carol Bardo	Jayne Webber
2008	Cassanova	Natalie Moore	Natalie Moore
2007	The Duke	Mrs S. Cuddy	Robert Oliver
2006	So Smart	Camila Neame	Robert Walker
2005	Robocop	Dr Bill Bardo and Dr Alan Ross	Jayne Webber
2004	Tom Firr	R. Rowley	Robert Walker
2003	Boy George	Tim Briggs	Robert Walker
2002	Will Scarlet	Sally Reed	A.J. Walker
2001	Telly Tubbs	Mrs Paulette Cooper	Simon Reynolds
2000	Rob Roy	Mr Russel Christie	Russel Christie
1999	Polaris	Baileys Horse Feeds	Lynn Russell
1998	Wallace	Mrs S. Kerfoot	Moggy Hennessy
1997	Milky Way	Miss E. M. Coomber	Liz Coomber
1996	Gilbraith Crack of Dawn	Mrs J. Pilkington	Robert Oliver
1995	Apollo	Baileys Horse Feeds	Lynn Russell
1994	Super Ted	Mrs H. Griffith	Robert Oliver
1993	Super Ted	Mrs H. Griffith	Robert Oliver
1992	Super Ted	Mrs H. Griffith	Robert Oliver
1991	Just William	Mr J. Dunlop	Roy Trigg
1990	Super Ted	Mrs H. Griffith	Robert Oliver
1989	Super Ted	Mrs H. Griffith	Robert Oliver
1988	Just William	Mr J. Dunlop	Roy Trigg
1987	Super Ted	Mrs H. Griffith	Robert Oliver
1986	Grandstand	K. Luxford	Roger Stack
1985	The Irish RM	J. Dewer	Vin Toulson
1984	Grandstand	K. Luxford	Roger Stack
1983	Grandstand	K. Luxford	Roger Stack
1982	Grandstand	K. Luxford	Roger Stack
1981	Ducklys Huggy Bear	Mrs V. Hurst	Roy Trigg
1980	Brock	W. S. Bryan	Bill Bryan
1979	Kempley	Mrs P. White and Mrs J. Daniel	Robert Oliver
1978	Kempley	Mrs P. White and Mrs J. Daniel	Robert Oliver
1977	Kempley	Mrs P. White and Mrs J. Daniel	Robert Oliver
1976	Cromwell	Major and Mrs McLean	Robert Oliver
1975	Grand View	Mr R. Page	Ruth McMullen
1974	Justin Time	Annette Landau	Sue Trigg
1973	Jonathon	Mrs A. Baldry	Roy Trigg
1972	Jonathon	Mrs A. Baldry	Roy Trigg
1971	Vodka	Mrs Z. S. Clark	N.R. Clark
1970	Jonathon	Mrs A. Baldry	Roy Trigg
1969	Jonathon	Mrs A. Baldry	Roy Trigg
1968	Sport	Mrs Z.S. Clark	N.R. Clark
1967	Sport	Mrs Z.S. Clark	N.R. Clark

Cob of the Year *continued*

Year	Horse	Owner	Rider
1966	Button	Mrs M. Hill	Mimi Hillman
1965	Sport	Mrs Z.S. Clark	N.R. Clark
1964	Sport	Mrs Z.S. Clark	N.R. Clark
1963	Sport	Mrs Z.S. Clark	Marshall Parkhill
1962	Sport	Mrs Z.S. Clark	N.R. Clark
1961	Charlie	Mrs W.A. Waring	
1960	Bronze Boy	R. Hugford	C. Bonner
1954	Tommy	Mrs C. Barber	C. Bonner
1953	Badger	Mrs J.M. Crotty	Major Crotty
1952	Alexander	Mrs R. Cooke	Rosemary Cooke
1951	George	Miss J. Cox	Major Crotty
1950	Nutmeg	Miss E. Profumo	Miss E. Profumo
1949	Knobby	Mrs R. Cooke	Rosemary Cooke

◄ Super Ted, six times Cob Champion at HOYS, and Supreme Champion of the show in 1990. This popular cob was owned by Heather Griffiths and ridden by Robert Oliver.

Hack of the Year

NB This class was not run in 1954 or 1955

Year	Horse	Owner	Rider
2010	Royal Angel	Mrs S. Wood	Michaela Wood
2009	Baydale Venus	Mrs Sheila Fenwick	Simon Charlesworth
2008	Silent Words II	Carmen Gridley	Robert Walker
2007	Silent Words II	Thoroughbred Developments	Robert Walker
2006	Almost Illegal	Mrs D. Stenett	Katie Jerram
2005	Daldorn State Melody	Lady Benton-Jones	Jo Jenkins
2004	Colbeach Starlight Express	Mr C. Fagan	Ali Fagan
2003	Royal Trooper	Mr & Mrs Underwood	Allister Hood
2002	Royal Trooper	Mr & Mrs Underwood	Allister Hood
2001	Jennifer's Diary	Natalie Cooper	Natalie Cooper
2000	Pencroft Blue Print	Vivienne Foster	Robert Walker
1999	Folkins Fern Owl	Mr & Mrs Underwood	Allister Hood
1998	Valentino	Mrs S. Nichol	Richard Ramsay
1997	Absolutely Fabulous	Mr & Mrs J. Keen	John Keen
1996	Valentino	Mrs S. Nichol	Richard Ramsay
1995	Treverva Verity	Mrs M. Jerram	Katie Jerram
1994	Nobility	Mrs J. Friswell	Lisa Friswell
1993	Mystic Minstrel	Carol Cooper	Carol Cooper
1992	Treverva Verity	Miss K. Jerram	Ruth McMullen
1991	Piran Pyca	Mr & Mrs M. Jerram	Katie Jerram
1990	Piran Pyca	Mr & Mrs M. Jerram	Katie Jerram
1989	Agar Heir Apparent	Mr D.R. Cronk	D.R. Cronk
1988	Formidable	Mr & Mrs J. Keen	John Keen
1987	Rye Tangle	Miss K. Birch	Robert Oliver
1986	Rye Tangle	Miss K. Birch	Robert Oliver
1985	Rye Tangle	Miss K. Birch	Robert Oliver
1984	Fair Change	Dr & Mrs Gilbert-Scott	Carol Gilbert-Scott
1983	Loch Lomond	Miss S. Cooper	Miss S. Cooper
1982	Brown Buzzard	Mr & Mrs C. Cooper	Cathryn Cooper
1981	Brown Buzzard	Mr & Mrs C. Cooper	Allister Hood
1980	Royal Return	Mrs J. Keen	Vicki Keen
1979	Tenterk	Mrs D. Goodall	Robert Oliver
1978	Tenterk	Mrs D. Goodall	Robert Oliver
1977	Sparkling Prince	Mrs M. Bonsor	Robert Oliver
1976	Lemington Moon River	Miss E. Profumo and Mrs W. Stirling	Jennie Loriston-Clarke
1975	Lemington Moon River	Miss E. Profumo	Jennie Loriston-Clarke
1974	Right Royal	Miss F. O'Neil	Fiona O'Neil
1973	Right Royal	Mrs R. Ramsay	Marjorie Ramsay
1972	Right Royal	Mr & Mrs T. Spencer-Cox	Vera Holden
1971	Right Royal	Mr & Mrs T. Spencer-Cox	Vicky Spencer-Cox
1970	Lady Teller	Mrs B. Samwells	David Tatlow
1969	Lady Teller	Mrs B. Samwells	David Tatlow
1968	Lady Teller	Mrs B. Samwells	David Tatlow
1967	Moonstrike	Miss V. De Quincey	Vanessa de Quincey

Hack of the Year *continued*

Year	Horse	Owner	Rider
1966	Feudal Knight	Mrs Lloyd	Donald Owen
1965	Berrydon Lad	Mrs A. Battine	Jane McHugh
1964	Smooth Talk	Miss E. Profumo	Jennie Bullen
1963	Mirage	Miss Z. Foxwell	Jennie Bullen
1962	Lucky Strike	H. Haldin	Anne Davy
1961	Desert Storm	Miss A. Stubbings	Jennie Bullen
1960	Juniper	Miss M. de Beaumont	Harry Tatlow
1959	Desert Storm	Miss A. Stubbings	Jennie Bullen
1958	Kavora Another Star	Miss K. Coates	Miss K. Coates
1957	Sea Breeze	J. Hindley	Miss S. Gilbert
1956	Regina	Mrs F. Kemp	Pat Kemp
1953	Lovely Boy	Miss P. Wainwright	Harry Tatlow
1952	Honeysuckle	Miss M. de Beaumont	Count Robert Orssich
1951	Festival Maid	Mrs F. Phelps-Penry	Mr Brine
1950	Liberty Light	Miss V. Evans	Count Robert Orssich
1949	Liberty Light	Selwyn Butcher	Count Robert Orssich

▲ Mr and Mrs M.R. Underwood's Royal Trooper, Champion Hack two years in a row (2002 and 2003).

▲ The 2010 Hack of the Year: Royal Angel, ridden by 18-year-old Michaela Wood who is presented with her trophy by sponsors of the Hack Championship, Julia and David Topham Barnes.

▲ Three champions at the 2001 show from the Ramsay's Yard: the Hack, Jennifer's Diary (Natalie Cooper), the Riding Horse, Soldier Brave (Jayne Webber) and the Intermediate Show Riding Type, Calder Impressionist (Lottie Fry).

Ladies Hunter of the Year

NB This class was not run between 1999 and 2001

Year	Horse	Owner	Rider
2010	Dunbeacon	Mrs J. Jerram	Katie Jerram
2009	Loch Smith	Mrs P. Underwood	Shelley Perham
2008	Tommy III	Mrs P. Underwood	Shelley Perham
2007	Tommy III	Mrs P. Underwood	Shelley Perham
2006	Lark Hill	Mrs P. Moon	Pippa Moon
2005	Bournebrook Golden Law	Rooks Nest Farms	Shelley Perham
2004	Bournebrook Golden Law	Rooks Nest Farms	Shelley Perham
2003	Bournebrook Golden Law	R. Walker	Lucy Killingbeck
2002	Fergie St George	Mrs J.L. Philips	Lucy Killingbeck
1998	Statesman	Mrs J.L. Dunlop	Mrs S. Rawding
1997	Money Mover	Mr P. Rackham	Jane Williams
1996	Trump Card	Tanya Nichol	Tanya Nichol
1995	Harristown	Mrs Roy Phillips	Sally Hennessy
1994	Sudden Flight	Waltons Restaurant, N. Swallow & R. Wren	Jayne Webber
1993	College Jester	Mr Roy Creber	Moggy Hennessy
1992	Trengwainton Manakin	Mrs A. Bolitho	Sue Rawding

▼ Dual Ladies Hunter Champion Tommy III, ridden by Shelley Perham who won the Ladies Hunter Championship five times in six years, with three different horses.

Riding Horse of the Year

Year	Horse	Owner	Rider
2010	Sirius II	Mrs V. Ramm	Vanessa Ramm
2009	The Philanderer	Carol Bardo	Jayne Webber
2008	The Philanderer	Carol Bardo	Jayne Webber
2007	Broadstone Doulton	Robert Walker	Robert Walker
2006	Captain Hastings	Miss Lucy Smith-Crallon	Allister Hood
2005	Gosh	Dell Park Stud	Natalie Lintott
2004	Soldier Brave	Carol Bardo	Jayne Webber
2003	Dallas Gazumpa	Jane Carter	Jane Carter
2002	Broadstone Dee	Broadstone Stud	Jo Bates
2001	Soldier Brave	Carol Bardo	Jayne Webber
2000	I'm Blue Chip Too	Mrs Claire Blaskey	Robert Walker
1999	I'm Blue Chip Too	Mrs Claire Blasky	Robert Walker
1998	Orlando	Carol Bardo	Richard Ramsay
1997	Original Sin	Mrs Creed-Miles	Richard Ramsay
1996	The Cisto Kid	Cooper Corporation	Allister Hood
1995	Meridiana	Mrs S.G.D. Rowe	Michael J. Gray
1994	Madam Victoria	Mrs C. Mackness	Jayne Webber
1993	Brown Sabre	Cooper Corporation	Allister Hood
1992	JCB	JCB Excavators Ltd	Mr Robert Oliver
1991	JCB	JCB Excavators Ltd	Mr Robert Oliver
1990	Earl Of Dudley	Mr and Mrs P. Lee Taylor	Angela Lee Taylor
1989	Fair Breeze	Mr J. Tierney	Nigel Hollings
1988	Burroprince	Mr and Mrs Burroughes	Allister Hood
1987	Burroprince	Mr and Mrs Burroughes	Allister Hood
1986	Meridian	Mrs S. Rowe	Richard Ramsay

SEIB Racehorse to Riding Horse Show Championship

Year	Horse	Owner	Rider
2010	Blue Java	T. Billington	Sonya Fitch-Peyton
2009	Ironman Muldoon	Amanda Bowlby	Jayne Webber
2008	Another Man	Mr and Mrs R.O. Hartland	Claire Oliver
2007	Lin P'estruval	Bailey Horse Feeds & Rider	Lynn Russell
2006	Gosh	Dell Park Stud	Natalie Lintott

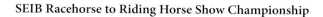

▶ ▲ (right, top) Jill Blundell and family, sponsors of the Riding Horse Championship, present Jayne Webber and The Philanderer with their championship award in 2009. It was the second time The Philanderer had won the championship, and he was also Supreme Horse of the Year.

▶ Richard and Lisha Leeman, sponsors of the Small Riding Horse class in 2010 and of the new Maxi Cob class in 2011, presenting the trophy to the 2010 winner of the Accumulator, Shane Breen riding Mullaghdrin Gold Rain.

Shire Horse of the Year

NB This class was not held at HOYS between 1999 and 2008

Year	Horse	Owner	Year	Horse	Owner
2010	Acle Sabrina	B. Banham	1979	Jim's Lucky Charm	J.B. Cooke
2009	Hainton Charlie Girl	J. Wilkinson	1978	Cowerslane Gem	T. Yates
2008	Acle Delma's Double D	P. & W. Bedford	1977	Cowerslane Truman	T. Yates
1999	Regis Jet	J. & V. Worthington	1976	Vyrnwy Lady	W. Livesey
1998	Trelow Antigone	R.L. Sandling	1975	Cowerslane Gem	T. Yates
1997	Craven Zara	P. & W. Bedford	1974	Lillingstone Again	Eady Robinson
1996	Arclid Rose Marie	A. Bull			
1995	Walton President	D. Worthington			
1994	Caerberllan Gold Gift	W.T. Jones			
1993	Bewholme Wendy	P. & W. Bedford			
1992	Bewholme Wendy	P. & W. Bedford			
1991	Gronant Charlie	C.J. & S. Leverett			
1990	Highbanks Heath Hendy	D. Worthington			
1989	St Vincents Royal	R. Coward			
1988	Landcliffe Laura	P. & W. Bedford			
1987	Landcliffe Laura	P. & W. Bedford			
1986	Landcliffe Laura	P. & W. Bedford			
1985	Landcliffe Laura	P. & W. Bedford			
1984	Jim's Chance	W.H. Griffith			
1983	Tremoelgoch Miss Fashion	G. Lloyd Owen			
1982	Jim's Lucky Charm	J.B. Cooke			
1981	Jim's Lucky Charm	J.B. Cooke			
1980	Decoy Royal Surprise	G.T. Ward & Sons			

▲ Landcliffe Laura, owned by Paul and Walter Bedford, winner of the Shire Horse of the Year four times in a row (1985–88).

Show Hunter of the Year

Year	Horse	Owner	Rider
2010	Pride and Joy II	Jill Day	Robert Walker
2009	Finn McCool III	J.L. Dunlop OBE	Guy Landau
2008	Finn McCool III	J.L. Dunlop OBE	Guy Landau
2007	Masterful	Jethro Bloodstock	Robert Oliver
2006	Imperator	Integrated Packaging Ltd	David Tatlow
2005	Principal Partner	Hilary le Moignan	Charles le Moignan
2004	Reaction	Mr & Mrs Rawding and Mr & Mrs Wilson	Sue Rawding
2003	Sunday Best	Osborne Refrigerators	Robert Oliver
2002	Rosenbright	Mrs Jerram & J. Moore	Katie Jerram
2001	Otter Point	G. A. Newall	David Tatlow
2000	King Street	Mr A. Belfield	Magnus Nicholson
1999	Guardsman V	Mrs C. Elwers	Guy Landau
1998	Red Hand	Mr J. Dunlop	Guy Landau
1997	Red Hand	Mr J. Dunlop	Guy Landau
1996	The Showman	Jill Ashmole	Bill Bryan
1995	Regal Max	Allister Hood	Allister Hood

Show Hunter of the Year *continued*

Year	Horse	Owner	Rider
1994	King's Warrior	Mrs. F. Rapson	Robert Oliver
1993	College Jester	Mr Roy Creber	Moggy Hennessy
1992	King's Warrior	Mr Roy Creber	Robert Oliver
1991	King's Warrior	Mr Roy Creber	Robert Oliver
1990	See Lightwater	Lightwater Valley Ltd	David Tatlow
1989	Mr Meade	Mrs N.J. Turner	David Tatlow
1988	Classic Tales	Miss V. White	Mrs G. Oliver
1987	Seabrook	Mrs J. Dewar	Vin Toulson
1986	Seabrook	Mrs J. Dewar	Vin Toulson
1985	Standing Ovation	W. Wood & N. Trevithick	Robert Oliver
1984	Seabrook	G. Buckingham-Bawden	Robert Oliver
1983	Elite	The South Essex Insurance Group	Vin Toulson
1982	Assurance	The South Essex Insurance Group	Vin Toulson
1981	Bayleaf III	Mrs G.L. Wathan	Allister Hood
1980	The Brigadier	Mrs R. Healy-Fenton	Robert Oliver
1979	Flashman	Mr P. White	Robert Oliver
1978	Bunowen	Mrs T.A. Bland	David Tatlow
1977	Bunowen	Mrs T.A. Bland	David Tatlow
1976	Bally Manor	L.S. Ivens and T.S. Tetley	L.S. Ivens
1975	Langton Orchid	Mr P. Rackham	Allister Hood
1974	Aristocrat	Miss M.A. Griffin	Roy Trigg
1973	Prince's Street	The South Essex Finance Group	Vin Toulson
1972	Admiral	Mr R.A. Bonnett	Roy Trigg
1971	Admiral	Mr R.A. Bonnett	Roy Trigg
1970	Top Notch	Mr N. Crow	Mr N. Crow
1969	Top Notch	Mr N. Crow	Mr N. Crow
1968	State Visit	David Tatlow	David Tatlow
1967	Tudor Line	Mrs S.J. Sexton	Mrs C. McHugh
1966	Monbra	Mrs R. Cooke and Miss E. Profumo	Mrs R. Cooke
1965	Spey Cast	W.F. Ransom	Mrs Ransom
1964	Romeo VI	Miss P. Morris	Bill Bryan
1963	Romeo VI	Miss P. Morris	Bill Bryan
1962	Viking	Mrs Dean	W. Donaldson
1961	Swagger	Lady Pascoe	Jane McHugh
1960	Gold Dust	Major C.S. Drabble	C.S. Drabble
1959	Toby	R. Farrow	Ray Lester
1958	Silverin	Mrs N.H. Tollit	Harry Bonner
1957	Gowran Boy	Ronald Marmont	Jack Gittens
1956	Mighty Grand	Miss P. Cope	Miss P. Cope
1955	Mighty Grand	Miss P. Cope	Miss P. Cope
1954	Cufflink	Ronald Marmont	Ronald Marmont
1953	Penny Royal	His Grace The Duke of Norfolk	The Duchess of Norfolk
1952	Rajah III	Ronald Marmont	Ronald Marmont
1951	Mighty Atom	W.H. Cooper Esq	Mr J. Daly
1950	Mighty Atom	W.H. Cooper Esq	Mr J. Daly
1949	Mighty Fine	J.R. Hindley	J.R. Hindley

Small Hunter of the Year

NB This class was not run in 1952 or 1953

Year	Horse	Owner	Rider
2010	Sir William John	Miss V. Clayton	Jack Cochrane
2009	Unlimited	Peter Bowdler	Charles Le Moignan
2008	Temple Bready Fear Not	Mrs V. Ramm MFH	Katie Jerram
2007	Temple Bready Fear Not	Mrs V. Ramm MFH	V. Ramm MFH
2006	Coppenagh Lad	Debbie Boylan	Debbie Boylan
2005	Harley Street	Jayne Carter	Robert Walker
2004	Red Alert	Mr and Mrs D. Curtis	Sarah Curtis
2003	Lord Oliver II	Mr Beamish and Mrs Parish	Katie Jerram
2002	Sporting Sam	Lady Kirkham	Simon Reynolds
2001	Sporting Sam	Lady Kirkham	Simon Reynolds
2000	Sporting Sam	Lady Kirkham	Simon Reynolds
1999	Sporting Sam	Lady Kirkham	Simon Reynolds
1998	Toy Boy	Mrs Jill Ashmole	Bill Bryan
1997	Astaire	Mrs Jill Ashmole	Allister Hood
1996	Brown Bob	Cooper Corp	Allister Hood
1995	Face the Music	Colchester Commission	Tracey Parrish
1994	Small Print	Mrs J. Hutchinson	Peter Richmond
1993	Small Print	Mrs J. Hutchinson	Peter Richmond
1992	Small Print	Mrs J. Hutchinson	Peter Richmond
1991	Manuscript	Mr I. Thomas LVO	Robert Oliver
1990	Manuscript	Mr I. Thomas LVO	Robert Oliver
1989	Small Print	Mrs J. Hutchinson	Peter Richmond
1988	Small Print	Mrs J. Hutchinson	Peter Richmond
1987	Swindon Wood	Miss J. Ashworth	Jane Crofts
1986	Little John	Miss J. Newberry	Jane Crofts
1985	Macbeth	Mrs C. Van Praagh	Allister Hood
1984	Little John	Mr and Mrs J.A. Crofts	Jane Crofts
1983	Statesman	Mr and Mrs A. McCowan	Peter Richmond
1982	Whitcroft Highland Bound	Mr D.J.C.P. Powell	Jane Hankey
1981	Sea Lord	Mr and Mrs M. Hilliard-Gosling	Susan Hilliard-Gosling
1980	Royal Gossip	Mr and Mrs Rogers	J. Rogers
1979	Statesman	Mr and Mrs A. McCowan	Mrs A. McCowan
1978	Misty Day	Mrs O. Jackson	Michael Poole
1977	Footpath	Miss J. Taylor	Robert Oliver
1976	Footpath	Miss J. Taylor	Robert Oliver
1975	Sporting Print	Jean Andrews	Jean Andrews
1974	Smasher	N.H. Gardener	Mrs Taylor
1973	Sporting Print	The Countess of Inchcape	Vin Toulson
1972	Roulette	Mrs J. Hunter-Blair	Jack Gittens
1971	Sportsman	Mrs J. Wallace & E.B. Parkinson	Mrs Hilliard-Gosling
1970	Lord Sorcerer	Major J. Helme	Robert Oliver
1969	Newton Belle	G.W. Dale Ltd	D. Owen
1968	May Queen	Ronald Marmont	Ronald Marmont
1967	Little Buzzard	Mrs J. Richardson	Mrs J. Stevens
1966	Some Gardener	Mrs R. Cooke	Mrs R. Cooke

▲ Small Hunter of the Year four times in a row: Lady Kirkham's Sporting Sam, ridden by Simon Reynolds.

Small Hunter of the Year *continued*

Year	Horse	Owner	Rider
1965	Some Gardener	Mrs R. Cooke	Mrs R. Cooke
1964	Savoya	Van de Vater	Van de Vater
1963	Pelicamp	F.M. Lawrey	Judith Lawrey
1962	Some Gardener	Mrs R. Cooke	Mrs R. Cooke
1961	Tom Boy	Mrs R. Cooke	Mrs R. Cooke
1960	Pelicamp	G.A. Hall	Ronald Marmont
1959	Burrough Hills	Ronald Marmont	Ronald Marmont
1958	Burrough Hills	Ronald Marmont	Ronald Marmont
1957	Burrough Hills	Ronald Marmont	Ronald Marmont
1956	Fonmon	Mrs D. Faber	
1955	Silver Streak	Mrs J. Skelton	Mrs P. Tozer
1954	Rightaway	The Hon. Mary Curzon	Mr J. Moss

Working Hunter of the Year

NB This class was not run in 1955 or 1956

Year	Horse	Owner	Rider
2010	Thor	J. Callwood	Jo Callwood
2009	Keep Talking	June Snedker	Jo Geddes
2008	Out of Sight	Sarah Gallagher	Louise Bell
2007	Mountain Ember	Jack Cochrane	Jack Cochrane
2006	Mountain Ember	Jack Cochrane	Jack Cochrane
2005	Barry Bug	Caroline Lyons	Kelly Lyons
2004	Zin Zan	Justine Armstrong-Small	Justine Armstrong-Small
2003	Zin Zan	Justine Armstrong-Small	Justine Armstrong-Small
2002	Out of Sight	Sarah Gallagher	Louise Bell
2001	Scotch The Rumours	Mr and Mrs T. Fairburn	Tim Fairburn
2000	Scotch The Rumours	Mr and Mrs T. Fairburn	Tim Fairburn
1999	Mendip Macho	Louise Bell	Robert Bell
1998	Little Sister	D. & G. Tatlow	Gillian Tatlow

▲ Louise Bell on her Champion Working Hunter, Out of Sight in 2008. The pair also won the championship in 2002, after Louise had fought back from horrendous injuries sustained in a road accident.

◄ Tim Fairburn riding Scotch The Rumours, Champion Working Hunter for two years in a row (2000 and 2001).

Working Hunter of the Year *continued*

Year	Horse	Owner	Rider
1997	Scotch the Rumours	Mr and Mrs T. Fairburn	Tim Fairburn
1996	Rocky IV	Louise Bell	Louise Bell
1995	Mexican Wave	Lisa Hales	Lisa Hales
1994	Falloon	Mr & Mrs Hastie, Nixon and Marshall	Gillian Tatlow
1993	Lightwater What Fun	David Bartram	David Bartram
1992	Tom Sawyer	Mr W.R. Barter	Tim Brown
1991	Constable Burton	David Bartram	David Bartram
1990	Bootleg	Mrs J. Harpham	Mrs Betty Robinson
1989	Bootleg	Mrs J. Harpham	Mrs Betty Robinson
1988	Boleyhill	Mr and Mrs J.A. Crofts	Mrs J. Crofts
1987	Lifeline	Miss G. Hancock	Gail Hancock
1986	Valindrie	Miss M. Sherrington	Jane Holderness-Roddam
1985	Supercoin	Mr E. Bristow	Marcus Chambers
1984	Threes are Wild	Mrs M.A. Baker	Mrs M.A. Baker
1983	Gibbert Hill	Track Marshall Ltd	Penny Whitelam
1982	Cartier	Mrs S.L. Tetley-Hall	Mrs S.L. Tetley-Hall
1981	Andeguy	Mr and Mrs P.N. Warcup	Mrs R. Thompson
1980	Dual Gold	Mrs P. White	Gillian Oliver
1979	Castlewellan	Judy Bradwell	Judy Bradwell
1978	Let's Go	Mr and Mrs F.M. Broome	Mary Broome
1977	Let's Go	Mr and Mrs F.M. Broome	Mary Broome
1976	Morning Glory	Roy Trigg	Roy Trigg
1975	Fidelio	Mrs R.C. Quinney	Miss S. MacIntosh
1974	Mister Perkins	Capt. Tyrwhitt-Drake	Miss G. Blakeway
1973	Slaney Valley	J. McGrath	M. Hickey
1972	Sporting Print	R.D.S. Carpendale	
1971	Someday	B. Cleminson	Miss C. Cleminson
1970	Upton	Mrs R.F. Daniel	Miss J. Ballard
1969	Goodwill	Miss R. Burch	Miss R. Burch
1968	Sebastian	Mrs F.A. Hall	D. Kent
1967	Snake	H.C. Straker	H.C. Straker
1966	Rupert	Miss J. Forwood	H.C. Straker
1965	Kittiwake	Mr & Mrs P. Robeson	Peter Robeson
1964	Sundew	Van de Vater	Van de Vater
1963	Rhythm	Deidre Butler	Deidre Butler
1962	Makeway	Miss R.P. Boughton	Miss R.P. Boughton
1961	Navan	Miss Deidre Butler	Deidre Butler
1960	Fintan	The Hon. Elizabeth Keyes	
1959	Ryebrooks	Miss J. Wykeham-Musgrave	Jane Kent
1958	Gowran Boy	Ronald Marmont	Ronald Marmont
1957	Gowran Boy	Ronald Marmont	Jack Gittens
1954	Pampas Cat	Mrs Bulkeley	Miss K. Taltham-Walker
1953	Rajah III	Ronald Marmont	Miss Murray Smith
1952	Lanhill	Mrs John Watney	
1951	Rajah III	Ronald Marmont	Ronald Marmont

PONIES

Intermediate Show Hunter of the Year

Year	Pony	Owner	Rider
2010	Utah II	Mr & Mrs M.R. Underwood	Hannah Horton
2009	Galtree Park	Mrs S. Cuddy	Yasmin Cuddy
2008	Twice as Smart	Mr C. Yates	Natasha Yates
2007	Eagle Moor	Mrs Thompson	Lillie Twitchett
2006	Guy Fawkes III	Amy Underwood	Amy Underwood
2005	Escapado	Mrs Abel	Sarah Fern
2004	Banjo II	Mrs M. Harwich and Ms J. Newbery	Peter Thomas
2003	Doctor Dolittle	Liz Strathern	Oliver Hood
2002	Baileys over Ice	Miss N. Moore	Miss N. Moore
2001	Baileys over Ice	Miss N. Moore	Miss N. Moore
2000	Traverston Trendmaker	Miss H. Cook	Susan Cornish
1999	Riverdance XII	Sarah Ambler	Sarah Ambler

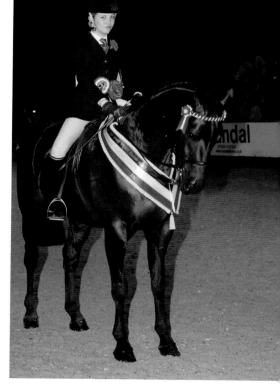

▼ The 2007 Reserve Champion of the Oggy Oggy Intermediate Show Riding Type of the Year: Mrs Doris Lacey's Radway All Talk, ridden by Emily Lacey.

Intermediate Show Riding Type of the Year

Year	Pony	Owner	Rider
2010	Opium Casa Leona	Mr A. Winbourne	Yasmin Cuddy
2009	Wilderness Carmen	Mrs W. & Miss L. Edgar	Louise Edgar
2008	Paschal High Flyer	Mesdames S. & H. Broom	Hazel Broom
2007	Marshbrook Sir George	Mrs D. Hesford	Victoria Hesford
2006	Mountcaulfield Freedom	Mrs D.L. Thomas	Gemma James
2005	Alpine Diplomat	Mrs A. Fowler	Alexandra Fowler
2004	Opium De Limges	Adam Winbourne	Adam Winbourne
2003	Spyanfly Storm Trooper	Sara Neachell	Sara Neachell
2002	Spyanfly Storm Trooper	Sara Neachell	Sara Neachell
2001	Calder Impressionist	Mrs A. Fry	Charlotte Fry
2000	Saran Lady Gayle	Mr and Mrs B. Williams	Sarah Butler
1999	Radway Small Talk	Mr R. Cockram, Mr and Mrs R.M. Clarke, and Dr and Mrs Gilbert-Scott	Melanie Packham

◄ Winners of the Intermediate Show Riding Type of the Year in 2010, Yasmin Cuddy with Mr. A. Winbourne's Opium Casa Leona.

Intermediate Working Hunter of the Year
(merged into Working Hunter Championship from 2008)

Year	Pony	Owner	Rider
2007	Noble Rockstar	Elaine Barnes	Callum Barnes
2006	Pebbly Goose	Miss S. Challinor	Sarah Challinor
2005	Cadre Noir Z	Mr A. Yaqub	Al-Jabar Yaqub
2004	Carnsdale Top Gun	Mrs P. Druggan	Katie Druggan
2003	Pebbly Tuff Stuff	Mrs Y. Dixon	Scott Dixon
2002	Profitable Gamble	Jane Beswick	Hayden Hankey
2001	Pebbly Tuff Stuff	Mrs R. Gredley	Tim Gredley
2000	Pebbly Tuff Stuff	Mrs R. Gredley	Tim Gredley
1999	Versalis	Mrs A. Phillipson	Katrina Phillipson

Lead Rein Pony of Hunter Type of the Year

Year		Pony	Owner	Rider
2010	Champion	Charn Secret Legend	Miss K. Fuge	Abbie Farmer
	Reserve	Wortley Celebration	Mrs S. Darlington	Kitty Jewson
2009	Champion	Waxwing Pringle	Sophie Manners	Millie Manners
	Reserve	Wortley Celebration	Mrs S. Darlington	Scarlett Jewson

Mini Mountain and Moorland of the Year

Year	Pony	Owner	Rider
2010	Ekens Fifer	Mrs A. Smalley	Eloise Pinnock
2009	Costone Cayti	Mr John Elliott	Joshua Blythe
2008	Abbeybells Queen Adelaide	Mrs K. Carter & Mrs M. Cartlidge	Poppy Marie Carter
2007	Waxwing Thumbs Up	Mrs G. Shuttleworth & Mrs L.D.P Leeming	Oliver Shuttleworth
2006	Waxwing Paintbrush	Mr Paul Starkie	Jack Starkie
2005	Gwauniarll Katie	Mr & Mrs R. Cambray	Daisy Cambray
2004	Wait With Connie	Mrs L. Stewart	Emily Skuse

► Five year old Eloise Pinnock riding Mrs A. Smalley's Dartmoor Ekens Fifer receives the Mini Mountain and Moorland of the Year trophy in 2010 from Christine Madeley and Ann Overton-Ablitt.

Mini Mountain and Moorland of the Year *continued*

Year	Pony	Owner	Rider
2003	Dykes Rosie Mead	Team Hollings	Alexandra Hollings
2002	Bryndefaid Patsy	K. Scott and A.J. Anderson	Catherine Scott
2001	Roseilse Tudor Melody	Mrs G.M.R. Homfray-Jones	Ryan Homfray-Jones
2000	Rowfantina Old Fashioned	Mrs Mandy Burchall-Small & Mrs J. Shemilt	Owen Small
1999	Brierdene Llewelyn	Gill Simpson	Daniel Simpson

▼ Alexandra Hollings with Elizabeth Stanleick's Trevaylor Tiger Lily, winning the First Ridden class in 2006, three years after the pair won the Mini Show Pony of the Year.

Mini Show Pony of the Year

Year	Pony	Owner	Rider
2010	Copybush Moon Sprite	Mr L. Bowen	Nicole Bowen
2009	Cosford Chartreuse	Cooper Corporation	Myles Cooper
2008	Chagford Lewis	Mrs K. Carter	Poppy Marie Carter
2007	Hightopps Dancing Bee	Mrs S. Dennison	Harriet Dennison
2006	Okewood Delightful	Mrs G. Kapadia	Clea Kapadia
2005	Chaseford Charisma	Mrs A. Fowler	Philippa Horton
2004	Harver Relativity	Mrs L. Fitzgerald	Alice Greenwood
2003	Trevaylor Tiger Lily	Mrs E. Stanleick	Alexandra Hollings
2002	Barkway Happy Returns	Mrs V. Derrick	Katie White
2001	Colne Heiress	Mrs M. Dent	Charlotte Dent
2000	Fenwick Virginia	Mrs S. Cuddy	Yasmin Cuddy
1999	Greylands Little Gem	Mrs H. Horton	Hannah Horton
1998	Colne Heiress	Mrs S.J. Rowland	Sophie Rowland
1997	Evandale Charisma	Mrs S. Cuddy	Yasmin Cuddy
1996	Nantcol Lady Julia	Mr and Mrs Rayner	H. Rayner
1995	Lechlade Melissa	Mr R. Kirk	Gemma Kirk
1994	Heaton Oscar	Mrs V. Swinburn	Julie Swinburn
1993	Firle Yasmina	Mr D. Smith	Caroline Smith
1992	Roseisle Bridesmaid	Mr & Mrs Milligan	Alexandra Grant

Miniature Horse of the Year

Year	Pony	Owner
2010	Zealshouse Black Jack	Mrs M. Foulkes
2009	M H B Apollo	Mrs W. Edgar
2008	Ujeniks Extasys Capiccino	Ujenik Pallatt Family
2007	M H B Apollo	Mrs W. Edgar
2006	Ujenik Extasys Alpine Boy	Pallatt Family
2005	M H Apollo	Mrs W. Edgar
2004	Jezabelles Famous Song	S. & A. Johnston
2003	Toyhorse Prince Dillion	Miss J. Domhill
2002	Royal Oaks Sparkling Confetti	Mrs J. Robinson
2001	Toyhorse Ice Fantasy	Denise Windsor
2000	Farthingwood Romeo	Sarah Hampton/ Snowbella Miniatures

► Zealshouse Black Jack and Maxine Foulkes after winning the Miniature Horse of the Year in 2010.

Mountain and Moorland Pony of the Year

Year	Pony	Owner	Rider
2010	Pumphill Buckthorn	Mrs S. Hughes	Sarah Challinor
2009	Dunedin Marksman	Anne Mitchell	Matthew Lawrence
2008	Drumacre Lloer Solo	Charlene Richardson	Charlene Richardson
2007	Menai Sparkling Imperial	Menai Stud	Gemma Paxford
2006	Southley Red Ember	Mrs D. Barr	Alice Barr
2005	Bunowen Castle RI	Mrs Jackie Webb	Matthew Lawrence
2004	Kilmannan Black Velvet	Mr W.R. Ireland	Richard Telford
2003	Rhydfendigaid Daniel	Ms J. Arnold	Chris Patrick
2002	Castle Comet	Vanessa Compton	Vanessa Compton
2001	Townend Breeze	Mrs M. Sweeney	Cara Sweeney
2000	Pantmanrs Jog-On	Mrs S. Darlington	Sam Darlington
1999	Rannock Of Trailtrow	Mrs H.E. Prescott	Heather Prescott

Mountain and Moorland Working Hunter Pony of the Year

Year	Pony	Owner	Rider
2010	Pumphill Buckthorn	Mrs S. Hughes	Sarah Challinor
2009	Willoway Lord of the Rings	Sally Carpenter	Charlotte Harlow
2008	Trefynys Princess Saskia	Barbara Williams	Louise Jones
2007	Halnaker Marten	Mrs Pearl Underwood	Lucy Loughton
2006	Moortown Honeyman	J.S. Barton	Petrina Theobald
2005	Quarry House Jasper	Mrs Chris Jowett	Sarah Drake
2004	Shilstone Rocks Rough Mountain	Sandy Barnett	Sasha Barnett
2003	Penwayn Ryan	Laura Collett	Laura Collet
2002	Gryngallt Playsome	Paul Keepe	Jennifer Keepe
2001	Shilstone Rocks Rough Mountain	Sandy Barnett	C. Barnett
2000	Dunedin Harris	Anne Mitchell	Joanna Jack
1999	Cwmbachstel Dion	Mrs Burchell-Small and Mrs Roberts	Samantha Roberts
1998	Llanina Malgwyn	Mrs R.G. Weller	Jayne Weller
1997	Ashfield Black Jack	Mrs Ann Wilson	Laura Wilson

► An historic double for the Dartmoor stallion Pumphill Buckthorn ridden by Sarah Challinor, winners of both the Mountain and Moorland Pony of the Year, and the Mountain and Moorland Working Hunter Pony of the Year in 2010. Pumphill Buckthorn is out of Pumphill Belladonna, the first Dartmoor to win the In-hand Championship (1999).

Mountain and Moorland Working Hunter Pony of the Year *continued*

Year	Pony	Owner	Rider
1996	Llanina Malgwyn	Mrs R.G. Weller	Jayne Weller
1995	Langshot Toytown	Mr J. Forsyth	Rebecca Greenwood
1994	Langshot Toytown	Mr J. Forsyth	Hugh Forsyth
1993	Tetworth Catelpa	Samantha Clark	Samantha Clark
1992	Lewcombe Rondeau	Miss A. Leonard	Melissa Broadfield

Show Hunter Pony of the Year

Year	Horse	Owner	Rider
2010	Wortley Celebration	Mrs S.J. Darlington	Georgia Darlington
2009	Greylands Maid in the Dark	Mrs D.L. Thomas	Katie Roberts
2008	Pretoria	Mrs L.M. Minchin	Kimberley Minchin
2007	Yealand Angelina	Alison & Tony Georgakis	Jack Starkie
2006	Fairholme Rossetta's Rhapsody	Mrs D. Moreton	Chloe Willett
2005	Crafton Waltz Of The Toreador	Mr C.R.W. Yates & Mrs D.L. Thomas	Nicholas Scofield
2004	Chiddock Over the Limit	Mrs D.L. Thomas & Ms J. Newbery	Nicholas Scofield
2003	Rathnaleen Fascination	Mrs S. Cuddy	Yasmin Cuddy
2002	Trewolla Denzil	Mr and Mrs R.D. Binks	Hannah Binks
2001	Chiddock Spot on	Mrs D.L. Thomas	Gemma James
2000	Fielding Tom Sawyer	Mrs A. Miller	Rebecca Miller
1999	J.B. Esquire	Mr M. Gibson	Lisa Gibson
1998	Highmead Mystic Man	Mr M. Gibson	Lisa Gibson
1997	Scottish Quest	Mr D. Parker	Sarian Turner
1996	Oliver Twist	Mrs R. Threlfall	Kate Threlfall
1995	Young Dragonara	Mr and Mrs Ryder-Phillips	Christopher Ryder-Phillips
1994	Small Land Moonwalk	Mr and Mrs D. Jackson	Peter Thomas
1993	Peter Rabbit	Mrs T.A. Smith	Kate Smith
1992	Towy Valley Jester	Mrs P. Haigh-Maynard	Peter Thomas

◄ ◄ (far left) The 2004 Show Hunter Pony Champion and Supreme Pony Chiddock Over the Limit, ridden by Nicholas Schofield, who is now a jockey.

◄ Harriet Dennison deputising for Katie Roberts on the 2009 Supreme Pony, Greylands Maid in the Dark. Katie rode Diptford Amazing Grace to win the Show Pony title, and both of these ponies were owned by Debbie Thomas.

Show Pony of the Year

Year	Pony	Owner	Rider
2010	Broadgrove Springtime	Mrs A. Fowler	Millie Wonnacott
2009	Diptford Amazing Grace	Mrs D.L. Thomas	Katie Roberts
2008	Rhos Emblem	Mr Harvey & Mrs Brewis	Rebecca Harvey
2007	Roseberry Highland Fling	Mrs S. Hinchcliffe	Charlotte Thompson
2006	Anton Princess Nadia	Mrs H. Brill & Mr S. Arrowsmith	Lauren Brill
2005	Broadgrove Chatterbox	Mrs A. Fowler	Jemima Walker
2004	Colbeach Salaman	Mrs Dent	Samantha Dent
2003	Rotherwood Take-a-Peep	P. Sowerby	Alix Coster
2002	Oldcourt Balilka	D.L. Thomas & Oldcourts Stud	Gemma James
2001	Jackets Maybe	Mrs J. Rucklidge and the Gilbert-Scotts	Melanie Packham
2000	Kavanaghs Dream	Mrs X. Barker Wild	Louise Blackwell
1999	Glenmoss Juliet	Mrs J. Sehne & the Gilbert-Scotts	Imogen Allison
1998	Bradmore Catkin	Mrs P. Greenleaf & the Gilbert-Scotts	Imogen Allison
1997	Ardenhall Royal Secret	D. Shawe	Charlotte Dujardin
1996	Trelawn Playboy	Mr and Mrs R. Templeton/Mrs K. McWilliams	Lisa Gibson
1995	Chinook Chantilly	Mr M. Davies	Mari Williams
1994	Ardenhall Royal Secret	Mrs J.K. Dujardin	Emma-Jayne Dujardin
1993	Cringle Laughter	Mrs L. Hillyard	Philip Cooper
1992	Drayton Penny Royal	N. Leheup, Ms R. Ball & Dr & Mrs Gilbert-Scott	Jilly Cooper
1991	Coveham Sensation	Mr and Mrs M.G. Hounsom	Hayden Hankey
1990	Sandbourne Royal Emblem	Mrs Commerford	Katie Rose
1989	Jackets Maysong	Mrs J. Rucklidge	Hayley Hankey
1988	Creden Keepsake	Mr & Mrs R.M. Clarke	Louisa Clarke
1987	Groundhills Amazing Grace	D. Champion	Katie Cartlidge
1986	Gaylord of Keston	Mrs P. Holden	Paula Holden
1985	Twylands Carillon	Mrs D.G. Jago and Mrs P. Carvosso	Poppy Peacock
1984	Coveham Fascination	Mrs D.G. Jago and Mrs P. Carvosso	Rachel Parker Dean
1983	Harmony Bubbling Champagne	Mr and Mrs C.R. Sandison	Antonia Sandison
1982	Runnings Park Hill Star	Mrs L. Lee	Louisa Lee
1981	Gunnerby Alborg Elegant	Mr and Mrs R.G. Owens	Lisa Owens
1980	Katslea Zindle	Mrs J. Hussey	Jane Hussey
1979	Ocean So Fair	Mrs N.A. Rogers	Camilla Gray
1978	Holly of Spring	Mr and Mrs C.A. Cooper	Cathryn Cooper
1977	Holly of Spring	Mr and Mrs C.A. Cooper	Cathryn Cooper
1976	Holly of Spring	Mr and Mrs C.A. Cooper	Cathryn Cooper
1975	Holly of Spring	Mr and Mrs C.A. Cooper	Cathryn Cooper
1974	Christmas Carol of Bennochy	Dr and Mrs Gilbert-Scott	Miss M. Coates
1973	Lennel Aurora	Dr and Mrs Gilbert-Scott	Miss J. Corrie
1972	Snailwell Charles	Mr and Mrs G. Hollings	Nigel Hollings
1971	Gems Signet	Miss A. Sangan	Sophie Waddilove
1970	Treharne Veronica	Mrs D. Egerton	Miss S.A. Rose
1969	Shandon	Miss S. Commerford	Miss S. Commerford
1968	Greenacres Twilight	Miss A. Massarella	Miss A. Massarella
1967	Favorita	Alicia Stubbings	Jane Soutar
1966	Cusop Pirouette	Dr and Mrs Gilbert-Scott	Jayne Williams

Show Pony of the Year *continued*

Year	Pony	Owner	Rider
1965	Shandon	Mrs H.M. Payn and Mrs K.V. Coates	Lucy Payn
1964	Creden Lucky Charm	P.H. Hall	Judy Bradwell
1963	Pollyanna	Albert Deptford	Aly Pattinson
1962	Cusop Quickstep	Lady Reiss	Virginia Booth-Jones
1961	Second Thoughts	Miss V. Froome	Vanessa Froome
1960	Arden Tittle Tattle	Miss Coates and Miss A. Stubbings	Mary Rose Peddie
1959	Arden Tittle Tattle	Miss Coates and Miss A. Stubbings	Mary Rose Peddie
1958	Enoch Arden	Lady Reiss	Virginia Booth-Jones
1957	Kavora Mr Crisp	Mrs K.V. Coates and Albert Deptford	Gaye Coates
1956	Royal Show	Miss A. Stubbings	Jennie Bullen
1955	Kavora My Pretty Maid	Mrs K.V. Coates	Christine Harries
1954	Hassan	Mr and Mrs Hinkley	Kay Hinkley
1953	Kavora My Pretty Maid	Mrs K.V. Coates	Christine Harries
1952	Royal Show	Lt.Col. & Mrs J.F.S. Bullen	Jennie Bullen
1951	Pretty Polly	Albert Deptford	Davina Lee-Smith
1950	Pretty Polly	Albert Deptford	Davina Lee-Smith
1949	Legend	Elizabeth Spencer	Elizabeth Spencer

▲ The 2008 Show Pony of the Year, Rhos Emblem, ridden by Rebecca Harvey.

Working Hunter Pony of the Year

Year	Pony	Owner	Rider
2010	Freckleton Maximus	Mr A. Brewster	Caroline Brewster
2009	Noble Bing	Mrs M.R. Underwood	Michelle Baker
2008	Kelsterton Merlin	Miss V. & Mrs B. White	Victoria White
2007	Folly II	Mr D. Wittrick	Alice McCullagh
2006	Oscar Charles	Sally Taylor	Emmie Collier
2005	Oscar Charles	Sally Taylor	Emmie Collier
2004	Boycott Tonic	Mrs R. Gredley	Polly Gredley
2003	Valepark Holiday	Mrs K. Farrar-Fry	Alexandra Farrar-Fry
2002	Black Monday	Mrs S. Smith	Jo Masterson
2001	Mytilene	Mrs S. Boldock	Charlene Leatham
2000	Tresilian Tempest	Mrs Sue Jones	Pippa Jones
1999	Roodlebats Robert	Yvonne Rayner	Holly Rayner
1998	Stambrook Pavarotti	Mr B. Lears	Sarah Lears
1997	Blainslie Wedding Breakfast	Lady Caroline Tyrell	Karene Miller
1996	Young Dragonara	Mr and Mrs J. Ryder-Phillips	Francoise Guillambert
1995	Roodlebats Robert	Mr B. Lewis	Sarah Lears
1994	Young Dragonara	Mr and Mrs J. Ryder-Phillips	Chris Ryder-Phillips
1993	Steady Freddie	Jane Marjorie Hankey	Hayden Hankey

MIXED CLASSES

Coloured Horse and Pony Championship

Year	Horse	Owner	Rider
2010	The Humdinger	Carol Bardo & Mandy Hughes	Jayne Webber
2009	The Humdinger	Carol Bardo & Mandy Hughes	Jayne Webber
2008	Red Andes	Elaine Place	Jayne Webber
2007	So Smart	Camilla Neame	Sarah Walker
2006	Brynteg Llywnay Daffodil	K. Pritchard and R. Maynard	Jessica Pritchard
2005	Electric Storm	Sally Mariani	Jane Beswick
2004	Florinda	Miss M. Toomes	Ben Martin
2003	Merrigan	Mrs C. Merrigan-Martin	Simon Charlesworth
2002	Mostock Sarrison Lad	Mr C. Willet	Chloe Willet
2001	LB's Legacy	Joanna Whiston	Joanna Whiston
2000	Mr Moses	Frank Slattery	Zoe Etherington
1999	Mostock Sarrison Lad	Mr C. Willet	Fiona Davis
1998	Lostock Huntsman	Mrs C.M. Hamilton	Zoe Bowden

SEIB Search for a Star Championship

Year	Horse	Owner	Rider
2010	I'm Clover Too	Miss A. Fisher	Angharad Fisher
2009	Archwood Romeo Gigle	Allison Hilton	Jessica Leigh Hilton
2008	Welton Archer	Aislinn McKibbin	Ciara McKibbin
2007	Fleet Water X Ecutive	Jordan Cook	Jordan Thomas Cook
2006	Chivers	Mr and Mrs J. Thornton	Jooli Thornton
2005	Rodham Sir Thomas	Skye Houldsworth	Mrs J. Maycock
2004	Atlantic Prospect	Jessica Bennett	Jessica Bennett
2003	Barney Rubble V	Graham Brierlay	Rebecca Brierlay
2002	Urishay	Elaine Place	Elaine Place
2001	Classic Court	R.A. Lee	Laura Lucas
2000	Early Edition	Mr & Mrs G.W. Handley	Anne Handley
1999	Class Performance	Wendy Aarons	Felicity Wells
1998	Barkway Black Magic	Miss N. Salvidge	Nicolai Boinville

Supreme In-hand Championship
NB: The championship was not held in 1970 and 1971.

Year	Horse	Owner
2010	Catwalk	Mr & Mrs J. Parkin
2009	Pinewell Bucks Fizz	Mrs A. Higgins
2008	Pinewell Bucks Fizz	Mrs A. Higgins
2007	Mountain Firefly	Jack Cochrane
2006	Waitwith West Wind	Mrs D. Barr
2005	Rotherwood Take-A-Peep	Mrs P. Sowerby
2004	Kingvean Gypsy Star	Miss S.E. Ferguson & Mr & Mrs B.P. Rennocks
2003	Broadgrove Chatterbox	Mrs A. Fowler

Supreme In-hand Championship *continued*

Year	Horse	Owner
2002	Jackets Maybe	Mrs J. Rutlidge
2001	Rosslyn Sweet Repose	David Ross
2000	Free Spirit	Miranda Skinner
1999	Pumphill Belladonna	Mr and Mrs R. Hinde
1998	Merriment Pussycat	S. Griffith
1997	Meridiana	Miss P. Allress
1996	Man Of Honour	J.I. Dunlop
1995	Free Spirit	M. Skinner
1994	Copybush Catchphrase	Miss S. Jewson
1993	High Road	Mrs M. Geake and Mrs C. Balding
1992	TSB Sheer Delight	Houston Bros
1991	Little Patch	Mr and Mrs J. Rawding
1990	Rasehaven Honeysuckle	Mr and Mrs P. Rennocks
1989	Hunting Eve	Miss A.J. Murray
1988	Hunting Eve	Miss A.J. Murray
1987	Hunting Eve	Miss A.J. Murray
1986	Chirk Wind Flower	Mrs M.E. Mansfield
1985	Celtic Ballad	Mrs D.E.M. Alexandrea
1984	Falledge Sundance	Mr and Mrs F.W. Furness
1983	Winneydene Satelite	Mr and Mrs T.W. Irving
1982	Mallard Court	Miss A.J. Murray
1981	Little Primrose	Mrs D. Nicholson
1980	Llanarth Flying Comet	University College of Wales
1979	Llanarth Flying Comet	University College of Wales
1978	Rosevean Eagle Hill	Miss S.E. Fergusen
1977	Three Wishes	Mr and Mrs A. McGowan
1976	Rosevean Eagle Hill	Miss S.E. Fergusen
1975	Clipston	Mrs V.A. Fergusen
1974	Sammy Dasher	L.S. Ivens & Mrs P. Jackson
1973	Whalton Ragtime	Mr and Mrs J.C. Alton
1972	Fresco	N. Crow
1969	Treharne Tomboy	Col. Rosser John
1968	Treharne Tomboy	Col. Rosser John
1967	Honyton Michael ap Braint	M. Isaac
1966	Carbrooke Surprise	Mrs Robert Crawford
1965	Prince's Grace	Mrs A.L. Wood

▲ Jack Cochrane leading his homebred Hunter brood mare Mountain Firefly – the Cuddy In-Hand Supreme Champion in 2007. The mare also won the Horse section and was reserve Cuddy champion to the Pony winner (Broadgrove Chatterbox) in 2003, as a 4 year old brood mare. Jack won the Working Hunter final for the second year running in 2007 with Firefly's half-brother Mountain Ember.

▼ Champion coloured horse for two years in a row, Carol Bardo and Mandy Hughes' The Humdinger, ridden by Jayne Webber.

Supreme Horse and Pony of the Year

NB This competition was split between horses and ponies in 2003. The class was not held in 1997.
Before that it was called Champion of Champions

Year		Horse	Owner	Rider
2010	Horse	Dunbeacon	Mrs J. Jerram	Katie Jerram
2010	Pony	Charn Secret Legend	Miss K. Fuge	Abbie Farmer
2009	Horse	The Philanderer	Carol Bardo	Jayne Webber
2009	Pony	Greylands Maid in the Dark	Mrs D.L. Thomas	Katie Roberts
2008	Horse	Finn McCool III	J.L. Dunlop OBE	Guy Landau
2008	Pony	Chagford Lewis	Mrs K. Carter	Poppy Marie Carter
2007	Horse	Broadstone Doulton	Robert Walker	Robert Walker
2007	Pony	Waxwing Thumbs Up	Mrs G. Shuttleworth & Mrs L.D.P. Leeming	Charlotte Dent
2006	Horse	So Smart	Camilla Neame	Robert Walker
2006	Pony	Fairholme Rossetta's Rhapsody	Mrs D. Moreton	Chloe Willett
2005	Horse	Bournebrook Golden Law	Rooksnest Farms	Shelley Perham
2005	Pony	Broadgrove Chatterbox	Mrs A. Fowler	Jemima Walker
2004	Horse	Soldier Brave	Carol Bardo	Jayne Webber
2004	Pony	Chiddock Over the Limit	Mrs D.L. Thomas and Ms J. Newbery	Nicholas Schofield
2003	Horse	Zin Zan	Justine Armstrong-Small	Justine Armstrong-Small
2003	Pony	Penwayn Ryan	Laura Collett	Laura Collett
2002		Castle Comet	Vanessa Compton	Vanessa Compton
2001		Chiddock Spot on	Mrs D.L. Thomas	Gemma James
2000		Fielding Tom Sawyer	A. Miller	Rebecca Miller
1999		Greylands Little Gem	Helen Horton	Hannah Horton
1998		Colne Heiress	Mrs S.J. Rowland	Sophie Rowland
1996		The Showman	Jill Ashmole	Bill Bryan
1993		College Jester	Mr R. Creber	Moggy Hennessy
1991		King's Warrior	Mr R. Creber	Robert Oliver
1990		Super Ted	Mrs H. Griffith	Robert Oliver
1989		Fair Breeze	Mr J. Tierney	Nigel Hollings
1988		Classic Tales	Miss V. White	Gill Oliver
1987		Rye Tangle	Miss K. Birch	Robert Oliver
1986		Rye Tangle	Miss K. Birch	Robert Oliver
1985		Macbeth	Mrs C. van Praagh	Allister Hood
1984		Fair Change	Dr and Mrs Gilbert-Scott	Carol Gilbert-Scott

FEATURE CLASSES

Driving

Double Harness Scurry Racing Championship

Year	Ponies	Owner	Driver
2010	Bow and Arrow	Pat Cooke	Sarah Cooke
2009	Code Pooh Bear and Piglet	Jemma Millman	Jemma Millman
2008	Code Pooh Bear and Piglet	Jemma Millman	Jemma Millman
2007	Darkhorse Fred and Barney	Gareth Roberts	Gareth Roberts
2006	Darkhorse Fred and Barney	Gareth Roberts	Gareth Roberts
2005	Whistle and Flute	Sally Mawer	Sally Mawer
2004	Whistle and Flute	Sally Mawer	Sally Mawer
2003	Topaz and Cally	Sally Mawer	Sally Mawer
2002	Sebastian and Co	Osborne Refrigerators Ltd	John Marson
2001	Touchwood and Whistle	Sally Mawer	Sally Mawer
2000	Pinky and Perky	Pro Mill Engineering	Sarah Cooke
1999	Marks and Sparks	Pro Mill Engineering	Sarah Cooke
1998	Lolly and Pop	Mr and Mrs D.E.G. Matthews	David Matthews
1997	Pinky and Perky	Pro Mill Engineering	Sarah Cooke
1996	Pinky and Perky	Pro Mill Engineering	Sarah Cooke
1995	Bits and Pieces	Mr and Mrs D.E.G. Matthews	David Matthews
1994	Bubble and Squeak	Robert Blake	Pat Cooke
1993	Lolly and Pop	Mr and Mrs D.E.G. Matthews	David Matthews Jnr
1992	Marks and Sparks	Pro Mill Engineering	Sarah Cooke
1991	Bubble and Squeak	Robert Blake	Pat Cooke
1990	Minnie and Fudge	Wednesbury Motor Services	Susie Lawrence
1989	Bits and Pieces	Mr and Mrs D.E.G. Matthews	David Matthews
1988	Dollar and Dime	Mr J.N. Swanson	Neil Swanson
1987	Mini and Sunlight	Osborne Refrigerators Ltd and C. Mason	John Marson
1986	Touch and Go	Robert Blake	Julie Blake
1985	Minnie and Fudge	Mrs J.N. Swanson	Neil Swanson
1984	Bubble and Squeak	Robert Blake	Robert Blake
1983	Pavlov and Peanuts	AGA Rayburn Team	Christine Dick
1982	Bubble and Squeak	Robert Blake	Robert Blake
1981	Bubble and Squeak	Robert Blake	Robert Blake
1980	Pavlov and Peanuts	Mr and Mrs J. Dick	Christine Dick
1979	Chalk and Cheese	Robert Blake	Robert Blake
1978	McTavish and Dooby Doo	A. Samuelson	B. Samuelson
1977	Pride and Prejudice	Pat Cooke	Pat Cooke
1976	Pavlov and Peanuts	Mr and Mrs J. Dick	Christine Dick
1975	Punch and Judy	Pat Cooke	Pat Cooke
1974	Friar Tuck and Jake	Robert Blake	Robert Blake
1973	Dandy and Don	J.P. Moore	Joe Moore
1972	Dandy and Don	J.P. Moore	Joe Moore
1971	Pinky and Perky	George Bowman	Robert Blake
1970	Whisky and Splash	Mrs P. Stewart-Smith	Mrs P. Stewart-Smith
1969	Revel Jon and Stoatley Moonlight	Miss A. Moit	Miss A. Moit
1968	Whisky and Splash	Mrs P. Stewart-Smith	Mrs P. Stewart-Smith

Harness and Concours d'Elegance

Year	Class	Horse	Owner	Driver
2010	Harness	Trehewyd Brenin Arthur	Nigel Fuller	Nigel Fuller
2009	Harness	Thorneyside the Foreman	M. Clarke	Minta Winn
2008	Harness	Royal Sunshine	Smith Bros	Lucy Smith
2007	Harness	Trehewyd Brenin Arthur	Nigel Fuller	Nigel Fuller
2006	Pony Harness	Trehewyd Brenin Arthur	Nigel Fuller	Nigel Fuller
	Horse Harness	Glenshane Prince	Jean Clayden	Jean Clayden
2005	Pony Harness	Lady Tara	Mick Corby	Jan Manning
	Horse Harness	Glenshane Prince	Jean Clayden	Jean Clayden
2004	Pony Harness	Wharley Pageboy	Mrs N.A. Blandin	N. Blandin
	Horse Harness	Glenshane Prince	Jean Clayden	Jean Clayden
2003	Pony Harness	Gunthwaite Tailrace	Mrs J. Manning	Jan Manning
	Horse Harness	Glenshane Prince	Jean Clayden	Jean Clayden
2002	Pony Harness	Wharley Pageboy	Mrs N.A. Blandin	N. Blandin
	Horse Harness	Glenshane Prince	Jean Clayden	Jean Clayden
2001	Pony Harness	Murdoch of Creag Dhubh	Mr and Mrs A.M. Steven	Elinor Steven
	Horse Harness	Thank-you Ovation and Thank-you Oh Wow	Sealmaster Fire, Draught and Weather Seals	David Barker
2000	Horse Harness	Wentworth Prince Regent	Mrs S.M. Murrell	Christine Dick
	Pony Harness	Ovington Xanadu	V.M. Neal	Vanessa Neal
1999	Horse Harness	Wentworth Prince Regent	Mrs S.M. Murrell	Christine Dick
	Pony Harness	Synod Guard	Mr and Mrs M.J. Edwards	Liz Edmonds
1998	Horse Harness	Garstons Lord George	Eddie Smith Snr	Eddie Smith Jnr
	Pony Harness	Vimpenny Lucky Strike	Ella McNinch	Ella McNinch
1997	Horse Harness	Thank-you Ovation and Thank-you Oh Wow	Tessa Reeve	Tessa Reeve
	Pony Harness	Black Diamond and Black Pearl	Mr and Mrs C.J. Powell	Betty Powell
1996	Horse Harness	Hugo and Ernest	Mark Broadbent	Mark Broadbent
	Pony Harness	Black Diamond and Black Pearl	Mr and Mrs C.J. Powell	Betty Powell
1995	Concours d'Elegance	Monnington Conductor	Sealmaster Fire, Draught and Weather Seals	Heidi Eagle
1994	Concours d'Elegance	Hurstwood Golden Girl	D. Clixby	Judy Clixby
1993	Concours d'Elegance	Wentworth Prince Regent	Mrs J.R. Dick	Christine Dick
1992	Concours d'Elegance	Welsh Pageant	Mrs Wray	Neil Wray
1991	Concours d'Elegance	Portsdown Knight Errant	A.P. Noble and M.E. Gould	Alan Noble
1990	Concours d'Elegance	Monnington Granados	Sealmaster Fire, Draught and Weather Seals	Valerie Beckum
1989	Concours d'Elegance	Portsdown Knight Errant	A.P. Noble and M.E. Gould	Alan Noble
1988	Concours d'Elegance	Wentworth Prince Regent	S. Murrell	Christine Dick
1987	Concours d'Elegance	Holypark Tarquinius	Eddie Buck	Eddie Buck
1986	Concours d'Elegance	Holypark Tarquinius	Eddie Buck	Eddie Buck
1985	Concours d'Elegance	Holypark Tarquinius	Eddie Buck	Eddie Buck
1984	Concours d'Elegance	Holypark Tarquinius	Eddie Buck	Eddie Buck
1983	Concours d'Elegance	Portsdown Knight Errant	A.P. Noble and M.E. Gould	Alan Noble
1982	Concours d'Elegance	Finesse	Elspeth Gill	Elspeth Gill
1981	Concours d'Elegance	Holypark Tarquinius	Eddie Buck	Eddie Buck
1980	Concours d'Elegance	Gatsby	Miss B. Sheldon	Miss B. Sheldon
1979	Concours d'Elegance	Hurstwood Mersul	Mr and Mrs W. Isaac	Joan Isaac
1978	Concours d'Elegance	Hurstwood Mersul	Mr and Mrs W. Isaac	Joan Isaac
1977	Concours d'Elegance	Cefnor Clansman	Mr and Mrs W. Isaac	A. Isaac
1976	Concours d'Elegance	Cambridge Proctor	Mrs L. Mills	Mrs L. Mills

◀ Nigel Fuller and Trehewyd Brenin Arthur claim their third Harness Championship in five years (2010).

Hackney Horse of the Year

NB This class was not run between 1960 and 1970

Year	Horse	Owner
1993	Whitehavens Step High	Mr and Mrs Vyse
1992	Forewood Commander	B. Bass
1991	Ingfield Black Prince	Jo Quigg
1990	Ingfield Black Prince	Jo Quigg
1989	Ingfield Black Prince	Jo Quigg
1988	Appleton Bay Duke	G. Vardy
1987	Whitehavens Step High	E. Vyse
1986	Bally May Queen	J. Wenham
1985	Ingfield Black Prince	S. Sparks
1984	Holypark What's Wanted	J.M. Neachell
1983	Whitehavens Step High	E. Vyse
1982	Eaglestone Arc Royal	D.C. Lunnon
1981	Eaglestone Arc Royal	D.C. Lunnon
1980	Hurstwood Director	J.A. McDougald
1979	Brookfield Harvest Moon	J. Peter
1978	Walton Revelation	M. Neachell
1977	Brookfield Harvest Moon	J. Peter
1976	Brook Acres Light Mist	K.G. Moss
1975	Brook Acres Light Mist	K.G. Moss
1974	Brook Acres Light Mist	K.G. Moss
1973	Brook Acres Light Mist	K.G. Moss
1972	Outwood Florescent	M.C. Hughes
1971	Outwood Florescent	M.C. Hughes
1959	Walton Searchlight	W.T. Barton
1958	Hurstwood Tarantella	Capt. R.S. de Quincey
1957	Walton Diplomat	W.T. Barton
1956	Walton Diplomat	W.T. Barton
1955	Cornishman	E.S. Philips
1954	Walton Diplomat	W.T. Barton
1953	Hurstwood Lonely Lady	Mrs B. Mellow
1952	Holywell Florette	W.T. Barton

Hackney Pony of the Year

NB This class was not run between 1960 and 1975

Year	Horse	Owner
1993	Woodside Kaspar	J. Wenham
1992	Flashwood Vulcan	J.H. Chicken
1991	Northbrook Handy Mac	Jo Quigg
1990	Flashwood Vulcan	J.H. Chicken
1989	Sunbeam Super Star	E. Vyse
1988	Sunbeam Super Star	E. Vyse
1987	Hurstwood Untouchable	S. Davidson
1986	Sunbeam Super Star	E. Vyse
1985	Barnfield Poldark	G. Haffenden
1984	Hurstwood Consort	F. Haydon
1983	Stapleford Duke	J.H. Chicken
1982	Stapleford Duke	J.H. Chicken
1981	Heathfield George	C.R. Cowan
1980	Heathfield George	C.R. Cowan
1979	Heathfield George	C.R. Cowan
1978	Hurstwood Consort	Miss R. Davidson
1977	Marden Little Swell	K.G. Moss
1976	Marden Little Swell	K.G. Moss
1959	Highstone Nicholas	The Hon. Mrs Ionides
1958	Highstone Nicholas	The Hon. Mrs Ionides
1957	Highstone Nicholas	The Hon. Mrs Ionides
1956	Oakwell Sir James	The Hon. Mrs Ionides
1955	Oakwell Sir James	Miss M. James
1954	Hurstwood Coronation	L. Hirst
1953	Oakwell Sir James	Miss M. James
1952	Bossy	Mr & Mrs G.C. Kimpton

▲ The victorious Devon & Somerset Branch of the Pony Club celebrate their win in the Pony Club Mounted Games 2010.

Pony Club and Riding Club Classes

Pony Club Mounted Games

2010	Devon & Somerset
2009	Percy Hunt
2008	Oakley Hunt West
2007	Atherstone
2006	Banwell
2005	Eglinton
2004	West Perthshire
2003	Wylye Valley
2002	Oakley Hunt West
2001	Oakley Hunt West
2000	Eglinton
1999	Poole & District
1998	Clydach
1997	Oakley Hunt West
1996	Eglinton Hunt
1995	Eglinton Hunt
1994	Eglinton Hunt
1993	Eglinton Hunt
1992	Eglinton Hunt
1991	Wyle Valley
1990	North Warwickshire
1989	Oakley Hunt West
1988	Eglinton Hunt
1987	Eglinton Hunt
1986	Wylye Valley Hunt
1985	Atherstone Hunt
1984	Eglinton Hunt
1983	Eglinton Hunt
1982	Eglinton Hunt
1981	Banwen & District
1980	Oakley Hunt
1979	Cheshire Hunt (North)
1978	Eglinton Hunt
1977	Banwen & District
1976	Wylye Valley Hunt
1975	Peak
1974	Kirkintiloch & Campsie
1973	Strathblane & District
1972	Strathblane & District
1971	Atherstone Hunt
1970	Atherstone Hunt
1969	Taunton Vale Hunt
1968	Angus
1967	Hurworth Hunt
1966	Woodland
1965	Blackmore Vale Hunt
1964	Atherstone Hunt
1963	Angus
1962	High Peak Hunt North
1961	Enfield Chase Hunt
1960	High Peak Hunt North
1959	High Peak Hunt North
1958	Cheshire Hunt North
1957	North West Kent

Riding Club Quadrilles

NB This competition ran between 1966 and 1990

1990	Wilmslow
1989	East Yorkshire
1988	South of England Agricultural Society
1987	East Grinstead
1986	Wilmslow
1985	East Grinstead
1984	Wilmslow
1983	Wilmslow
1982	Hailsham
1981	West Surrey
1980	Rudgwick & District
1979	West Surrey
1978	East Grinstead
1977	West Surrey
1976	York & District
1975	The Chiltern
1974	South Shropshire
1973	Chiltern
1972	East Grinstead
1971	Old Berkeley
1970	Newcastle
1969	Chiltern
1968	Evenlode
1967	Chiltern
1966	Household Cavalry

OTHER RESULTS

Combined Training

NB This class ran between 1952 and 1988

Year	Horse	Owner	Rider
1988	Canworthy Ivonsun	S. Ivins	J. Spring
1987	Poshpaws	Mrs J. Cammaerts	Mrs J. Cammaerts
1986	Poshpaws	Mrs J. Cammaerts	Mrs J. Cammaerts
1985	Catherston Dutch Bid	Masterlock Recruitment	Jennie Loriston-Clarke
1984	Dutch Gold	Mr D.R. Bannocks	Jennie Loriston-Clarke
1983	Mystic Minstrel	Rachel Bayliss	Rachel Bayliss
1982	Waterscot	Mrs N. Routledge	Mrs E. de Haan
1981	Early Dawn	Richard Walker	Richard Walker
1980	Welton Louis	S. Barr	Mrs J. Mansfield
1979	Castlewellen	Judy Bradwell	Judy Bradwell
1978	Watertight	Mrs C.D. Collins	Mrs C.D. Collins
1977	Persian Holiday	Capt. Mark Phillips	Capt. Mark Phillips
1976	Gurgle the Greek	Rachel Bayliss	Rachel Bayliss
1975	Royal Slam	Mrs P.A. & Miss J.P. Pointer	Miss J.P. Pointer
1974	Olivia	Mrs M. Hance	Miss A. Pattinson
1973	Goodwill	H.M. The Queen	H.R.H. Princess Anne
1972	Xenocles	Jennie Loriston-Clarke	Jennie Loriston-Clarke
1971	Ripalong	Pamela Sivewright	Pamela Sivewright
1970	Pasha	Richard Walker	Richard Walker
1969	Johnny Walker	Mrs M.G. Holland	Mrs M.G. Holland
1968	Fair and Square	Sheila Willcox	Sheila Willcox
1967	Xenocles	Mr & Mrs Loriston-Clarke and Miss A. Stubbings	Jennie Loriston-Clarke
1966	Johnny Walker	Mrs R. Sutton	
1965	Fulmer Featherweight	Angela Martin-Bird	Angela Martin-Bird
1964	Japhet	The Hon. Mrs D. Allhusen	
1963	Lotti	The Hon. Mrs D. Allhusen	Shelagh Keslar
1962	Japhet	The Hon. Mrs D. Allhusen	
1961	Merely-a-Monarch	Anneli Drummond-Hay	Anneli Drummond-Hay
1960	Merely-a-Monarch	Anneli Drummond-Hay	Anneli Drummond-Hay
1959	Perhaps	Anneli Drummond-Hay	Anneli Drummond-Hay
1958	Laurien	The Hon. Mrs D Allhusen	
1957	High and Mighty	Sheila Willcox	Sheila Wilcox
1956	High and Mighty	Sheila Willcox	Sheila Wilcox
1955	Tramella	Diana Mason	Diana Mason
1954	Tramella	Diana Mason	Diana Mason
1953	Bright Prospect	The Benenden Riding Establishment	Miss C. Kendall
1952	Tosca		Pat Smythe

Police Horse of the Year

NB This class ran between 1962 and 1996

Year	Horse	Rider	Year	Horse	Rider
1996	Illustrious	Merseyside Police	1978	Marquess	Lancashire Constabulary
1995	Vincent	Metropolitan Police	1977	Ediscombe	Durham Constabulary
1994	Steele	Avon & Somerset Constabulary	1976	Ashton	Avon & Somerset Constabulary
1993	Pascal	West Midlands Police	1975	Dalesman II	West Yorkshire Metropolitan Police
1992	Pascal	West Midlands Police	1974	Sandown	Metropolitan Police
1991	Pascal	West Midlands Police	1973	Avon	Bristol Constabulary
1990	Illustrious	Merseyside Police	1972	Sandown	Metropolitan Police
1989	Centaur	Avon & Somerset Constabulary	1971	Sandown	Metropolitan Police
1988	Steele	Avon & Somerset Constabulary	1970	Pennie Way	West Yorkshire Constabulary
1987	Steele	Avon & Somerset Constabulary	1969	Belmont	Lancashire Constabulary
1986	Steele	Avon & Somerset Constabulary	1968	Sultan II	Birmingham City Police
1985	Kingweston	Avon & Somerset Constabulary	1967	Redcliffe	Bristol City Police
1984	Steele	Avon & Somerset Constabulary	1966	Redcliffe	Bristol City Police
1983	Steele	Avon & Somerset Constabulary	1965	Don	Bradford City Police
1982	Steele	Avon & Somerset Constabulary	1964	Grey Mist	Staffordshire County Police
1981	Steele	Avon & Somerset Constabulary	1963	Angus IV	Bradford City Police
1980	Marquess	Lancashire Constabulary	1962	Grey Sky	Birmingham City PoliceAga, cleaning 28–9
1979	Marquess	Lancashire Constabulary			

◄ Sandy Anderson, Chairman, Grandstand Media Ltd, presenting the Vinopolis Trophy to Linda Heed in 2008.

Susan George: A Tribute to Simon MacCorkindale

'Give of your best endeavours and reap the rewards and, when "Auld Lang Syne" rings out once more, relish the fact that we will all be back together again next year.'

These are my words of welcome in the HOYS brochure at the start of our 2010 show, and at the time they conveyed everything I wanted and firmly believed. Little could I have conceived the thought that my husband, best friend and partner for twenty-eight years, Simon MacCorkindale, my one in a million husband, would not be with me and us in 2011 to recite the ode that he had made entirely his own for the past eleven years.

He was an amazingly talented and masterful actor, well versed in Shakespeare and the classics, achieving outstanding fame throughout his career. America remembers him as Jane Wyman's handsome lawyer in the glamorous TV series 'Falcon Crest', but fans in Britain will remember him, I know, for his eight-year run as super surgeon Harry Harper in 'Casualty'.

Horse of the Year Show will remember him for his incredible commitment, never missing a show, and once flying back from filming in the States to perform on the last night and, as always, be at my side. He had time for everyone. He was admired by all for his generosity, genuine personality, grace and presence, and his exceptional velvet voice, which echoed around the main arena for our finale every year as he made us weep with the words, 'Ladies and gentlemen, I give to you the Horse.'

Rest in peace my darling Simon.

Susan George
Honorary President of HOYS

INDEX

Note: Page numbers in **bold** refer to illustrations